C000060235

MENTAL HEALTH AND SCOTS LAW
IN PRACTICE

AUSTRALIA
Law Book Co.
Sydney

CANADA and USA
Carswell
Toronto

HONG KONG
Sweet & Maxwell Asia

NEW ZEALAND
Brookers
Wellington

SINGAPORE and MALAYSIA
Sweet & Maxwell Asia
Singapore and Kuala Lumpur

MENTAL HEALTH AND SCOTS LAW
IN PRACTICE

by

J.J. McManus, LL.B., Ph.D.
Professor of Criminal Justice, Glasgow Caledonian University

&

Dr Lindsay D.G. Thomson,
M.B., Ch.B., MRCPsych, MPhil, M.D.
Senior Lecturer in Forensic Psychiatry, University of Edinburgh and
Honorary Consultant Forensic Psychiatry, The State Hospital

THOMSON

™

W. GREEN

Published in 2005 by
W. Green & Son Ltd
21 Alva Street
Edinburgh EH2 4PS

www.wgreen.thomson.com

Reprinted 2006

Typeset by LBJ Typesetting Ltd, Kingsclere

Printed and bound in Great Britain by
TJI Digital, Padstow, Cornwall

No natural forests were destroyed to make this product;
only farmed timber was used and replanted

A CIP catalogue record for this book is available from
the British Library.

ISBN 0414 01475 8

ACKNOWLEDGEMENTS

The editors acknowledge with grateful thanks the contribution of Sheila McLennan, Malcolm Macleod and James Thomson to this book.

FOREWORD

By Dr Derek Chiswick, Consultant Forensic Psychiatrist, Royal Edinburgh Hospital and The Right Honorable Lord Maclean, Senator of the College of Justice.

Psychiatry and the law have never been comfortable working companions. Each has its own language, arcane working practices, responsibilities and ethical standards. There are, however, many areas in which the two are required to work together. The most important areas are in the criminal justice system and in measures for compulsory admission to hospital. In the last decade there has been a huge expansion of legal interest in mental health procedures. There has been very recent legislation both in the criminal justice field and in the field of mental health. There have been legal judgments delivered in United Kingdom courts and in the European Court of Human Rights that have been of profound importance for the practice of psychiatry.

Practitioners in this area of law and psychiatry are from diverse professions including lawyers, doctors, social workers, police, prison authorities and mental health staff. It is not easy to locate a solid resource that can explain in terms understandable to all concerned the salient features of the subject. It is even more difficult for practitioners working in Scotland to find such materials. In this book Lindsay Thomson and Jim McManus have set out to provide an authoritative, readable and comprehensible text that is immediately accessible to the range of practitioners who have responsibilities for dealing with mentally disordered people. We feel they have fulfilled their aim with credit. We hope that Mental Health and Scots Law in Practice will become the standard source for practitioners seeking to gain an understanding of the law in Scotland as it applies to mental health issues. The fact that it is written in clear and comprehensible language will help practitioners to share a common and agreed understanding of this complex and sometimes contentious area.

Derek Chiswick   Ranald Maclean

November 2004

PREFACE

The Mental Health (Care and Treatment) (Scotland) Act 2003 is the first radical overhaul of the law relating to mental health in Scotland since the Mental Health (Scotland) Acts of 1960 and 1984. As all practitioners will be aware, there have been many developments in research, practice and, perhaps, philosophy relating to mental health in this period.

From the lawyers' perspective, the Human Rights Act 1998 actually summed up, rather than created, the environment which most demanded a new mental health law. Nonetheless, that Act has ensured that domestic courts are empowered to examine cases which previously would have perished on the way to Strasbourg, not because they were not worthy of consideration by the European Court of Human Rights but because the time, dedication and financial commitment required would have deterred all but the most persistent litigant somewhere along the line. It is not just the availability of a domestic remedy which has highlighted the issues; it is also a change in the culture of rights which has ensured that previously marginalised groups in our society now obtain the protection of the law which they have always deserved. Unfortunately, our history has rendered it less than likely that the average legal practitioner has the skills, knowledge and experience to fully and properly serve the client group involved.

From the perspective of mental health practitioners, the new Act presents both an opportunity and a challenge. Its fundamental principles, uncoupling of hospital detention and compulsory measures in the community, and its statutory basis to patient representation can be used by a knowledgeable practitioner to improve patient care and to promote service development. The reciprocity principle is worthy of particular note. It ensures the provision of appropriate services to a person who is subject to a certificate or order under the Act; and provision of continuing care when the Act is no longer being used. The Act is, however, lengthy, difficult to follow and brings in a variety of new working methods, in particular mental health tribunals. There will be a steep learning curve for all involved but it is essential that all doctors, mental health officers and mental health practitioners are familiar with the Act's basic provisions to ensure safe patient care.

Accordingly, we felt that a book like this would serve the needs of all the professionals potentially involved in ensuring the success of the new Act and the Adults with Incapacity (Scotland) Act 2000. Each of the contributors is fully involved in different aspects of practice in areas covered by the new law. Under the direction of the editors, each has attempted to outline the requirements of that law, as far as can be anticipated at this time. The editors have added general introductory chapters on Mental Illness and the Scottish Legal System so that those from divergent disciplines might have the required basic knowledge to follow the rest of the text. These introductory chapters can, of course, be skipped by readers well versed in either—or both—discipline(s), but we have been struck by the number of both legal and mental health professionals who have sought this kind of statement of basic facts, and thought it best to make the text a complete introduction to the scene. This book provides practitioners with a systematic guide to the provisions of the new Act, setting out their conditions of use, implementation process, available powers, exclusion criteria, and revocation and appeal procedures with clinical examples as illustrations. In addition, it describes in detail services for mentally disordered offenders, the process of risk assessment and management, psychiatric defences, legislation for mentally disordered offenders, and the means by which a mental health practitioner's opinion may be obtained and communicated in written or verbal format to the courts. The high prevalence of mental disorder in those in contact with the criminal justice system makes such information relevant not only to mental health and legal practitioners but also to police officers, prosecution services, criminal justice social workers and prison officers. These chapters rely heavily on the experience of their authors, albeit sometimes in anticipation of how practice will work under the Act. Much of that will depend on the actions of all the professionals involved. We trust that this text will assist you to make the most of what the new law offers, to improve both the treatment and protection of mentally ill people in Scotland and advance public understanding of the issues involved.

Jim McManus   Lindsay Thomson

CONTENTS

CHAPTER 3 CIVIL MENTAL HEALTH LEGISLATION 40

*Chapter Author: Dr Lindsay D.G. Thomson M.D., Senior Lecturer
    in Forensic Psychiatry, University of Edinburgh*

CHAPTER 4 ADULTS WITH INCAPACITY 93

Chapter Author: Dr John Crichton, PhD, Consultant Forensic
Psychiatrist, Orchard Clinic, Edinburgh

CHAPTER 6 PSYCHIATRIC DEFENCES   161

*Chapter Author: Dr Rajan Darjee MPhil, Lecturer in Forensic
     Psychiatry, University of Edinburgh*

CHAPTER 8 COURT REPORTS AND THE EXPERT WITNESS

*Chapter Author: Dr Lindsay D.G. Thomson M.D., Senior Lecturer
    in Forensic Psychiatry, University of Edinburgh*

TABLE OF CASES

TABLE OF STATUTES

TABLE OF ACTS OF THE SCOTTISH PARLIAMENT

TABLE OF STATUTORY INSTRUMENTS

TABLE OF SCOTTISH STATUTORY INSTRUMENTS

MENTAL DISORDER AND PSYCHIATRIC SERVICES

An Introduction to Mental Disorder

This basic guide describes mental disorders from a clinical and legal **1–01**
perspective. An understanding of the concept of mental disorder will
assist practitioners in the criminal justice system in the appropriate
management of offenders. It is not necessary, or indeed desirable, for
you to make a diagnosis but rather that your index of suspicion is raised
concerning the possible presence of a mental disorder.

Detailed information on mental disorders, including their prevalence,
cause, course, treatment and outcome, can be found in textbooks of
psychiatry such as the *Companion to Psychiatric Studies*[2].

Clinical Definitions of Mental Disorder

A mental disorder is a disorder of the brain and mind. There are **1–02**
different types of mental disorder and these are classified in the
International Classification of Diseases (ICD-10)[3] and the Diagnostic
and Statistical Manual IV (DSM-IV),[4] produced by the World Health
Organisation and the American Psychiatric Association respectively.
These manuals classify disorders into groups and describe, using narrative or specific diagnostic criteria, the different diagnostic categories
within each group and their subtypes. For example, Alzheimer's disease
is a subtype of dementia and a form of organic mental disorder.

The major clinical diagnostic groups are shown in Box 1.

Box 1: Clinical Diagnostic Hierarchy

Mental Disorder	Example
Organic Mental Disorder	Epilepsy, learning disability, dementia
Functional Disorder	Schizophrenia, manic depression, major depressive disorder

---

[1] Chapter author: Dr Lindsay D.G. Thomson, M.D.

[2] Johnstone, E.C *et al*, *Companion to Psychiatric Studies* (7th ed., Churchill Livingstone, 2004).

[3] WHO (1992) *The ICD-10 classification of mental and behavioural disorders: clinical descriptions and diagnostic guidelines*, World Health Organisation, Geneva.

[4] APA (1994) *Diagnostic and statistical manual of mental disorders*, 4th ed. (DSM-IV), American Psychiatric Association, Washington, DC.

Mental Disorder	Example
Neurotic Mental Disorder	Anxiety states, phobia, depression, obsessive-compulsive disorder, post traumatic stress disorder (PTSD), adjustment disorder
Eating Disorders	Anorexia nervosa, bulimia nervosa
Substance Misuse Disorder	Alcohol and/or drug intoxication, harmful use or dependence
Personality Disorder	Dissocial, paranoid, schizoid, emotionally unstable (impulsive or borderline), histrionic, obsessive-compulsive, anxious (or avoidant), dependent
Disorders of Childhood/ Adolescence/Development	Attention deficit hyperactivity disorder (ADHD), conduct disorder, autism

Organic Mental Disorder

1–03 There are a number of organic mental disorders. Delirium and dementia are common presentations.

Acute Confusion or Delirium

1–04   In this condition a person's consciousness is clouded, and there is impairment of recent memory and disorientation in time, place or person. The sleep pattern is disturbed and he may turn day into night, not sleep, or have nightmares or hallucinations when awake. Symptoms fluctuate and are often worse at night. He may be frightened or perplexed. Acute confusional states most commonly occur in the elderly, secondary to a physical illness such as a chest or urinary tract infection. Treatment is primarily of the underlying cause with reassurance, sedation, adequate hydration and good nursing care in a well-lit room.

Dementia

1–05   In dementia a person's memory and intellect decline, and there are changes in personality. Depression is common in the early stages. The individual's ability to think and to judge situations and tasks are impaired. He may become apathetic, irritable, emotionally labile and unable to function socially. Speech becomes more difficult and in the latter stages the person may be unable to walk and become incontinent. It is a terminal condition and death usually occurs within ten years. It occurs in five per cent of people over the age of 65 and 20 per cent over the age of 80. There are multiple causes of dementia and some are reversible, for example dementia secondary to hypothyroidism. The commonest causes of dementia are degenerative (senile dementia of Alzheimer type) and vascular (multi-infarct dementia). Any reversible cause must be treated. A new type of drug, an acetylcholinesterase, does slow the progress of Alzheimer's disease in its initial stages but doubt remains about the clinical benefit of this. The mainstay of treatment is a practical support package to the sufferer and his carer. This includes access to memory aids, home-helps, meals on wheels, lunch clubs, day centres and respite care. Residential care may be required, especially in the latter stages.

Learning Disability

There are two components to learning disability: firstly, low intelligence (I.Q. mild 50–69; moderate 35–49; severe 20–34; profound <20) and, secondly, poor social and behavioural functioning. Approximately five per cent of the population has an intelligence quotient (I.Q.) of less than 70. The origin in many cases is unknown but recognised causes include infection (such as rubella) in mother's pregnancy, hypoxia at birth, metabolic abnormalities such as hypothyroidism or phenylketonuria, and genetic variations with chromosomal abnormalities as occur in Down's Syndrome. Treatment varies depending on the medical and social needs of the individual but may include input from teachers, social workers, speech therapists, physiotherapists, occupational therapists, psychologists, nurses, paediatricians and psychiatrists. A multidisciplinary approach is essential. **1–06**

Functional Disorder

Schizophrenia

Schizophrenia is a major mental disorder characterised by a significant disturbance in thought processes, loss of contact with reality and changes in emotional responses. It affects just under one per cent of the population worldwide often at a young age, typically late teens or early twenties for men and five years later for women. The course of the illness varies with 10 per cent making a full recovery, 10 per cent becoming severely disabled and the majority having intermittent delusions and hallucinations, lack of motivation, and reduced social and occupational functioning. **1–07**

A delusion is a false, fixed idea that cannot be argued against and which is out of keeping with cultural norms. A hallucination occurs when an individual perceives a sight, sound, taste, touch or smell without it being present.

Symptoms of schizophrenia include delusions of being controlled (passivity phenomena); persecutory, grandiose or religious delusions, or delusions of reference (for example that the TV is sending personal messages to the patient); and hallucinations, typically of voices giving a running commentary on the patient's actions, discussing the patient with each other (third person auditory hallucinations), or speaking to the patient, often in a derogatory manner. An individual may believe that his thoughts are being broadcast out loud, or that thoughts are being inserted into or withdrawn from his brain. The sufferer may appear flat or incongruous in his mood, for example giggling inappropriately. His thoughts may be disordered and his speech very difficult to follow.

Schizophrenia is likely to lead to reduced social functioning with loss of relationships and job. Antipsychotic medication is the mainstay of treatment and can successfully control delusions and hallucinations. Education of patients and carers, establishing regular, low-stress life routines and social support are also important.

Mood Disorders

1–08   An individual's mood varies according to day-to-day events. For example, sitting a driving test may cause anxiety, passing may result in happiness and relief, and failing may cause disappointment and sadness. Everyone has these ups and downs. For some people however, these highs and lows are extreme and the individual is no longer able to function in a normal way. These mood disorders, mania and depression, are not normal but pathological. These disorders are often referred to as bipolar (manic depression) or unipolar (depression alone). The lifetime risk of bipolar disorder is 1.2 per cent and it is found slightly more commonly in women and more frequently in higher social classes. Unipolar depression is twice as common in women than men and approximately five per cent of the population will suffer from it at any one time.

Mania

1–09   In mania an individual will typically experience elevated mood or irritability; increased libido; decreased need for sleep; weight loss; increased but unfocussed activity; racing thoughts; pressure of speech; flight of ideas (jumping from one subject to another) or grandiose delusions, for example believing that you have the power to heal. The term "hypomania" is used to describe a milder episode of mania. Mania is managed using mood stabilising medication such as lithium, valproate or carbamazepine; and antipsychotic medication. Recurrence is common but the sufferer is usually able to return to a full level of normal functioning in between episodes.

Depression

1–10   In depression an individual experiences abnormally low mood almost constantly. Symptoms can include a disturbance of sleep typically with early morning wakening; a change in appetite either increased or decreased; poor concentration; indecisiveness; loss of interest and anhedonia; anxiety; agitation or retardation; lack of confidence and self esteem; rumination on death or suicide; self harm; or feelings of guilt. Depressive episodes are often described as mild, moderate, or severe depending upon the symptoms presented. In a severe depressive episode, an individual may be psychotic and have hallucinations or delusions that are related to their low mood, for example the belief that the world is coming to an end or that the sufferer has a terminal illness. Depression is typically treated using antidepressant medication, augmented with a mood stabiliser if required; or cognitive behavioural therapy or interpersonal psychotherapy. Electroconvulsive therapy (ECT) is used in severe treatment-resistant or life threatening cases. Without adequate treatment 50 per cent of patients will relapse. Antidepressant medication is therefore usually recommended for six months following recovery.

Neurotic Mental Disorder

In a neurotic illness the individual has insight into their symptoms and 1–11
unimpaired reality testing. Typical symptoms include anxiety, depression,
complaints of physical ill health, repetitive thoughts or actions, and
avoidance. Neurotic disorders affect approximately 15 per cent of the
UK population and are more common in women. They are treated using
antidepressant or anxiolytic medication, and behavioural or cognitive
behavioural therapies. Common neurotic disorders include:

Panic Attacks

Panic attacks are episodes of intense, short lived anxiety with 1–12
breathlessness, palpitations, sweating, trembling, feelings of unreality,
and fear of collapse and loss of control.

Phobias

A phobia is a specific fear of an object or situation that is out of 1–13
proportion to any possible threat. The fear cannot be reasoned away, is
beyond voluntary control and leads to avoidance of the feared situation.
Typical phobias include agoraphobia (fear of open spaces), social phobia
(fear of social attention), and animal phobias (snakes, spiders).

Obsessive-Compulsive Disorder

In obsessive-compulsive disorder individuals experience repetitive and 1–14
persistent ideas, thoughts, impulses or images that appear intrusive and
senseless but which cause anxiety. They try to ignore or suppress these
with an alternative thought or action which may reduce anxiety on a
temporary basis. This may lead to the development of a compulsion.
These are repetitive, purposeful and intentional acts designed to deal
with an obsessional thought. For example, fear of contamination may
lead to repetitive hand washing.

Post Traumatic Stress Disorder (PTSD)

Post traumatic stress disorder may follow exposure to an exceptionally 1–15
threatening or catastrophic event likely to cause distress in anyone, for
example, an oil rig disaster or a war. Symptoms include flashbacks,
dreams, vivid memories or distress on exposure to a trigger reminiscent
of the event; avoidance of any triggers reminiscent of the event; sleep
problems, irritability, anger, poor concentration and hypervigilance.

Adjustment Disorders

In these disorders symptoms, typically of anxiety and depression, are 1–16
found in response to an identifiable, but not exceptional or catastrophic,
stressor. Anger and aggressive or regressive behaviour can occur.

Eating Disorders

Anorexia Nervosa

In anorexia nervosa the sufferer, usually female, believes that she is 1–17
too fat. This leads to deliberate weight loss of more than 15 per cent
below the norm for age and height. There may be self-induced vomiting

or purging, excessive exercising and use of appetite suppressants and/or diuretics. It occurs in less than one per cent of the female population and can be life-threatening. Treatment consists of normalising eating patterns, increasing self-esteem, improving body image, and building positive roles and relationships.

Bulimia Nervosa

1–18   Recurrent episodes of binge eating with a preoccupation with food and a compulsion to eat are key features of bulimia nervosa. In addition the sufferer will induce vomiting, diet and may use appetite suppressants. It is found in approximately one per cent of young females at any time. Treatment consists of cognitive behavioural therapy, interpersonal psychotherapy, group therapy and drug treatment with high dose serotonin reuptake inhibitors.

Substance Misuse Disorder

1–19   Alcohol and drug problems range from occasional intoxication or illegal use to dependence and life-threatening complications such as delirium tremens or cirrhosis. Symptoms of alcohol dependence are found in almost five per cent of the UK adult population per year and are three times more common in men. Approximately three per cent of the adult population in the UK uses an illegal drug in any one year. Any abuse of a substance resulting in the involvement of the police is clearly a problem. Treatment includes the use of medication for detoxification; medication to reduce craving or to cause an unpleasant reaction following alcohol consumption (antabuse); substitute prescribing; motivational interviewing; group therapy for support, education and awareness; self help or voluntary groups such as Alcoholics Anonymous; social skills training; and relapse prevention. Specific substance abuse problems include:

Alcohol Intoxication

1–20   The features of alcohol intoxication include recent consumption of alcohol, poor behavioural control with disinhibition or aggression; psychological changes such as impaired judgement or attention, or lability of mood; slurred speech; incoordination; unsteadiness; poor memory; and coma.

Alcohol Dependence

1–21   Alcohol dependence is marked by a reduction in types of alcohol consumed, an awareness of drink-seeking behaviour, increased tolerance, withdrawal symptoms, drinking to avoid withdrawal, a compulsion to drink, and recurrence after abstinence.

Alcohol Withdrawal

1–22   Symptoms of alcohol withdrawal include sweating, racing heart (tachycardia), insomnia, nausea, vomiting, agitation, anxiety, hallucinations and seizures.

Drug Intoxication

In drug intoxication there must be evidence that a substance has been **1–23** taken in an amount and within a timescale likely to cause intoxication. The presenting features must be consistent with the known actions of the drug and lead to a significant deterioration in behaviour, emotional state or intellectual functioning, hallucinations or coma. The symptoms of drug intoxication vary with the substance consumed. For example, opiate intoxication causes apathy and sedation whereas intoxication due to cocaine use causes euphoria and a sensation of increased energy.

Drug Dependence Syndrome

In drug dependence there is a loss of control over the pattern of **1–24** substance taking; compulsion to use drugs; preoccupation with drug use resulting in neglect of family, work, health and finances; increased tolerance; withdrawal symptoms and drug use to avoid withdrawal.

Drug-Induced Psychosis

Symptoms of a drug-induced psychosis must commence within two **1–25** weeks of substance use and stop within six months. Common psychotic symptoms include delusions and hallucinations.

Personality Disorders

The personality is formed during childhood and adolescence and it is **1–26** the features of an individual's personality, both emotional and cognitive, which make him or her identifiable to family and friends, and characterise their response to varying situations. A personality disorder consists of a deeply ingrained maladaptive pattern of behaviour recognisable from adolescence or earlier. It continues throughout adult life and causes suffering to that individual or others. The term remains controversial and can be viewed as vague and pejorative. Approximately 10 per cent of the general population have a personality disorder and between 30–50 per cent of psychiatric patients. There are different types of personality disorder including paranoid, schizoid, dissocial, emotionally unstable (impulsive or borderline), histrionic, obsessive-compulsive, anxious, or dependent. There is not a specific treatment for a personality disorder but clinicians may attempt to treat individual components of the disorder, for example by the use of anger management in dissocial personality disorder. Such treatments are dependent on the willingness of an individual to co-operate and will be prolonged. Dialectical behaviour therapy has been used in the treatment of people with borderline personality disorder. Cognitive behavioural therapy and medication are also utilised.

Antisocial Personality Disorder, Dissocial Personality Disorder and Psychopathy

Antisocial personality disorder is the personality disorder most often **1–27** found in mentally disordered offenders. It was diagnosed in over 80 per cent of prisoners in a study carried out in HMP Barlinnie[5]. The diagnosis is primarily made on the presentation of specific behaviours commonly seen in prisoners. For example, a history of truancy; running away in childhood; fighting; using weapons; forcing sexual activities on others; physical cruelty to animals or to people; destruction of property; stealing with or without confrontation of a victim; inability to sustain consistent work; breaking the law; irritability and aggression; failure to honour financial obligations; failure to plan ahead; impulsivity; lack of regard for the truth; recklessness; lack of ability to function as a parent; inability to sustain a monogamous relationship for more than one year; and lack of remorse.

The term "dissocial personality disorder" is now in use in ICD-10 and it concentrates more on emotional rather than behavioural factors. It is diagnosed in people who present with a callous lack of concern for others; gross and persistent irresponsibility and disregard for social norms, rules and obligations; an ability to establish but incapacity to maintain enduring relationships; very low tolerance to frustration and a low threshold for discharge of aggression; incapacity to experience guilt, or to profit from adverse experience, particularly punishment; and marked proneness to blame others, or to offer plausible rationalisations for the behaviour that has brought the individual into conflict with society.

The term "psychopathy" or "psychopath" does not feature in modern psychiatric classification systems. Cleckley, in his 1941 book *Mask of Sanity*, used the term "psychopath" to describe a cold, callous, predatory and impulsive individual. The Psychopathy Checklist—Revised (PCL-R)[6] is based on this concept. It encompasses both personality and behavioural components. See Box 2.

Antisocial personality disorder, dissocial personality disorder and psychopathy can be viewed as a diagnostic spectrum ranging from antisocial behaviours to cold, callous acts. It is important not to equate these disorders but to understand an individual's position on this spectrum.

Box 2: Psychopathy Checklist—Revised (PCL-R) Items

Personality Variables (Factor 1)	Anti-social Behaviour (Factor 2)
Glibness/superficial charm	Proneness to boredom
Grandiose sense of self-worth	Parasitic lifestyle
Pathological lying	Poor behavioural controls
Conning/manipulative	Early behavioural problems

[5] Bartlett K., Thomson L.D.G. and Johnstone E.C. (2001) *Mentally disordered offenders: an evaluation of the "Open Doors" Programme at HM Prison, Barlinnie*, Scottish Prison Service, Occasional Paper Series No. 2/2001.

[6] Hare R.D. (1991) *The Hare Psychopathy Checklist—Revised*, Multi-Health Systems, Toronto.

Personality Variables (Factor 1)	Anti-social Behaviour (Factor 2)
Lack of remorse or guilt	Lack of realistic plans
Shallow affect	Impulsivity
Callous/lack of empathy	Irresponsibility
Failure to accept responsibility for own actions	Frequent marital relations
	Juvenile delinquency
	Recall
	Criminal versatility
	Promiscuity

LEGAL DEFINITIONS OF MENTAL DISORDER

Mental disorder is defined under the Mental Health (Care and Treatment) (Scotland) Act 2003 as "any mental illness, personality disorder or learning disability however caused or manifested." A person is not mentally disordered only on account of sexual orientation; sexual deviancy; transsexualism; transvestism; dependence on, or use of, alcohol or drugs; behaviour that causes, or is likely to cause, harassment, alarm or distress to another person; or acting as no prudent person would act. **1–28**

Mental health legislation exists because people with mental disorder may lack insight into their illness, that is an understanding that they are ill and require treatment, or the ability to exercise their judgement in a considered way. They may therefore require protection of their rights and property, or detention and treatment. Almost 90 per cent of admissions to psychiatric hospitals are voluntary. The criteria for use of mental health legislation are set out in Chapter 3.

MENTAL DISORDER AND OFFENDING BEHAVIOUR

During the last 15 years a number of studies have demonstrated a clear association between major mental disorder and violence. The methodologies of these studies vary but include patient and population based studies. The results are summarised in Table 1. Major mental disorder is usually applied to schizophrenia, mania and major depressive episodes. **1–29**

Table 1: Association between Mental Disorder and Violence

Authors	Study Population	Increased Risk of Violence Associated with:
Swanson *et al*[7]	USA: Epidemiological catchment area survey	Schizophrenia (x4) Substance Abuse (x10) Comorbid schizophrenia and substance abuse (x15)
Eronen *et al*[8]	Finnish homicide cohort (male)	Schizophrenia (x6) ASPD (x10) Alcohol abuse (x11)
Hodgins *et al*[9]	Danish birth cohort (male)	Major mental disorder (x4) ASPD (x8) Drug misuse (x9) Alcohol misuse (x7)
Wessely[10]	UK: Patient cohort	Schizophrenia (x2)
Tiihonen *et al*[11]	Finnish birth cohort	Schizophrenia and alcohol abuse (x4)
Steadman *et al*[12]	USA: Longitudinal case controlled study—discharged patients	Comorbid substance abuse and major mental disorder (x2) Comorbid substance abuse and personality disorder or adjustment disorder (x3)

The actual number of offenders perpetrating serious violence with a major mental illness is, however, small. On average, some 15 people per year are sent from Scottish Courts to hospital with a restriction order on account of their mental disorder, serious index offence, past behaviour and perceived risk. The risk of suicide is much greater (10–15 per cent) than the risk of harm to others. Where violence does occur, the victim is seldom a stranger and much more likely to be a family member or carer.

---

[7] Swanson J., Holzer C.E., Ganju V.K. and Jono R.T. (1990) *Violence and psychiatric disorder in the community: evidence from the epidemiological catchment area surveys*, Hospital and Community Psychiatry 41, 761–770.

[8] Eronen M., Hakola P. and Tiihonen J. (1996) *Mental disorder and homicidal behaviour in Finland*, Archives of General Psychiatry 53, 497–501.

[9] Hodgins S., Mednick S.A., Brennan P.A., Schulsinger F and Engberg M (1996) *Mental disorder and crime: evidence form a Danish birth cohort*, Archives of General Psychiatry 53, 489–96.

[10] Wessely S. (1997) *The epidemiology of crime, violence, and schizophrenia*, British Journal of Psychiatry 172, 11–18.

[11] Tiihonen J., Isohanni M., Rasanen P., Koiranen M. and Moring J. (1997) *Specific major mental disorder and criminality: 26 year prospective study of the 1966 Northern Finland birth cohort*, American Journal of Psychiatry 154, 840–5.

[12] Steadman H.J., Mulvey E.P., Monahan J., Robbins P.C., Appelbaum P.S., Grisso T., Roth L.H. and Silver E. (1998) *Violence by people discharged from acute psychiatric inpatient facilities and by others in the same neighbourhood*, Archives of general psychiatry 55(5), 393–401.

Other disorders can lead to offending. Learning disability has a small association with arson and sexual offending. Organic disorders can cause disinhibited behaviour, aggression or offending secondary to forgetfulness, for example shoplifting. Substance abuse is associated with offending for financial gain to fund the purchase of the substance of choice, as well as violence. Bulimia nervosa can lead to shoplifting to obtain food for binge eating.

PSYCHIATRIC SERVICES

The blueprint for psychiatric services is set out in the Framework for **1–30** Mental Health Services in Scotland[13]. There are 15 Health Board areas in Scotland and, within these, services are organised on a divisional basis. Psychiatric services assess and treat people with mental disorder and encompass outpatient, day hospital and inpatient care. Staff work in multi-disciplinary teams which should ideally include a psychiatrist, psychiatric nurses, an occupational therapist, a social worker and a clinical psychologist. In reality, many teams function with medical and nursing staff. Social workers involved in psychiatric care are often specially trained mental health officers. They have a specific role under mental health legislation. The Mental Welfare Commission has a duty to protect people with mental disorders and to visit and report on psychiatric services. It is a major protective mechanism for patients. Its role is fully described in Chapter 3.

Forensic psychiatric services are purchased and administered by Health Boards under the Framework. In 2002 the Scottish Executive established the Forensic Mental Health Services Managed Care Network to oversee the development and organisation of forensic mental health services in Scotland[14]. It has no direct managerial control over services or purchasing power. Its role is to encourage and coordinate the development of services and to promote their consistency throughout the country.

PSYCHIATRIC HOSPITALS

There were 3,553 psychiatric beds in Scotland in 2001[15] for patients with **1–31** a mental illness, excluding the elderly and learning disabled. This number has fallen by 45 per cent since 1991 with the development of community care. There is tremendous pressure on these beds and, commonly, only patients who are acutely psychotic or suicidal are admitted to acute adult general psychiatry beds. There were over 28,000 admissions to psychiatric hospitals in 2001 and almost 90 per cent of patients were admitted on a voluntary basis.

---

[13] Scottish Office (1997) Framework for Mental Health Services in Scotland. NHS MEL (1997) 62; SWSG Circular 30/97; SODD Circular 30/97.
[14] Scottish Executive (2002) *The Right Place, the Right Time: Improving the patient journey for those who need secure mental health care.*
[15] Information and Services Division (ISD, 2004) Scottish Health Statistics: Mental Health, NHS National Services Scotland.

Different levels of secure psychiatric inpatient provision exist ranging from open wards, through locked wards and intensive psychiatric care units, to medium and high security facilities.

Intensive Psychiatric Care Units (IPCU)

1–32   IPCUs are designed to care for acutely disturbed patients and have higher staff/patient ratios. These units vary in their degree of sophistication; many are only a standard ward with a locked door, others are purposefully designed with good vision and security of staff and patients in mind, alarm systems, two locked doors operated as an air lock system and special furnishing. Usually patients in IPCUs are formally detained under mental health legislation and the average length of stay is short. Some of these units, however, are used in the rehabilitation of mentally disordered offenders who require a secure environment on a longer term basis but who are no longer acutely disturbed. This occurs in the absence of an appropriate facility elsewhere and is recognised to be highly unsatisfactory and to increase the risk of relapse and violence in a mentally disordered offender.

Smith and Humphreys[16] examined patients transferred to one such unit, the IPCU at the Royal Edinburgh Hospital, in 1991. There were 131 transfer episodes involving 97 patients of whom one-third were women. Just over half the patients had a diagnosis of schizophrenia, a quarter of hypomania and under a tenth of personality disorder. The reasons for transfer included physical violence (30 per cent), attempting to abscond (19 per cent), verbal threat (17 per cent), disruptive behaviour (16 per cent), self-harm (12 per cent) and damage to property (4 per cent). Seventy percent spent less than two weeks in that setting.

There are approximately 300 IPCU or low secure beds in Scotland.

Low Secure Units

1–33   In some areas of Scotland, notably Aberdeen, Glasgow and Perth, there are low secure units for mentally disordered offenders. These vary from a purpose-built facility at the Blair Unit in Aberdeen to adapted wards in the Murray Royal Hospital in Perth.

Medium Secure Units

1–34   In January 2001, Scotland opened its first medium secure unit in Edinburgh. The Orchard Clinic provides treatment for 50 mentally disordered offenders or others requiring similar services. It is a purpose-built unit situated in the grounds of the Royal Edinburgh Hospital[17]. It has three wards, one acute and two rehabilitation, all with single, en-suite rooms. The clinic provides a forensic psychiatry service to Lothian, Borders and Forth Valley Health Board Areas and will consider out of area transfers.

---

[16] Smith, A. (1997) *Survey of locked facilities in Scottish psychiatric hospitals*, Psychiatric Bulletin 21, 77–79.

[17] Nelson, D. (2003) *Service innovations: The Orchard Clinic: Scotland's first medium secure unit*, Psychiatric Bulletin 27(4), 105–107.

It admits patients usually aged 18 or over who are untried, unsentenced or convicted mentally disordered offenders liable to detention under the Mental Health (Care and Treatment) (Scotland) Act 2003 or the Criminal Procedure (Scotland) Act 1995. Occasionally it will accept non offence-related patients who require medium security because of major behavioural problems often posing a serious risk to others. All patients must require assessment or treatment of a mental illness and should not have an established principle diagnosis of learning disability, traumatic brain injury or personality disorder. They must present a risk to others or themselves arising from their mental illness such that medium secure care is the most appropriate and least restrictive treatment setting. The expected need for this treatment should not exceed two years.

Assessment and treatment are provided by multidisciplinary teams led by a consultant forensic psychiatrist. Each patient has a care plan which is regularly reviewed with risk assessment and management being an integral part. Discharge planning commences early in the process with liaison with local psychiatric and social work services. The clinic does not yet have a dedicated community-based team or a day care service. Throughput of patients is largely dependent on good communication and contact with adult general psychiatric services.

The development of three further medium secure units in Glasgow, the west and north of Scotland is expected and much needed. A medium secure unit for Northern Ireland (the Shannon Clinic) opened in 2005.

High Security Psychiatric Hospitals

There are four high security psychiatric hospitals in the United **1–35** Kingdom: Broadmoor Hospital in Berkshire (founded in 1863); Rampton Hospital in Nottinghamshire (1914); Ashworth Hospital in Merseyside (1990), which opened following the amalgamation of Park Lane (1974) and Mosside Hospitals (1913); and the State Hospital at Carstairs in Lanarkshire (1948). The first three hospitals serve England and Wales. The State Hospital offers a special security service, combining high and medium secure care, for the whole of Scotland and Northern Ireland. With the development of medium secure units elsewhere this remit is likely to change. A major difference between high and medium secure units is the presence of perimeter security.

The State Hospital provides care for patients who require to be detained in hospital under conditions of special security because of their "dangerous, violent or criminal propensities"[18]. All patients are legally detained under the Mental Health (Care and Treatment) (Scotland) Act 2003, the Criminal Procedure (Scotland) Act 1995 or the Crime and Punishment (Scotland) Act 1997. The State Hospital has 240 beds and 11 wards: one male admission, one female, one for patients with a primary diagnosis of learning disability, two rehabilitation and six generic continuing care male wards. Each patient in this setting requires ongoing assessment of his illness and potential risk. The assessment of risk examines violent episodes, or threatened actions, and considers any

---

[18] National Health Service (Scotland) Act 1978, s.102(2).

precipitating factors including deterioration in mental state, life events, substance misuse, non-compliance with treatment and social instability. A major aim of staff within the hospital is to prevent violent episodes and to de-escalate those in progress. High quality training is essential.

The population of the State Hospital has been studied extensively[19]. Patients were on average 34 years old and had spent 9 years in psychiatric hospitals. Seventy percent had a principle diagnosis of schizophrenia, and 15 per cent of learning disability. Secondary drug and alcohol problems were common. Although only five per cent had a primary diagnosis of antisocial personality disorder, this was a secondary diagnosis in a third of all patients. Approximately half were admitted following an offence, usually of a serious nature. A fifth of patients were transferred from prison and a third came from local psychiatric hospitals following incidents of violence, menace, self-harm, absconding, fire-raising or sexually inappropriate behaviour. Physical health problems were present in more than half the patients and adverse childhood events were frequently reported. Psychotic symptoms continued to occur in 50 per cent of patients and more than half were said not to require the full security of the State Hospital. In general this population was severely ill, relatively young and likely to require considerable care in the future in a variety of settings. Follow-up research on the population with schizophrenia has shown that 75 per cent remain in hospital.

The patient's management is organised by a multidisciplinary team comprising psychiatric, nursing, social work, psychology, occupational therapy and security staff. Regular case conferences are held, and reviews of detention carried out or formal reports on restricted patients prepared for the Scottish Executive. Patients receive a restriction order because of the nature of their index offence, previous behaviour and potential risk to the public. All movement outwith the hospital by restricted patients must be approved by the Scottish Executive. The Mental Health Tribunal reviews the restriction order. The progress of these patients is monitored by the Scottish Executive under guidance prepared by the Department of Health in the Memorandum of Procedure on Restricted Patients.

Treatment plans are developed at case conferences and aim to: improve the patient's mental state, social functioning, self care and self esteem; reduce aggressive or challenging behaviour; promote the use of coping techniques; encourage community links; and establish ongoing analysis of risk following each intervention.

The State Hospital is an institution and patients can spend prolonged periods there (four years on average). There is, therefore, considerable risk that institutionalised behaviour will develop and this is known to have a deleterious effect on the prognosis of mental disorder. Patients require access to activities, structure to their day and the opportunity to act as an individual. In order to provide this activity, the State Hospital has occupational departments such as woodwork, arts and crafts, gardens and laundry. Patients are given a choice as to which departments they

---

[19] Thomson, L.D.G., Bogue, J.P., Humphreys, M.S. and Johnstone, E.C. (1997) *The State Hospital Survey: a description of psychiatric patients in conditions of special security in Scotland*, Journal of Forensic Psychiatry, Vol. 8(2), 263–284.

would like to attend. In addition there are education and recreation departments.

Within the hospital there are psychotherapeutic groups on anger management, anxiety management, relaxation, drug and alcohol awareness and relapse prevention, coping with mental illness, communication skills, social skills training, assertiveness training and practical skills. There are specific programmes to address sexual and general offending. Alcoholics Anonymous hold meetings within the hospital.

Each year approximately one-quarter of patients leave the State Hospital. It is essential that good communication is established between the transferring and receiving teams. Ideally a pre-transfer case conference will take place and a treatment plan will be agreed.

Day Hospital

Day hospitals exist for those patients resident in the community who 1–36 require further support. Their use may avoid admission to hospital or assist in the rehabilitation of a patient moving from hospital into the community. Day hospitals offer assessment and treatment in the form of medication, psychotherapeutic groups, and occupational therapies.

Private Facilities

In May 2004, the first private secure psychiatric facility for patients 1–37 with mental illness (Churchill Clinic) opened in Scotland. It has 24 low secure beds divided between an intensive psychiatric care unit and a secure unit. In addition, there is a low secure unit for patients with learning disability in Dundee.

OUTPATIENT PSYCHIATRIC SERVICE AND CARE IN THE COMMUNITY

In 2001 there were over 350,000 psychiatric outpatient appointments in 1–38 Scotland. Patients who require ongoing care are supported by a Community Mental Health Team. People with mental disorders in the community require accommodation and access to employment schemes, social care, advocacy, a community mental health team, and specialist services, for example for drug and alcohol problems.

Community care provides support for people who need help to cope with life as independently and safely as possible. The NHS and Community Care Act 1990 provided a legal basis for this. Individuals are entitled to an assessment of their needs carried out by a local social work department. Successful care in the community requires continuity of care from hospital to the community, readily accessible services, and the provision of support in proportion to need. A detailed care plan records what services are in place, where they are provided and by whom, when they will be reviewed and, where appropriate, costs.

Mentally disordered offenders have access to general psychiatric day hospitals and community mental health teams. Ongoing liaison between general and forensic psychiatry is essential to ensure a continuous, rather than parallel, system of patient care. Serious offenders, however, with a moderate to high risk of future violence, often remain under the care of forensic psychiatry. Comprehensive forensic mental health services extending into the community, such as the day hospital for mentally disordered offenders in Perth or the community forensic mental health team in Forth Valley, are rare. These require to be developed.

Care Programme Approach

1–39   The Care Programme Approach (CPA) is a form of care planning designed to ensure structured arrangements for health and social care for patients with major mental disorders. CPA is used if a patient is detained under mental health legislation, has had a prolonged admission or requires a complex package of care. Planning begins well before discharge to ensure that the individual has satisfactory accommodation, social care and mental health services. A care manager or keyworker is identified as a focal contact point in each case. Meetings are held involving the person concerned, their relatives, carers or advocacy where appropriate, and staff from the relevant professions. Services are agreed, review dates set and clear lines of communication established so that if problems arise, action is taken. Coordinators oversee the whole CPA process and ensure that meetings take place and documentation is updated. Some areas use the concept of augmented CPA for patients identified as particularly vulnerable, or a risk to themselves or others.

THE SCOTTISH LEGAL SYSTEM

INTRODUCTION

In order to carry out the varied range of professional duties incumbent **2–01** upon mental health professionals, it is important that they have a general understanding of the operation of the Scottish legal system in the areas in which they may be involved. This chapter sets out the main component elements of interest to mental health professionals and provides references to further works where more details about each aspect can be found.

CIVIL AND CRIMINAL LAW

Lawyers generally divide the law into two distinct areas, at least for the **2–02** purposes of procedure. Civil law governs the relationships between individuals and between individuals and the state in areas like taxation, contract, debt, damages, company law, partnership, marriage, adoption, capacity and, of course, civil detention under mental health legislation. Criminal law in Scotland, on the other hand, consists almost exclusively of the State taking action against a person or a company on the grounds that the person or company is alleged to have committed a crime or offence. There can be overlaps; thus, for example, failure to fence a dangerous machine in a factory can lead to a criminal prosecution and a civil action for damages by any person injured by the machine. Equally, a criminal assault can lead to a criminal court awarding a compensation order to the victim, or to separate action by the victim in a civil court.

Generally, however, the two are kept apart and have different forms of procedure and different courts for the resolution of problems.

Psychiatrists can become involved in both types of procedure as expert witnesses and may initiate action in the civil courts seeking power compulsorily to detain and treat a patient. Actions for the detention of patients, a species of civil action, are considered in Chapter 3.

The Civil Courts

There are two levels of civil court in Scotland: Sheriff courts and the **2–03** Court of Session. Sheriff courts are organised on a regional basis, called sheriffdoms. There are 6 sheriffdoms: Grampian, Highlands and Islands; Tayside, Central and Fife; Lothian and Borders; North Strathclyde;

---

[1] Chapter author: Prof. J.J. McManus LL.B., Ph.D.

Glasgow and Strathkelvin; South Strathclyde, Dumfries and Galloway. Each sheriffdom has a sheriff principal and a number of sheriffs depending on the size of the area. In civil matters, but not in criminal, appeal lies from the sheriff to the sheriff principal, or to the Court of Session. All full-time and part-time sheriffs are legally qualified people, with a minimum of 10 years' experience as advocates or solicitors. Vacancies are now publicly advertised and candidates are interviewed by the Judicial Appointments Board[2], which makes recommendations to the First Minister. Appointments are made by the Queen on the recommendation of the First Minister. Appointments are made to a specific sheriffdom, with a small number of "floating" sheriffs, who can sit anywhere in Scotland. Sheriffs can only be dismissed for inability, neglect of duty or misbehaviour. In general, sheriffdoms can only deal with matters which arise within, or concern a defender resident within, their geographical area.

Sheriff courts have exclusive jurisdiction in civil cases where the amount of money involved is less than £1500. In most cases involving sums above this amount, the parties can choose whether to initiate proceedings in the Sheriff Court or in the Court of Session. Certain cases, for example petitions for the winding up of companies with a share capital of more than £120,000, can only be heard in the Court of Session. The Court of Session sits only in Edinburgh and has jurisdiction throughout Scotland. It is composed of the Senators of the College of Justice, of whom there are about to be 34 in all, each appointed by the Queen on the recommendation of the First Minister after a recommendation from the Judicial Appointments Board. All are qualified lawyers, with a minimum of five years' experience as a sheriff, sheriff principal or with right of audience in the Court of Session, and are protected from dismissal except for inability, neglect of duty or misbehaviour and subject to a retiral age of 70. The Lord President and the Lord Justice Clerk, Scotland's most senior two judges, are appointed by the Crown on the advice of the Prime Minister. Technically, the Court of Session is a *collegiate* court, which means that all judges have equal powers. The judges are, however, divided into an Inner House and an Outer House, with the Inner House further subdivided into a First and Second division. The Inner House consists of the more senior judges and generally deals with appeals. The Inner House may call in judges from the Outer House if required. The Outer House deals with cases at first instance (that is, as the first court to deal with the matter). Maintaining the notion of collegiality, the process by which a decision of the Outer House can be challenged is called a reclaiming motion rather than an appeal. Such motions are heard by a minimum of three judges, again sitting in Edinburgh. In difficult, complex or novel cases, the number of judges can be increased and the greater the number of judges, the more authoritative the decision. Further appeal lies to the House of Lords in London, where convention usually ensures a minimum of one Scottish judge sits when a case from Scotland is being considered. In a normal year, fewer than 10 cases go from Scotland to the House of Lords.

---

[2] The Judicial Appointments Board, composed of senior judges and lay people, was established in 2001 in order to render the appointment process more transparent and independent of government.

The hierarchy of civil courts can be presented diagrammatically thus:

Fig. 1:

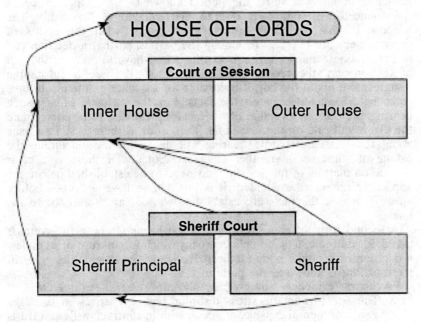

Scottish Civil Courts

HOUSE OF LORDS

Court of Session

Inner House

Outer House

Sheriff Court

Sheriff Principal

Sheriff

Arrows indicate lines of appeal

Judges in civil cases generally sit without a jury. There are provisions for juries in civil cases in the Court of Session and when used they consist of 12 members. The commonest kind of case in which a jury is used is actions for personal injury.

Civil Procedure

Parties to most civil cases are known as the pursuer (the person, **2–04** company or local or central government department initiating the action) and the defender (the party against whom or which the action is brought). Minor civil cases, *i.e.* those involving actions for sums less than £1500, are initiated by service of a summons in standard form. Other cases involve the issue of a summons which consists three parts:

(a) The *Conclusion* (in the Court of Session) or *Crave* (in the sheriff court): a statement of what the pursuer is asking the court to order.
(b) The *Condescendence*: a detailed statement of all the alleged facts which the pursuer will rely on to show that the order requested should be given.

(c) The *Pleas in Law*: the pursuer's understanding of the law which should lead to the conclusion being sought in the face of the facts alleged.

After the summons has been served, the defender is entitled to provide answers to the statements made under each of these heads. The provision of answers starts the period known as the "Open Record" (pronounced with emphasis on the first syllable of "record"). The purpose of this period is to determine exactly what the points of disagreement are between or among the parties, so that a decision can be made about what form the proceedings may have to take. At the end of the process, the record is "closed". Then, if there is substantial disagreement about the law, it is possible for a debate on the law to take place before any hearing on the facts. For the purpose of any such hearing, the pursuer's version of the facts is presumed to be correct and the Court will rule on the law alone. Thereafter, if there is still an issue about the facts, a separate hearing will deal with this, including the calling of witnesses and other evidence. Equally, if there is a clear dispute on matters of fact, or the facts need to be established before the applicable law can be decided, it is possible to have a "proof before answer", where the facts are established without any reference to the law.

A second form of civil procedure is the *petition*, where the court is asked, for example, to wind up a company which is bankrupt or to review a decision of a public body (Judicial Review). The originating party in these actions is known as the petitioner.

Psychiatric evidence may be crucially important in several types of case. Thus post-traumatic stress disorder regularly arises in damages cases; issues of mental capacity are dealt with in contract, wills and trusts cases; mental health issues may be important in adoption and matrimonial cases, as well as in the appointment of trustees. In all such cases, psychiatric evidence is evidence about a matter of fact in the eyes of the law. Your crucial contribution may thus be to the condescendence at the Open Record stage and to the hearing of evidence if the case goes the full length. Many, indeed most, civil cases are settled out of court by agreement between the parties. You should therefore not be surprised if you hear nothing further about a case in which you have been asked to provide an opinion. Equally, some cases can take an inordinate time to reach the final stages, so it is not safe to assume that a case is over simply because you have heard nothing about it for a long time. You should maintain all records until you hear from whoever commissioned your report that the matter has been concluded. There are no time limits once civil proceedings have been started, though there are limits which apply between any event giving rise to a claim and the claim being intimated.

The standard of proof in civil cases is generally "on the balance of probabilities" and thus lower than the criminal standard of "beyond reasonable doubt". The precise meaning of these standards is not absolutely clear, but it is evident that the standard of proof required is lower in civil cases than in criminal. In all civil cases, the burden of proof falls on the person initiating the action.

When a case goes to court, judges will usually take time to consider their decision—in the normal Scottish terminology, "take it to avizandum". Civil judgments order, forbid or refuse to order or forbid certain conduct on the part of parties, grant or refuse damages to a party for the breach of their legal rights or declare what a party's legal rights, duties or status were, are or are to become in the eyes of the law. Commonly the court will award *expenses* to the winning party so that the losing party has to pay the costs of both sides to the action.

Judicial Review is a special procedure for challenging any decision-making body whose powers are given by statute, agreement or other document when the challenger (*the petitioner*) alleges that the body has exceeded or abused its powers, acted unreasonably or failed to exercise its discretion properly. Cases are heard by a single judge, in the Court of Session only, and the procedure is expedited in order to give a real remedy to the petitioner. An *interim order* (an order demanding or forbidding particular action immediately, pending a full hearing of the case) may be made at first hearing to safeguard the petitioner's position. The role of the court is, however, to review the process by which the decision was taken rather than to consider an appeal against the decision. Thus it is not concerned with the merits of the decision (unless the decision was so unreasonable that no reasonable body could have reached it) and cases mostly proceed by way of legal debate alone, the facts having been agreed between the parties in advance of the hearing. The availability of this form of hearing since 1985 has contributed greatly to the awareness of those exercising public powers of the need to act in compliance with the rules of natural justice, and in particular the need to be seen to act fairly.

Scots Criminal Law

Criminal courts deal almost exclusively with allegations brought on **2–05** behalf of the state that a person or body has breached the criminal law. (There is still the possibility of a private criminal prosecution, with the consent of the Lord Advocate or the court, but in practice this happens very rarely.) Much of Scotland's criminal law remains in the form of Common Law—*i.e.* it is not written down in the form of Acts of Parliament—and the courts retain the power to declare that conduct not previously prosecuted as criminal can be so. It is also the case that the maximum sentence for all violations of the common law is life imprisonment, although, as will be seen, each court in the system has its own maximum power. The terms "crime" and "offence" are not terms of art in Scots law. "Offence" is generally used to refer to less serious matters, or to matters rendered criminal by statute, but the use is not precise. There is a strong presumption that all crimes and offences must consist of two parts, the *actus reus* and the *mens rea*. The *actus reus* is the physical requirements of the crime—the removal of property without authorisation in the case of a theft. The *mens rea*, or *dole* (an older Scots term, derived from the Latin *dolum*, thought by many to be a more accurate term than *mens rea*), is the mental element required to make the action criminal for the individual accused—the knowledge that authorisation was lacking, the intention permanently to deprive the authorised possessor of possession and the ability to control one's actions in accordance with one's will. Conviction generally requires proof beyond reasonable doubt of both *actus reus* and *mens rea*. Where an

accused lacks *mens rea* because of a mental illness, the appropriate
verdict is "not guilty by reason of insanity", rather than the illogical
"guilty but insane". The very notion of guilt requires some connection
between the actor's mind and the action which the actor was able to
control at the time.

There is an irrebuttable presumption that a child under the age of
eight cannot form *mens rea* (the age of criminal responsibility being
eight, one of the youngest ages in Europe).

The Criminal Process

2–06   The body technically responsible for the investigation of crime in
Scotland is the *Procurator Fiscal Service*, under the authority of the Lord
Advocate. In practice, of course, it is the police who carry out investigations, but they report to the procurator fiscal, who can, and does, ask the
police to gather further evidence.

The police in Scotland are organised into eight forces. Each chief
constable has a considerable amount of autonomy in the allocation of
officers and in setting priorities for the force area. Individual police
officers exercise considerable discretion in performing their roles and it
may be that good relationships build up between officers and psychiatric
services which encourage officers to think more often of direct referral
to such services in appropriate circumstances.

The *Crown Office*, headed by the *Lord Advocate*, is responsible for all
criminal justice policy in Scotland and for the operation of the criminal
justice system. The Lord Advocate and the Solicitor General are
members of the Scottish Executive, appointed by the Queen on the
advice of the First Minister and with the approval of the Scottish
Parliament. As a political appointee, the Lord Advocate has the
important role of advising the Scottish Executive on all legal matters and
is accountable to the Scottish Parliament for the actions of the Office. By
convention, individual decisions about prosecutions are not questioned
in public. As head of the prosecution system, the Lord Advocate
appoints a number of advocates depute (or Crown Counsel) to assist in
the matter of deciding on prosecutions and actually carrying out these
prosecutions in the highest courts. The Lord Advocate will also appear
in court in particularly important cases (for example in the case against
the alleged Lockerbie bombers). Advocates depute are part-time temporary appointees, who may continue with other work as advocates. The
Crown Office develops policy in relation to prosecution decisions and
provides general guidelines to the Procurator Fiscal Service.

The Procurator Fiscal Service is the local agent of the Crown Office,
spread throughout Scotland on a regional basis, with the Regions
corresponding to the sheriffdoms described above. Each Region has a
Regional Procurator Fiscal, who is assisted by a number of procurators
fiscal reflecting the volume of work in the area. All fiscals are legally
qualified as advocates or solicitors and are civil servants. Acting on
instructions from the Crown Office, they are charged with exercising
discretion in relation to all reports forwarded to them by the police. In
serious cases, they refer to the Crown Office for the instructions of the
advocates depute or the Lord Advocate. In all other cases they make
important decisions themselves about whether to prosecute, what to
prosecute for and where to prosecute.

In making these decisions, procurators fiscal have regard to two main factors:

1. Is there enough evidence to justify prosecution?
2. Is prosecution in the public interest?

The evidence test is a reasonably simple one. All relevant components of the charge have to be proved beyond reasonable doubt. Traditionally this means that in Scotland *corroboration* is required for each material fact. Corroboration means that there has to be a minimum of two independent pieces of evidence confirming something—not necessarily two witnesses, but two different bits of evidence. Thus, for example, an eye witness and fingerprints in a particular location could amount to corroboration in a case of housebreaking. The fiscal then assesses the credibility of the evidence available and makes a decision on whether there is enough credible evidence to support a conviction on any charge.

Assessing the public interest in the matter is a more difficult task. In some areas, there may be instructions from the Crown Office that certain types of offence should—or should not—routinely be prosecuted when the evidence test is met. Thus, for example, there was a period when homosexual conduct in private between consenting adults was still illegal in Scotland, though not in England. It is widely thought that there was a policy of not prosecuting such behaviour in the period leading up to the law change in Scotland. Equally, there was for a while a policy of not prosecuting travelling people for illegal camping in areas where there was no provision of local authority, or other, sites for them. Clearly, such policies are usually kept confidential—it should not be the function of the Crown Office to change the criminal law by stealth—but it is also sensible that there is a mechanism for bringing common sense into play in the operation of criminal justice.

Public interest considerations can also apply to decisions in relation to individuals alleged to have broken the law. Thus, for example, it might be thought that prosecuting the elderly, female, first offender shoplifter is unlikely to make much of a contribution to protecting the public; or bringing further minor charges against someone who is already in prison serving a lengthy sentence; or prosecuting someone who is clearly suffering from a mental illness and who is being offered, and is prepared to accept, appropriate treatment from the health services. Accordingly, this is an area in which mental health services may have a significant input. Indeed, in some areas there are formally established *diversion from prosecution* schemes under which fiscals or the police refer cases they consider possibly appropriate for assessment by psychiatrists before a decision on prosecution is made. If the psychiatrist considers that the person could benefit from mental health intervention, a service is available and the person consents to accept it, the fiscal may then decide not to proceed with a prosecution. This process can ensure that the person obtains treatment quickly, that the public is protected and that the costs of prosecution, including possible adverse effects on the mental health of the alleged offender, are avoided.

The process of decision making by fiscals is called *marking*. The first decision is whether or not to proceed at all. When it is decided not to bring proceedings, the papers are marked "No Proceedings", leading to the common abbreviation "No Pros". While the rate of such markings varies throughout the country, it is not uncommon for 30–35 per cent of cases to be disposed of in this way. Fiscals rarely give reasons in public for their decisions, so it is not known for sure why this figure is reached.

If a case is to be prosecuted, several other decisions need to be made. The most important is whether to prosecute on *indictment* or on *complaint*. An indictment leads to *Solemn Procedure*, before a judge and jury, and is used in more serious cases; a complaint leads to *Summary Procedure*, before a judge on his own, and can only result in relatively minor punishments. There are two courts available in each of solemn and summary procedure, one with greater power than the other, and the fiscal must decide which of the two to use. Some crimes and offences can only be prosecuted in one way. Thus, murder, rape and treason can only be prosecuted on indictment and in the High Court, while many statutory offences can only be dealt with summarily. For most of our crimes, however, a choice must be made and, given the massive potential difference in the punishments available, the decision is a very important one. Some conventions, as well as the law itself, have built up to assist the decision makers. Thus, assaults not involving broken limbs or stab wounds normally go to the lowest court; those involving broken bones and cuts requiring stitches to the second level; and those involving weapons, severe injury or permanent disfigurement to the highest court. Two major factors are taken into account—the nature of the alleged conduct and the previous criminal record of the alleged offender. Again, however, information about the personal circumstances of the alleged offender may influence the decision and thus there is room for input from mental health practitioners.

The next important decision is about what charge(s) should be brought. The same circumstances might support a variety of charges. Thus a serious assault can be charged as attempted murder or assault to severe injury, permanent disfigurement and/or danger of life. The exact nature of the charge will have a considerable bearing on the level of punishment awarded if a conviction is secured. It is the discretion available in this regard which creates the possibility of *Plea Negotiation* in Scotland. It should be noted that we do not have plea bargaining— that process involves the judge and a deal being done about the sentence which will be imposed if the person pleads guilty to a charge. The Scottish practice involves the defence and the prosecution negotiating the precise terms of the charge with a view to reaching an agreement about a guilty plea and avoiding the full trial process with all its attendant expense and inconvenience for witnesses and juries. Obviously, the defence is looking for a reduction in the seriousness of the charge, either by reducing the charge from, say, rape to sexual assault, or by deleting reference to aggravating factors in the narrative of the charge. There is a limit to what the prosecution will accept, but there might also be pressure on the prosecution to obtain a guilty plea to assist the protection of a vulnerable witness or avoid the expense of a trial. Often negotiations take place at the very last minute, resulting in cases which were thought to be going to trial, and for which jurors and witnesses have already been cited, being cancelled on the day of the hearing. This causes much understandable anger, but it may result from the fact that it is only at this stage that both prosecution and defence are fully prepared for the case. Attempts have been made, by the introduction of inter-mediate diets in summary cases and first diets in sheriff solemn cases, to reduce the incidence of last minute changes of plea, but the problem is still with us.

Once a decision is made to prosecute, the relevant summons or indictment must be served on the accused and proceedings commence. While there is no common law time limit for bringing prosecutions, in solemn proceedings the trial must start within 12 months of the person's first appearance in court. If the person is in custody, the indictment must be served within 80 days of full committal and the trial must commence within 110 days of that committal. There are provisions for extending these time limits, but they are generally strictly adhered to, giving Scotland one of the shortest average periods in custody pending trial in the world. Summary proceedings must commence within six months of the alleged offence (there are some statutory offences with different time limits), and the trial of a person held in custody must commence within 40 days of committal. Persons who are admitted to bail (*i.e.* not kept in custody pending trial) do not benefit from these time limits and it is possible for the court to admit someone to bail close to the expiry of a time limit and continue with proceedings thereafter.

A further discretion available pre-trial relates to which, if any, previous convictions of the accused person should be *libelled* (listed along with the charge and to be presented to the judge in the event of a conviction, but not before). An accused must be given advance notice of any previous convictions which are to be presented to the court, but the fiscal may only libel the ones relevant to the particular charge now being brought (or the major or recent ones). Since previous convictions can be taken into account in sentencing a convicted person, this can be an important decision.

The Criminal Courts

(a) Summary Courts

The lower level of summary criminal court is the District Court. Each **2–07** of Scotland's former District and Islands authorities was empowered to establish a court to replace the former Burgh Police courts and Justice of the Peace courts. The judges in these courts are lay people (with the exception of the Stipendiary Magistrates, legally qualified judges who sit in Glasgow District Court, appointed by the local authority, and have the same powers as a sheriff sitting summarily) who have been appointed as Justices of the Peace and undertaken a course of training before sitting in court. Appointments of JPs are made by the Crown on the advice of the First Minister. They sit, either on their own or in benches of three depending on the area, with a legally qualified clerk of court to advise them on legal issues. The maximum sentencing power of the court is a fine of level four (currently £2500) and imprisonment for a maximum of 60 days. Prosecutions are conducted by the procurator fiscal and legal aid is available for accused persons. These courts deal with many motoring offences, public order offences and minor thefts and assaults. They provide a relatively cheap and efficient method of local justice, allowing communities to respond appropriately to minor offences within the local area. Appeals from the District Court go directly to the High Court of Criminal Appeal in Edinburgh.

The higher summary court is the Sheriff Court. The same judges who sit in civil matters, within the same geographical boundaries, have criminal jurisdiction, with the only difference being that the sheriffs principal have no appellate jurisdiction. A sheriff, sitting without a jury, has the power to sentence a convicted person to a fine up to level five (currently £5000) and imprisonment up to three months (six months in the case of second or subsequent conviction for some offences and nine months and a year under particular statutes). Appeal lies directly to the High Court of Criminal Appeal in Edinburgh.

(b) Solemn Courts

2–08   The lower level of solemn courts is the Sheriff Court. Now sitting with a jury (of 15 persons) the same sheriffs can hear cases on indictment, where their sentencing powers are unlimited in terms of fines and up to five years imprisonment. Appeals from this court go to the High Court of Criminal Appeal in Edinburgh.

The higher court is the High Court of Justiciary, as a court of first instance. It consists of the same senators of the college of justice who sit in the Court of Session, though they wear different robes when sitting in criminal cases and are called Lords Commissioners of Justiciary. The court can sit anywhere throughout Scotland (and, in special circumstances, it seems, even The Hague can be declared a part of Scotland!). At first instance, there is a single judge and a jury of 15 people. The Court has unlimited sentencing powers. Appeal lies to the High Court as the Court of Criminal Appeal.

(c) The Appeal Court

2–09   As has been noted, all criminal appeals in Scotland go to the High Court as the court of criminal appeal. This court sits only in Edinburgh and consists of a minimum of three judges, sitting without a jury. A greater number of judges can be called in in cases where a particularly difficult or novel point of law has arisen. The larger the court, the more authoritative is its judgment. When dealing with appeals against sentence, the High Court can increase as well as decrease the sentence.

There is no further appeal on criminal matters in Scotland—the House of Lords has no jurisdiction in Scottish criminal law, unlike the position in civil law. The criminal courts can be presented diagrammatically as follows:

Fig. 2:

Scottish Criminal Courts

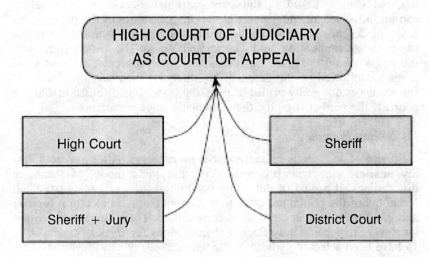

Arrows indicate lines of appeal

SOLEMN COURTS   SUMMARY COURTS

Criminal Procedure

In preparation of a case, witnesses are often asked to attend at the **2–10** office of the defence solicitor or the procurator fiscal to be precognosed (interviewed in relation to the evidence they have of relevance to the case). Attendance for precognition can be enforced, with penalties available for refusal to attend or failure to reveal relevant evidence. If the witness fails to co-operate with informal requests, resort is had to formal citations to attend for precognition. It is thus best, if you are asked to attend for precognition, to agree to attend and attempt to find a time and venue mutually suitable. At any such meeting, the psychiatrist will wish to restrict discussion to the details of any pre-prepared report.

(a) Summary Procedure

Summary cases start with the issue of a summons, requiring the person **2–11** to be brought from custody or to appear in person before the court. After the accused is identified, the charge is read and the accused is asked to plead to the charge. If a guilty plea is entered (as happens in most cases), the procurator fiscal is asked to provide a statement of the details of the crime and will also lodge any previous convictions relating to the offender (of which the offender will have been given prior notice). The offender or his lawyer is then invited to present a plea in mitigation and the court moves on to sentencing.

If a plea of not guilty is entered, the case moves on to trial, usually at a later date. Each trial commences with the prosecution evidence, without opening speeches, which are a feature of English trials. Each witness is examined by the prosecution first, then subject to cross-examination by the defence and re-examination by the prosecution. Different rules apply to each stage of the examination. Thus, leading questions are disallowed in the examination-in-chief, the first questioning, but can be asked in the cross-examination. The re-examination cannot introduce any new material. At the conclusion of the prosecution case, the defence may lead its own witnesses, who are then subject to the same cross-examination and re-examination as the prosecution witnesses. When all the evidence is complete, the prosecutor addresses the judge(s), followed by the defence. The judge(s) then reach a verdict. If the verdict is not guilty or not proven, the accused is dismissed from the court. If the verdict is guilty, the sentencing stage commences.

(b) Solemn Procedure

2–12   Service of an indictment commences proceedings. After any preliminary hearings, the trial proceeds along the same model as summary proceedings. If a plea of not guilty is adhered to, a jury is empanelled. Members of the public are chosen at random from the electoral register and cited to appear in court on a certain date. Their names are written on slips of paper and are selected at random by the clerk of court. Once 15 have been selected without challenge (and challenges must now show a valid cause), they are invited to swear an oath to try the case fairly and proceedings begin. The only difference from summary proceedings is at the end, when the trial judge "charges" the jury, that is instructs them on matters of law, before they adjourn to reach their decision.

(c) Verdicts

2–13   As is well known, Scottish criminal courts have three verdicts available to them, guilty, not guilty and not proven. This is a hangover from the olden days, when the verdicts were simply "proven" or "not proven", on the basis that the court was asked to rule on whether the Crown had succeeded in proving the charge brought against the accused. Not guilty and not proven have the same effect these days, with the accused being released from court. Scottish juries are only required to provide majority verdicts—a minimum of eight must vote for guilty before a guilty verdict can be reached. (This is unlike the position in England, where a jury, of 12 people, must first attempt to reach a unanimous verdict and only if they fail in this attempt to obtain at least a 10–2 verdict.)

Sentencing[3]

2–14   When a person has pled, or been found by a judge or jury, guilty of any charge, the court cannot proceed to sentence in solemn proceedings until and unless the Crown, in the person of the fiscal or the advocate depute, "moves for sentence". This is normally done automatically, and is generally taken for granted in summary proceedings, but there may be

---

[3] The matter of sentencing in Scotland is regulated, albeit with a light touch, by the Criminal Procedure (Scotland) Act 1995, as amended on many occasions (hereafter, "the 1995 Act"). Anyone consulting the Act should ensure that they are dealing with the most up-to-date version of the text.

circumstances in which the Crown decides that no sentence is necessary in the public interest. Thus, for example, if the guilty person is very ill, or if the charge actually proved is much less serious than the one alleged, it may be thought inappropriate to move for sentence. In normal circumstances, however, the move follows conviction. The prosecutor generally says very little, emphasising perhaps the nature of the offence and presenting (or "libelling") the convicted person's previous convictions, notice of which must have been given to the accused person beforehand. The defence is then asked if it wishes to make a plea in mitigation, giving an opportunity to stress any points which might be in the favour of the convicted person. If the defence raises any points in the plea in mitigation which the prosecution dispute, the court may order a *proof in mitigation*. This is a formal hearing, in open court, where evidence is led by the defence and the prosecution in relation to the claims made in the plea in mitigation. Thus, it is possible that psychiatric evidence could be led at this stage if the convicted person claims, for example, that he is undertaking treatment for a relevant illness. Proofs in mitigation are not frequently held, though some sheriffs in particular make use of them to stop routine pleas in mitigation claiming unrealistic future plans for the convicted person. With or without a proof in mitigation, sentence is then a matter for the judge to decide.

Sentencing judges in Scotland have a wide discretion when it comes to sentencing. There is no sentencing statute which lays down general guidelines; the High Court has the power to establish such guidelines[4], but has been very reluctant to exercise this power; even the training system for judges, which, save for that covering the lay justices in the District Courts, is of comparatively recent origin, does not attempt to be too definitive on the matter. Indeed, judges treasure their independence in sentencing as in all matters. The result is a system, if such it can be called, which is unpredictable, varied and sometimes confusing. Each court, as described above, has its own maximum powers. Sheriff solemn courts have the discretion to remit cases to the High Court when the sheriff considers that the case requires a sentence beyond the sheriff's powers. Individual statutes lay down maximum sentences for particular offences, and only rarely set out minimum sentences. The mandatory sentence for murder is established by statute as life imprisonment, with the judge now required to set a minimum period which must be served before the person can be considered for release on licence by the Parole Board. In establishing this period the judge must only have reference to the nature of the offence, the offender's previous convictions and the stage, if any, at which the person pled guilty. Judges are explicitly forbidden to take into account issues of public protection in sentencing to life imprisonment. The main other mandatory sentence is in the Road Traffic Act 1988, where persons convicted of driving under the influence of alcohol must, save in very exceptional circumstances, be banned from driving. An attempt has also been made, by an amendment to the 1995 Act introduced by s.2 of the Crime and Punishment (Scotland) Act 1997, to impose a minimum sentence, of seven years, on persons convicted for the third time of trafficking in class A drugs. However, judges are given

---

[4] s.118(7) of the 1995 Act.

discretion to look at any circumstances which "relate to any of the offences or to the offender and which would make that sentence unjust"[5]. In all other cases, the judges have discretion, with the result that the outcome can be very much dependent on the personality of the judge.

All courts have the discretion to adjourn before sentence and to order that the person be remanded in custody, on bail or simply ordained to appear, usually with a view to obtaining reports on the person. Reports must be obtained when a court is considering imposing a custodial sentence on a person under 21, or a person over 21 who has not previously been sentenced directly to custody. Equally, reports are required before probation or community service can be used as disposals, but the courts have discretion to seek reports in any circumstances. Custodial remands are subject to a maximum period of three weeks, with two weeks being the most common period. Non-custodial remands are subject to a maximum of four weeks, though this can be extended to eight weeks in some circumstances. If the court wishes to obtain reports specifically about the offender's mental health, it will continue the case, for a maximum of three weeks, with the person remanded in custody, on bail or committed to hospital. A hospital committal can only be ordered on the evidence of a medical practitioner that the convicted person appears to be suffering from a mental disorder and that a suitable bed is available for the person in hospital. Psychiatric opinion may also be sought as part of any other report for the court, and must be sought if psychiatric treatment is to be a condition of any probation order. Psychological reports may also be sought in any case.

The commonest reports sought are "Social Enquiry Reports" (SERs), written by Local Authority social workers. The worker will provide a full background on the person and, usually, an assessment of the suitability of any community-based resources as a disposal for the case. The worker may thus wish to investigate the availability of mental health services in appropriate cases.

Courts may also defer sentence, for any period they consider appropriate (as long as the person is not in custody) and subject to such conditions as they see fit[6]. If the person is remanded in custody for the period of deferral, the maximum period of remand is three weeks. The power of deferral can be used to allow a convicted person released on bail the opportunity to show good conduct or to make amends for the crime committed; it might also be used to enable the person to show willingness to engage in treatment or remedial work for any condition or habit which led to the criminality. Thus, sentence may be deferred to see if the convicted person will co-operate with psychiatric intervention or drug treatment or counselling. Conditions attached to a deferred sentence cannot be directly enforced. However, failure to keep to any such conditions can certainly be taken into account when the person returns for final disposal by the court, as can good co-operation with the conditions. This is an extremely flexible mechanism which leaves all of the powers of the court available while allowing a period of testing for

---

[5] s.205B(3) of the 1995 Act.
[6] s.202 of the 1995 Act.

the convicted person. It should not be confused with the English suspended sentence, where a sentence is passed but its implementation is suspended subject to certain conditions. Scotland knows not the suspended sentence.

Main Sentences Available to Scottish Courts

(a) *Absolute Discharge*: the lightest disposal available to the courts, **2–15** an absolute discharge is given in circumstances where the court considers it inexpedient to impose any punishment. In summary cases, the court does not proceed to conviction. The only circumstances in which an absolute discharge can be used against a person are when subsequent criminal proceedings are taken against that person.

(b) *Admonition*: next in seriousness is the admonition, where the **2–16** court simply gives the person a telling-off. This counts as a conviction for all purposes.

(c) *Fines*: fines account for some 78 per cent of all court disposals. **2–17** Maximum fines for statutory crimes and offences are laid down in the statute, while those for common law offences are set by the power of the sentencing court. Maxima are now expressed in levels, to allow for inflation-related upgrades without the necessity of amending each single piece of legislation. The levels are currently:

> Level 1 £200
> Level 2 £500
> Level 3 £1000
> Level 4 £2500
> Level 5 £5000

In imposing a fine, the court must have regard to the means of the offender, insofar as these are known to the court. Normally, it must also allow time to pay the fine (unless the person does not wish time to pay, or appears not to need such time, or does not have a fixed address or for "some other special reason" the court considers that time should not be allowed). The ultimate sanction for non-payment of a fine is the imposition of a period in custody, though the alternative of supervised attendance orders is being developed throughout the country[7].

(d) *Probation*[8]: any court other than the district court may dispose **2–18** of a case by means of a probation order instead of a sentence, if it has obtained reports on the offender and considers this an appropriate disposal in the circumstances of the offence and the offender. The order requires the person to be under the supervision of a named local authority and to comply with all the conditions of the order. Conditions can include anything the court thinks appropriate—for example, to attend drug or

---

[7] s.235 of the 1995 Act.
[8] s.228 of the 1995 Act.

alcohol counselling, to perform unpaid work for the community, to make compensation payments to any victim and to reside in any specified place for a maximum of 12 months. Under s.230 of the 1995 Act, a condition requiring the person to submit to treatment for a mental condition may be imposed in the order, but only where a doctor approved for the purpose by a Health Board gives evidence that the offender's condition requires, and may be susceptible to, such treatment and does not warrant detention under a hospital order. The court must specify if the treatment is to be in- or outpatient, must be sure that the treatment is available and must name the doctor or chartered psychologist in charge of the treatment. The treatment order can last for the duration of the probation order. The overall probation order must last between six months and three years in total and can be varied or discharged on application to the court at any time. Breach of probation can lead to another sentence being imposed for the original offence, a fine for the breach itself, the addition of a community service order to the probation order or variation in the order, subject to the maximum three year period. The full details of the order must be explained to the person and the acceptance of the person obtained.

2–19   (e) *Community Service Order*: where a person is convicted of a crime or offence which could be dealt with by means of a custodial sentence, the court may impose as an alternative an order requiring the person to perform unpaid community work for between 80 and 240 hours in summary cases or 300 hours in solemn cases. The court must be satisfied that there is work available, that the person is suitable and that the person agrees to perform the work. The work must be completed within 12 months of the order. Proceedings for failure to comply with an order are very similar to those for breach of probation.

2–20   (f) *Drug Treatment and Testing Order*[9]: in dealing with anyone over the age of 16 convicted of any offence (not necessarily drug-related), the court may, instead of sentencing the person, make a drug treatment and testing order (DTTO). There must be suitable arrangements for the order in the area and the court must be satisfied that the offender is suitable for, and agrees to, the order. The order lasts for between six months and three years, may involve in- or outpatient treatment and requires the offender to provide samples in order to show drug usage. Regular reviews are carried out on progress, at least on a monthly basis. These may involve the offender attending at court and the court can cancel the order if it is satisfied that the offender is not co-operating with it. These are relatively new powers and initial experience seems to be positive.

2–21   (g) *Restriction of Liberty Orders*: Introduced by the Crime and Punishment (Scotland) Act 1997, these orders require an offender to be present for up to 12 hours per day in a certain

---

[9] s.234B of the 1995 Act.

place or to absent themselves from any specified place at any specified times. They are enforced by means of electronic monitoring or "tagging" and are currently only available in some parts of the country. The maximum duration of an order is 12 months and the offender must give consent to the imposition of an order. Breach of an order is dealt with in the same way as breach of probation.

(h) *Custodial Disposals*: these are known as imprisonment when the person is over 21 years old and detention when the person is under that age. No sentence of detention, nor any sentence of imprisonment where a person has not previously been sentenced to a custodial sentence anywhere in the UK, can be imposed unless the court is of the opinion that no other disposal is appropriate. Summary courts must give reasons for their decision that no other sentence is appropriate. In principle then, custodial sentences should be reserved for the most serious circumstances. Nonetheless, they account for approximately 11 per cent of all disposals per year. In relation to release provisions, custodial sentences are of four kinds: **2–22**

(i) Life sentences: Since 2001, all persons sentenced to an indeterminate sentence must have a "punishment part" set by the presiding judge. Only after this period has been served can the case be referred to the Parole Board for Scotland and the Board must be satisfied that the release of the person would not pose an unacceptable risk to the public before it can order release. Persons sentenced to life imprisonment or detention without limit of time before October 2001 have now had their cases referred back to the sentencing court for the setting of a punishment part. In dealing with these cases, the Parole Board sits as a tribunal of three, with a legally qualified chairperson, and hears evidence from witnesses as well as having the usual parole dossier in advance of the hearing. It is thus possible that mental health staff may be called to give evidence at such tribunals, and, indeed, routine when the person is subject to a hospital order. Release, if ordered, is subject to licence for life and the licence will include any conditions which the parole board considers necessary for the management of risk in the community. There may thus be conditions relating to co-operation with psychiatric treatment. Any breach of licence can result in recall to custody, and such recall lasts unless and until the Board decides that it is safe to re-release the person. **2–23**

(ii) Long-term sentences: Any determinate sentence of four years or more is classified as a long-term sentence. On serving one half of such a sentence, a prisoner is entitled to be reviewed for release on parole. The Parole Board considers the case on the basis of a dossier of reports prepared for Scottish Ministers by those who have had contact with the prisoner during sentence and a home-based social worker from the Authority which would be **2–24** responsible for supervision if the person is released. The Board may grant parole subject to such conditions as it thinks necessary for the protection of the public from risk. Such conditions may again include co-operation with psychiatric input. A long-term prisoner not released on parole will be released on non-parole licence after completing two-thirds of the total sentence. This release is also on licence, with the licence conditions, determined by the parole board, also potentially including reference to psychiatric input. Both parole and non-parole licencees can be recalled by the parole board for any breach of licence. Recall can last until the sentence expiry date of the original sentence.

2–25   (iii) Short-term sentences: persons sentenced to less than four years are automatically released on serving half their sentence. The only circumstances in which the second half of the sentence can be given effect are if the person is convicted of a further offence during the second half of the original sentence and the court decides to order the person to serve part or the entire sentence outstanding at the date of the new offence.

2–26   (iv) Extended sentences: Section 210A of the 1995 Act allows a court, in sentencing a person convicted of a serious violent or sexual offence, to impose an extended sentence. Such a sentence consists of a custodial part followed by a period of supervision in the community which extends beyond the normal period of supervision following a long-term sentence, or requires supervision on release from a short-term sentence. During the period of supervision, the person is liable to be recalled to custody, but is entitled to challenge any recall before a tribunal of the Parole board in the same way as a life sentence prisoner. A new section 210AA was inserted into the 1995 Act by the Criminal Justice (Scotland) Act 2003 extending the range of crimes for which an extended sentence may be imposed. This section also requires that the court must take into account any information before it concerning the person's physical and mental condition before imposing an extended sentence and, if the case is on indictment, a report from a chartered clinical psychologist or chartered forensic psychologist. This section has not yet been brought into force.

Order for Lifelong Restriction of Liberty (OLR)

2–27   A new sentence is to be made available to the High Court under the Criminal Justice (Scotland) Act 2003, allowing the court to impose a sentence of lifelong restriction of liberty in cases where a risk assessment holds that the person poses a high risk to public safety. While the details of this disposal remain to be worked out in practice, the legislative provisions allow us to know generally what will be involved.

The sentence will be available for offences other than murder which are sexual offences, violent offences, offences which endanger life, or offences the nature of which or circumstances of the commission of which are such that it appears to the court that the person has a propensity to commit a sexual, violent or life-endangering offence. In any of these circumstances, the court, at its own instance or on the motion of the prosecutor, if notice has been given to the person in advance, must make a *risk assessment order*. Such an order commits the person for a maximum of 90 days, with a possible further 90 days and, exceptionally as a further extension, to a place to be determined in the order so that an assessment of the risk posed can be made. The details of places, persons who carry out the assessment and assessment forms are to be decided by the *Risk Management Authority*. This body, which commenced work in late 2004, is charged with accrediting practitioners, assessment strategies and management plans as well as overseeing the management of individual cases and promoting research and dissemination of information about risk assessment and management.

The risk assessment report to the court will classify the person as posing a "high, medium or low" risk to the safety of the public at large if the person is at liberty. The person may commission an independent risk assessment and there is the opportunity for a court hearing to decide what the final categorisation of the risk should be. Section 210E of the 1995 Act, as inserted by the Criminal Justice (Scotland) Act 2003, states:

> ". . . the risk criteria are that the nature of, or the circumstances of the commission of, the offence of which the convicted person has been found guilty either in themselves or as part of a pattern of behaviour are such as to demonstrate that there is a likelihood that he, if at liberty, will seriously endanger the lives, or physical or psychological well-being, of members of the public at large."

If the court is satisfied on the basis of the evidence before it that, on a balance of probabilities, the risk criteria are met, it must impose an order for lifelong restriction in the case. This order renders the person liable for imprisonment or detention for an indeterminate period. If the court decides that the risk criteria are not met, it may impose any other disposal available for the offence except life imprisonment or detention.

A person sentenced to an OLR must have a risk management plan drawn up for them within nine months of the sentence being passed. Thereafter the plan must be reviewed regularly. Review is the task of the "lead agency" which may be a prison, a hospital or a local authority, depending on where the person is located at the time of the review. Release from prison or from hospital will be determined by the Parole Board, to which the person's case must be referred when the punishment part of the sentence, set by the original court, has expired. The Parole Board must have regard to any risk management plans in reaching a decision about release. The person will remain on life licence, subject to recall by the Board or Scottish Ministers, until death.

This new disposal was introduced as a result of a recommendation by the MacLean Committee[10], which itself was set up after public concern about a small number of dangerous repeat offenders. It remains to be

---

[10] Scottish Executive, *Serious Violent and Sexual Offenders*, SE/2000/68.

seen how often the courts do use such orders and what policies the Risk Management Authority adopts in relation to the growing literature on risk assessment and management. It does, however, seem clear that both psychiatry and psychology will have considerable input into these arrangements.

Victims

2–28   As criminal procedure has developed over the last two centuries in Scotland, as in many countries, the role of the alleged victim of the crime or offence became effectively that of a witness rather than party in any meaningful sense of the word. Thus the Crown is master of the instance throughout proceedings and has power to drop or amend charges at any stage without consulting, or even informing, the victim. Equally, a victim cannot withdraw charges in Scotland—once a report has been made to the fiscal, it is purely a matter for the fiscal what proceedings take place. Of course it might be very difficult to proceed with an uncooperative witness, but the decision is one for the Crown. Various attempts have been made over the last few years to improve the treatment of victims in the criminal justice process. They are provided with much more information about proceedings, are assisted in understanding what happens in court and can, if vulnerable, have arrangements made to give their evidence by video link. Further rights are accorded to victims by the Criminal Justice (Scotland) Act 2003. In particular, victims who register with the Scottish Executive have the right to be told when any offender against them sentenced to a long-term or life sentence in prison is to be released, dies, is transferred outwith Scotland or is unlawfully at large. Victims who wish may also make representations to the Parole Board when it is considering the release of the person who offended against that victim.

The Human Rights Act 1998

2–29   The United Kingdom government, in a significant departure from traditional British legal practice, incorporated into British law most of the European Convention on Human Rights and Fundamental Freedoms (1950). In effect, this binds both government and public authorities, including courts, to comply with the Convention in all their actions (with some exceptions for Parliament). The Act has had a profound effect not just on the practices of public bodies but also on the attitudes of officials in both procedural and substantive issues.

Section 6 of the Act makes it unlawful for a public authority to act in a way incompatible with Convention rights. Included within public bodies are courts, tribunals and any other body exercising a public function. Thus hospitals, local authorities and anyone acting on their behalf must ensure that all actions comply with the provisions of the Convention. Particular attention has to be paid when restrictions are being imposed on the liberty of anyone. Such restrictions must be no more than are reasonably required and the procedures adopted for decision making must be fair and open to scrutiny. It is fair to say that the Act and the principles behind it have driven many of the changes incorporated in the new mental health legislation, but it is also important that all actors within the system have an understanding of the demands of the law.

Recent cases making use of the law have challenged the independence of temporary sheriffs and the physical conditions in Scottish prisons. Steps have also been taken, most notably in the Convention Rights (Compliance) (Scotland) Act 2001 to change, for example, parole procedures to ensure that they fully respect the rights of those being considered by the Board.

Other Courts and Tribunals of Interest to Mental Health Professionals

(1) *The European Court of Justice*: sitting in Luxembourg, this is the **2–30** supreme court of the European Union. It sits as a court of first instance, dealing with staff cases, cases involving Community institutions and cases alleging breach of community obligations. Of more interest to us is its role under Article 177 of the EEC. This article allows any national court in the EU to remit a question on the validity or interpretation of Community law to the court and the court provides a definitive answer. The court in this role does not concern itself with any issue other than that of the law. There is one judge from each member state of the EU.

(2) *The European Court of Human Rights*: sitting in Strasbourg, this **2–31** court deals with cases under the European Convention on Human Rights and is a Council of Europe body. The Council of Europe now has some 44 member states, including almost all of the former USSR countries. The Court has jurisdiction to adjudicate on cases brought by member states or by individuals when the member state has accepted the right of individual petition. All domestic remedies in the country of origin of the case must have been exhausted before the court can hear the case and a preliminary sift is carried out to ensure that the case is eligible for consideration. Judgments of the court are definitive in the interpretation of the Convention and have a very strong impact throughout the member states. Under the Human Rights Act 1998, domestic courts in the UK are now obliged to have regard to the judgments of the European Court of Human Rights in reaching their decisions.

(3) *Fatal Accident Inquiries*: the procurator fiscal has discretion to **2–32** order a Fatal Accident Inquiry (FAI) into any sudden or unexplained death in Scotland, but must order such an inquiry where the deceased appears to have died in the course of employment or while engaged in an occupation, or where the deceased was in lawful custody at the time of death. Hearings take place in the sheriff court and can be presided over by a sheriff or sheriff principal. The relatives of the deceased can be separately represented and issues of the deceased's mental health may well arise. Mental health professionals may thus be called to give evidence at such inquiries.

(4) *Children*: no child under the age of eight can be prosecuted for **2–33** a crime or offence in Scotland; they are irrebuttably presumed to lack the capacity for *mens rea*. Children between the ages of 8 and 16 can, with the approval of the Lord Advocate, be proceeded against in the ordinary criminal courts. This is

normally only done when the allegation is of a particularly serious crime or where a co-accused over the age of 16 is involved. Summary courts can impose detention in residential care provided by the Local Authority, probation, a fine, admonition or absolute discharge. Solemn courts can impose detention, in a place to be decided by Scottish Ministers, probation, fines, absolute discharge or admonition. Children under 16 can only be detained in penal establishments when they are certified as "unruly". Courts can also order parents of children found guilty of crimes to lodge "caution" for the child's good behaviour. Courts may choose to remit cases to Childrens Hearings for advice before sentencing or for the Hearing to decide on disposal.

The vast majority of cases involving children are, however, dealt with by Children's Hearings. An official, known as the Reporter, receives reports from many sources, including the police and the procurator fiscal, with evidence that a child may be in need of "compulsory measures of care". Such a need can be evidenced by a variety of factors: the child may be beyond parental control, in need of care and protection or be alleged to have offended. If the reporter considers that there are grounds for taking compulsory measures of care for the child, the case is referred to a panel of three trained lay persons for a determination. If the child or parents do not accept the grounds for referral, the case goes to the sheriff court for proof of the grounds. If the sheriff finds the grounds proved, the case is remitted back to the panel for disposal. Proceedings at the panel are informal. Reports are obtained from anyone with dealings with the child, including schools, social workers and medical personnel. The panel may conclude that no compulsory measures of care are necessary (often because the child and family are prepared to co-operate with intervention), that compulsory measures are necessary but can be taken with the child at home or that the child requires residential supervision. The interests of the child are paramount at all hearings. Panel orders must be reviewed at least annually and can continue until the young person is 18 years old. An appeal against an order can be taken to the sheriff and subsequently to the Court of Session, thus stressing that the proceedings are civil rather than criminal in nature.

2–34   (5) *Tribunals*: A substantial range of tribunals has been established to provide specialist mechanisms for resolving disputes in areas like employment, education, immigration and social security. In general these tribunals are staffed by a legally qualified chair and two lay persons and the procedures adopted are less formal than in traditional courts. Though the procedures may be less formal, it is still crucial that any reports sought by a tribunal are prepared with the same professional attention to detail as any court report.

Further Reading

This Chapter provides only a very general introduction to the subject **2–35** matter. Readers are referred to the following for further detail on each area of the chapter.

Legal System

Paterson, Bates and Poustie, *The Legal System of Scotland: Cases and Materials* (4th ed., W. Green, 1999)
Walker, *The Scottish Legal System* (8th ed., W. Green, 2001)
White and Willock, *The Scottish Legal System* (3rd ed., Lexis Nexis, 2003)

Civil Procedure

Hennessy, *Civil Procedure and Practice* (W. Green, 2000)

Criminal Procedure

Brown, *Criminal Evidence and Procedure* (2nd ed., Butterworths, 2002)
Stewart, *The Scottish Criminal Courts in Action* (2nd ed., Butterworths, 1997)

Sentencing

Nicholson, *Sentencing Law and Practice in Scotland* (2nd ed., W. Green, 1992)

Criminal Law

Gordon, *The Criminal Law of Scotland* (3rd ed., W. Green, 2000)
Jones and Christie, *Criminal Law* (3rd ed., W. Green, 2003)

Human Rights

Reed and Murdoch, *A Guide to Human Rights Law in Scotland* (Butterworths, 2001)
In addition, *The Laws of Scotland: Stair Memorial Encyclopaedia* (Law Society of Scotland/Butterworths) provides a regularly updated comprehensive coverage of the whole of Scots Law and practice.

CHAPTER 31

CIVIL MENTAL HEALTH LEGISLATION

Introduction

3–01 Civil legislation to detain and treat people with mental disorders has been in place in Scotland since the Lunacy (Scotland) Act 1857. Prior to this, Sheriffs were responsible for protecting the interests of the insane. Mental health legislation exists because it is recognised that people with major mental disorders may lack the realisation and understanding (or insight) that they are ill, and because the disorder may have impaired their judgement and reasoning regarding their need for treatment. Mental health legislation has two major functions: it creates powers to detain and/or treat people with mental disorders; and, very importantly, it establishes mechanisms and bodies to ensure that the rights of these individuals are protected.

In Scotland, new mental health legislation was passed by the Scottish Parliament in March 2003: The Mental Health (Care and Treatment) (Scotland) Act 2003[2]. It comes into effect in October 2005 and a Code of Practice[3] and relevant regulations[4], currently in draft format, will be available. The proposals for a new Mental Health Act came about largely because of changes in psychiatric practice. The 1960 and 1984 Mental Health (Scotland) Acts combined detention and treatment in a psychiatric hospital but, with the move towards community care and the closure of many psychiatric beds, this was no longer appropriate. In addition, over the years, anomalies within the 1984 Act had been identified and additional legislation, for example to create Community Care Orders, made the law complex and confusing.

This chapter describes the major civil legislation set out in the new Act for the care and treatment of people with mental disorders. Legislation for mentally disordered offenders is described in Chapter 7 although any reference to the 1995 Act refers to the Criminal Procedure (Scotland) Act 1995. It is essential for mental health, social work, criminal justice and legal professionals to have a clear understanding of the provisions of the new Act and their role in applying them.

---

[1] Chapter author: Dr Lindsay D. G. Thomson, M.D.
[2] Mental Health (Care and Treatment) (Scotland) Act 2003, The Stationery Office, Edinburgh.
[3] Health Department (2004) *Draft Code of Practice for the Mental Health (Care and Treatment) (Scotland) Act 2003*, Vol.1, Scottish Executive.
[4] Health Department (2004) *Mental Health (Care and Treatment) (Scotland) Act 2003: Regulations*, Policy Proposals Consultation Document, Scottish Executive.

THE MENTAL HEALTH (CARE AND TREATMENT) (SCOTLAND) ACT 2003

The committee established to review the Mental Health (Scotland) Act **3–02** 1984 suggested a number of basic principles on which the new Act should be based[5]. These principles appear in a somewhat diluted form but their existence is crucial in establishing the basis on which patients are to be approached.

Principles

Any person using the provisions of the Act, including decisions to take **3–03** no action or to discharge from the Act, must:

Participation
- Consider the present and past wishes and feelings of the patient **3–04** unless it is unreasonable or impracticable to do so. This includes the use of human or mechanical aids to assist communication.
- Allow the patient to participate as fully as possible.
- Provide support and information in a readily understandable format to enable the patient to participate.

Respect for Carers
- Consider the views of the patient's named person; and any **3–05** carer, guardian, or welfare attorney of the patient.
- Consider any known relevant needs and circumstances of a carer (except when making decisions about medical treatment); and the importance of providing information to any carer to assist them in caring for the patient.

Informal Care
- Consider the range of options available in the patient's case **3–06** and use informal care wherever possible.

Benefit
- Have regard to the importance of providing the maximum **3–07** benefit to the patient from use of the Act.

Non-discrimination
- Ensure that the patient is not treated in a way that is less **3–08** favourable than a person who is not a patient might be treated in a comparable situation, unless it can be shown to be justified.

Respect for Diversity
- Have regard to the patient's abilities, background and charac- **3–09** teristics without prejudice to the patient's age, sex, sexual orientation, religious persuasion, racial origin, cultural and linguistic background, and membership of any ethnic group.

---

[5] Scottish Executive (2001) *New Directions: Report on the review of the Mental Health (Scotland) Act 1984*, SE/2001/56.

Least Restrictive Alternative

3–10
- Do so in a manner that involves the minimum restriction on the freedom of the patient that is necessary in the circumstances.

Reciprocity

3–11
- Ensure the provision of appropriate services to the person who is subject to a certificate or order under the Act; and provision of continuing care when the Act is no longer being used.

Child Welfare

3–12
- Consider the welfare of any child (under 18 years of age) with mental disorder paramount in making any decision.

Equality

3–13
- Encourage equal opportunities and observe equal opportunity legislation.

Definitions

3–14   The Act specifies legal definitions of certain terms. Some of the basic, regularly applied terms are described here.

Mental Disorder[6]

3–15   "Mental disorder" means any mental illness, personality disorder or learning disability however caused or manifested.

A person is not mentally disordered by reason *only* of any of the following:

- Sexual orientation
- Sexual deviancy
- Transsexualism
- Transvestism
- Dependence on, or use of, alcohol or drugs
- Behaviour that causes, or is likely to cause, harassment, alarm or distress to any other person
- Acting as no prudent person would act.

Carer[7]

3–16   A "carer" is a person who provides on a regular basis a substantial amount of care for, and support to, the patient, including a person who did this before the patient's admission to hospital. It excludes people who do this as an employee or as a volunteer with a voluntary organisation.

Guardian[8]

3–17   A "guardian" is a person appointed under the Adults with Incapacity (Scotland) Act 2000, to look after the personal welfare of an individual.

---

[6] Mental Health (Care and Treatment) (Scotland) Act 2003, s.328.
[7] *ibid.*, s.329.
[8] Adults with Incapacity (Scotland) Act 2000, s.64(1)(a) or (b).

Welfare Attorney[9]

A "welfare attorney" is an individual authorised to act as such by a **3–18** welfare power of attorney granted under the Adults with Incapacity (Scotland) Act 2000.

Approved Medical Practitioner[10]

An "approved medical practitioner" (AMP) is a doctor who has **3–19** special experience in the diagnosis and treatment of mental disorder, and who has the qualifications and experience and has undergone training as specified by Scottish Ministers. Consultant psychiatrists and specialist registrars in psychiatry will obtain AMP status. This status allows doctors to carry out certain tasks and to utilise certain powers under the Act. Each health board must compile and maintain a list of approved medical practitioners.

Responsible Medical Officer[11]

The "Responsible Medical Officer" (RMO) is the AMP designated by **3–20** hospital managers for a particular patient.

Mental Health Officer[12]

A "Mental Health Officer" (MHO) is an officer of a local authority **3–21** with the necessary registration, education and training, experience and competence as respects people who have or have had a mental disorder. These are usually specially trained social workers.

INSTITUTIONS AND FUNCTIONS

The Mental Welfare Commission for Scotland

The Act legislates for the continued existence of the Mental Welfare **3–22** Commission.[13] This is one of the major protective mechanisms to ensure that patients are well cared for and that the legislation is properly utilised. The role of the Commission is:

- To promote best practice
- To report on general issues regarding the welfare of people with mental disorder
- To provide advice
- To highlight individual case issues involving unlawful detention; ill-treatment, neglect or some other deficiency in care or treatment; damage or loss of property or risk of such; or patients living alone or without care and unable to look after themselves, or their property or financial affairs

---

[9] Adults with Incapacity (Scotland) Act 2000, ss.16 and 19.
[10] Mental Health (Care and Treatment) (Scotland) Act 2003, s.22.
[11] *ibid.*, s.230.
[12] *ibid.*, s.32.
[13] *ibid.*, Pt 2 and Sch. 1.

- To carry out investigations into any individual case issues using a formal inquiry if required
- To visit patients subject to the provisions of this Act, the 1995 Act or the Adults with Incapacity (Scotland) Act 2000, and to inspect premises where patients may be resident, use facilities or receive medical treatment
- To publish an annual report, advice, the findings of routine visits and the outcome of any investigations

The Mental Health Tribunal for Scotland

3–23   The Act establishes the new body of a Mental Health Tribunal for Scotland. Primarily it will replace the Sheriff Court in considering longer-term detention and conditions for community residence. Such Tribunals have been in existence for some time in England and Wales. Instinctively it appears desirable to move such proceedings out of court to a more informal setting but the reality has been that these tribunals have often been prolonged and extremely adversarial. Whilst it is important to ensure that evidence is properly considered it will be detrimental to patient, carer and staff relationships if this occurs. The role of the Tribunal chair will therefore be crucial in ensuring that proceedings are fair, courteous and not prolonged. The Tribunal's composition, organisation, procedure and reporting mechanism are set out in Schedule 2 of the Act. Tribunal members will be appointed by Scottish Ministers and will include lawyers, psychiatrists, and others with qualifications, training, skills and experience in caring for, or providing services to, people with a mental disorder. It will be led by a President and a lawyer will convene each local tribunal. The logistical problems regarding the staffing of Tribunals are not insignificant due to the additional workload for legal and medical practitioners. The Tribunal may require any person to attend for the purpose of giving evidence or producing documents. It will produce an annual report.

Unlawful Detention

3–24   The Tribunal has a particular role to play with voluntary patients. An application can be made to the Tribunal for an order requiring hospital managers to cease to detain a patient if he is an inpatient not detained under this Act or the 1995 Act and is being given treatment primarily for mental disorder[14]. The patient, the patient's named person, an MHO, the Commission, any guardian, any welfare attorney or a person having an interest in the welfare of the patient may apply. The Tribunal may make an order requiring the managers of the hospital to cease to detain the patient if satisfied that the detention is unlawful.

Health Board and Local Authority Functions

3–25   Specific health board and local authority functions are described in Part 4 of the Act. Notable is the requirement for Health Boards to provide adequate services and accommodation to children and young

---

[14] Mental Health (Care and Treatment) (Scotland) Act 2003, s.291.

people for their needs[15]. This will prevent the current regular occurrence of young people being inappropriately treated in adult psychiatric wards due to lack of suitable facilities. Similarly, a Health Board must provide services and accommodation for mothers with babies[16]. Any mother with a child less than one year old normally in her care can, if she wishes, look after the child in hospital, if she is not likely to endanger the health or welfare of the child, and has been admitted to hospital for treatment of post-natal depression.

Similar obligations are placed on local authorities for the provision of care and support services for people with a current or past mental disorder living in the community[17]. These services are expected to minimise the effect of the mental disorder and give people the opportunity to lead lives which are as normal as possible. They include residential accommodation, and personal care and support but not nursing care. In addition a local authority must provide services which are designed to promote well-being and social development: these include social, cultural and recreational activities; and training and assistance to find and undertake employment. The local authority must provide assistance with travel for those engaging in such activities where necessary. A local authority may, but does not have to, provide any of the above for persons who are in hospital.

Duty to Inquire into Individual Cases

A local authority has a duty to inquire[18] if a person with a mental **3–26** disorder living in their area out of hospital and 16 years or over, may:

- currently or in the past have been ill-treated, neglected, or received deficient care and treatment
- now, or previously, have suffered or been at risk of suffering loss or damage to their property because of a mental disorder
- be living alone or without care and unable to look after his property or financial affairs; or
- be a risk to the safety of others because of mental disorder

The local authority may request assistance from the Commission, the Public Guardian, the Scottish Commission for the Regulation of Care, a Health Board, and an NHS Trust with these inquiries. The MHO appointed by the relevant local authority should interview the individual, visit his residence, consult with relevant professionals and ensure that there will be protection and promotion of his welfare in the future. It may be that no further action is required, or that informal care and support under the Social Work (Scotland) Act 1968 is needed, or that the provisions of the Adults with Incapacity (Scotland) Act 2000 or detention and/or treatment under the Mental Health (Care and Treatment) (Scotland) Act 2003 are required. A report on each investigation should be made.

---

[15] Mental Health (Care and Treatment) (Scotland) Act 2003, s.23.

[16] *ibid.*, s.24.

[17] *ibid.*, ss.25–27.

[18] *ibid.*, s.33.

An MHO may apply to a Sheriff or Justice of the Peace for the area where the person in question is currently located for a warrant[19] to carry out this duty to inquire in the following circumstances:

- If the MHO is unable to gain entry to premises where that person resides. A warrant will authorise the MHO, any other specified persons and any constable of the relevant police force to enter those premises, using force if necessary, within eight days of the day on which it was granted.
- To obtain a medical examination of that person if the MHO cannot obtain consent. The medical practitioner must be specified on the warrant and the person concerned can be detained for up to three hours to allow a medical examination to be carried out.
- To obtain access to the medical records by a medical practitioner of the individual subject to the inquiry, if the MHO is unable to gain consent of that individual.

The Sheriff or Justice of the Peace must be satisfied by an MHO's evidence on oath in order to grant the warrant. There is no statutory form. The Commission must be informed of any application for a warrant and its outcome. There is no appeal process regarding any decision taken. This warrant does not authorise the patient's removal to a place of safety.

Assessment of Needs

3–27 Part 14 of the Act imposes a duty on local authorities to carry out a needs assessment of community care services for patients identified by MHOs[20]. A needs assessment can also be requested by the patient, their named person or primary carer for community care and/or health services[21].

POWERS OF DETENTION AND COMPULSORY MEASURES

3–28 The process, timescales and powers of emergency or short-term detention under the Act are recognisable as developments from the 1984 Act. There are two major differences between the 1984 and 2003 Acts: firstly, short-term detention can be commenced directly without an initial emergency certificate and, indeed, this is the preferred course of action; and secondly, the introduction of the Compulsory Treatment Order (CTO). This is a longer-term measure of compulsion and in most respects other than timescale, the CTO is very different from its predecessor. Table 1 provides a summary of the powers of detention and compulsion in the United Kingdom and a comparison of the 1984 and 2003 Scottish Acts. Under the 1984 Act there were 3,689 episodes of

---

[19] Mental Health (Care and Treatment) (Scotland) Act 2003, s.35.
[20] *ibid.*, s.227.
[21] *ibid.*, s.228.

emergency detention, 2,795 episodes of short-term detention and 1,154 episodes of long-term detention in 2002–03. It will be interesting to see if the new legislation results in more or fewer episodes of detention and compulsion. A draft Mental Health Bill for England and Wales was published in September 2004[22]. A previous draft bill published in 2002 met with uniform opposition but the current draft bill is not dissimilar.

In carrying out functions under the Act there must be no conflict of interest for a medical practitioner in relation to the medical examination. For example, doctors must not treat themselves or family members, or have a pecuniary interest in an admission to hospital.

Table 1: Mental Health Legislation in the United Kingdom

Jurisdiction	England and Wales	Northern Ireland	Scotland	
			Previous Act	New Act
Legislation	Mental Health Act 1983	Mental Health (Northern Ireland) Order 1986	Mental Health (Scotland) Act 1984	Mental Health (Care and Treatment) (Scotland) Act 2003
Definition of Mental Disorder	Mental disorder means mental illness, arrested or incomplete development of mind, psychopathic disorder, and any other disorder or disability of mind	Mental disorder means mental illness, mental handicap and any other disorder or disability of mind	Mental disorder means mental illness or mental handicap however caused or manifested	Mental disorder means any mental illness, personality disorder or learning disability however caused or manifested

---

[22] Department of Health (2004) Draft Mental Health Bill, HMSO.

Jurisdiction	England and Wales	Northern Ireland	Scotland	
			Previous Act	New Act
Exclusions— relevant when the exclusion category listed is the *only* factor	Promiscuity Other immoral conduct Sexual deviancy Dependence on alcohol or drugs	Personality disorder Promiscuity Other immoral conduct Sexual deviancy Dependence on alcohol or drugs	Promiscuity Other immoral conduct Sexual deviancy Dependence on alcohol or drugs	Sexual orientation Sexual deviancy Transsexualism Transvestism Dependence on, or use of, alcohol or drugs. Behaviour that causes, or is likely to cause, harassment, alarm or distress to any other person. Acting as no prudent person would act
Emergency detention— duration	Outpatient s.4 Inpatient s.5(2) 72 hours	Inpatient art.7(2) 48 hours	Outpatient s.24 Inpatient s.25(1) 72 hours	s.36(1) 72 hours
Short-term detention— duration	Admission for Assessment s.2 28 days	Admission for Assessment art.4 7–14 days	s.26 28 days	s.44(1) 28 days
Long-term —initial duration	Detention for Treatment s.3 6 months	Detention for Treatment art.12 6 months	Detention for Treatment s.18 6 months	Compulsory Treatment Order s.64(4) 6 months
Nurses' Holding Power— duration	s.5(4) 6 hours	art.7(3) 6 hours	s.25(2) 2 hours	s.299 2 hours

s.=section, art.=article

Emergency Detention

3–29   An emergency detention certificate[23] allows a patient to be detained in hospital for up to 72 hours for the purpose of assessment of a person's mental state. A child can be detained but preferably in a specialist child

---

[23] Mental Health (Care and Treatment) (Scotland) Act 2003, Pt 5, s.36(1).

and adolescent unit. A short-term detention certificate is the preferred "gateway order" and should be used if an approved medical practitioner and MHO are available.

Conditions

The following conditions must be fulfilled to allow an emergency **3–30** detention certificate to be completed:

- It is likely that the patient has a mental disorder
- It is likely that the patient's ability to make decisions about the provision of medical treatment is significantly impaired because of mental disorder
- It is necessary as a matter of urgency to detain the patient in hospital for the purpose of determining what medical treatment requires to be provided
- If the patient were not detained in hospital there would be a significant risk to his health, safety or welfare; or to the safety of any other person
- There would be an undesirable delay in making arrangements for a short-term detention certificate

Process

The Code of Practice recommends that local agencies and services **3–31** agree on a "Psychiatric Emergency Plan" to facilitate proceedings in urgent circumstances, including arrangements for transfer to hospital.

First, a medical practitioner must carry out an examination of a patient and may grant an emergency detention certificate within the day on which the examination took place, or within four hours if the examination is completed after 8pm. The medical practitioner must consider that the conditions for certification are met. Assessment of significantly impaired decision-making ability involves consideration of the extent to which an individual's mental disorder interferes with their ability to accept, comprehend and retain information about their care and treatment, to take decisions based on that information and to communicate those decisions to others.

Second, the medical practitioner must consult with an MHO and obtain consent to the granting of an emergency detention certificate unless it is impracticable to do so. The MHO can only consent by telephone if he has recently seen the patient and knows the background details. If an MHO refuses consent there must be a viable and safe alternative to detention, a contingency plan in case the proposed arrangements break down and a written record of the decision to be given to the patient's GP, RMO and the Commission.

Third, the emergency detention certificate must state the medical practitioner's reasons for believing that the grounds for detention are met and must be signed. The certificate must be given to the hospital managers before the patient can be admitted and detained; or as soon as practicable after granting the certificate for current inpatients.

Fourth, a medical practitioner who grants an emergency detention certificate must, when the certificate is given to the hospital managers or as soon as practicable after that time, explain and record:

- the reason for granting the certificate
- whether the consent of an MHO was obtained
- if MHO consent was not obtained, the reason why it was impracticable to consult an MHO
- the alternatives to granting the certificate that were considered, and
- the reason for determining that any such alternative was inappropriate

Fifth, the hospital managers must, as soon as practical after the period of emergency detention begins, make arrangements for an approved medical practitioner to carry out a medical examination of the patient.

Sixth, the MHO giving consent to detention should ensure:

- that the patient is aware of his status and rights
- that the patient has access to information on representation and advocacy and, where necessary, is assisted in contacting these
- that the patient has access to interpretation and translation services where required
- the safety of the patient's children or other dependants
- the security of the patient's home and belongings
- that the patient's named person and/or nearest relative has been informed
- that the ward medical staff are aware of the patient's views on consent to treatment, including any advance statements
- that the medical staff have MHO and named person/carer details
- that a written record of the MHO's decision to give consent is included in the patient's records, where practicable
- that the patient and his carers and dependants have MHO contact details

Finally, the hospital managers must, within 12 hours of receiving the certificate, inform the Commission, the patient's nearest relative and/or any person who resides with the patient (if the nearest relative does not), and the patient's named person of the certification; and, within 7 days, the local authority in which the patient resides or, if unknown, in which the hospital is situated, if the certificate was granted without the consent of an MHO. The hospital managers must provide the patient with information on his rights and appoint an approved medical practitioner to act as the patient's RMO.

Box 1: Emergency Detention Process Summary

Doctor	: Examine patient
	: Consider conditions for emergency detention
	: Consult MHO
MHO	: Interview patient
Doctor	: Obtain MHO consent
	: Complete emergency detention certificate
Hospital Managers	: Arrange patient examination/appoint RMO
	: Inform Commission, nearest relative and named person within 12 hours of emergency detention
	: Inform Local Authority within 7 days
	: Inform patient of his rights
MHO = Mental Health Officer	

Powers

An emergency detention certificate permits: **3–32**

(a) The removal of the patient to hospital within a period of 72 hours beginning with the granting of the emergency detention certificate.

(b) The detention of the patient in hospital for a period of 72 hours beginning with the first admission under authority of the certificate of the patient to hospital; or the granting of the certificate for inpatients at the time of detention.

The emergency detention certificate does not confer the power to administer treatment although this can be done in an urgent situation under s.243 of the Act.

The authority to detain can be suspended by the patient's RMO[24]. The RMO can grant a certificate specifying a period during which the emergency detention certificate does not authorise the power to detain for an event or series of events and any associated travel. If the RMO considers it necessary in the interests of the patient or for the protection of any other person, the certificate may set out conditions specified by the RMO including that the patient be kept in the charge of a person authorised in writing for the purpose by the RMO. This certificate can be revoked by the RMO in the interests of the patient or for the protection of any other person[25]. This suspension of detention was previously known as leave of absence.

Any measures authorised by a compulsory treatment order cease during the period in which a patient is subject to an emergency detention certificate, except any specified medical treatment.

Exclusions

A patient is excluded from emergency detention if, immediately **3–33** before the medical examination, the patient is detained in hospital under the authority of:

---

[24] Mental Health (Care and Treatment) (Scotland) Act 2003, s.41.
[25] *ibid.*, s.42.

- A current emergency detention certificate[26]
- A short-term detention certificate[27]
- An extension of a short-term detention certificate pending application for a compulsory treatment order[28]
- An extension of short-term detention pending determination by the Tribunal of an application for a compulsory treatment order[29]
- A compulsory treatment order—detention pending review or application for variation following non-compliance with a compulsory treatment order[30]; or an interim compulsory treatment order—detention pending further procedure following non-compliance with a compulsory treatment order[31]

Revocation of an emergency detention certificate

3–34   The approved medical practitioner must revoke the certificate[32] if, following examination of the patient, he is not satisfied that the grounds for detention, excluding the conditions of urgency and undesirable delay in making arrangements for a short-term detention certificate, continue to be met, and that it continues to be necessary for the patient's detention in hospital to be authorised by certificate.

Any existing emergency detention certificate is revoked on the granting of the short-term detention certificate.

Appeal

3–35   Given its short duration there is no appeal process for an emergency detention certificate.

Example

A 22-year-old man was brought to see his general practitioner by his parents. He had become more withdrawn in the last few months and had recently been behaving in a bizarre manner, placing silver foil over the television, radio and telephone to prevent aliens from monitoring his family in the home he shared with his parents. On the day of his assessment, he had challenged his mother believing that she had been taken over by an alien. He agreed to see a doctor because his father told him that it would be possible to get his mother checked out to see if she was an alien. The patient had a history of intermittent cannabis use. He was examined by a doctor and considered to be psychotic and a differential diagnosis of schizophrenia or drug-induced psychosis was made. In view of the possible risk to his mother, admission to hospital was considered necessary and urgent. The patient adamantly refused voluntary admission to hospital and did not believe that he was unwell.

---

[26] Mental Health (Care and Treatment) (Scotland) Act 2003, s.36(1).
[27] *ibid.*, s.44(1).
[28] *ibid.*, s.47(1).
[29] *ibid.*, s.68.
[30] *ibid.*, s.114(2).
[31] *ibid.*, s.115(2).
[32] *ibid.*, s.39.

An MHO was consulted, interviewed the patient and gave consent for an emergency detention certificate. The patient was subsequently admitted to hospital under this certificate.

Table 2: Emergency Detention Certificate

Section	Conditions	Duration	Signatories/ Consent	Revocation	Appeal
36(1)	Mental disorder Significantly impaired ability to make decisions about treatment Urgent Significant risk to health, safety or welfare; or safety of others Undesirable delay for short-term detention certificate	Up to 72 hours	One fully registered doctor/ MHO if practicable	By an approved medical practitioner	Nil

Short-Term Detention

A short-term detention certificate[33] allows the patient to be detained **3–36** in hospital for up to 28 days to determine his/her medical needs and to be given medical treatment. It can be used as the first measure of detention or follow an emergency detention certificate.

Conditions

An approved medical practitioner must consider that: **3–37**

- It is likely that the patient has a mental disorder
- It is likely that the patient's ability to make decisions about the provision of medical treatment is significantly impaired because of that mental disorder
- It is necessary to detain the patient in hospital for the purpose of determining what medical treatment should be given to the patient; or giving medical treatment to the patient
- If the patient was not detained in hospital there would be a significant risk to his health, safety or welfare; or to the safety of any other person
- The granting of a short-term detention certificate is necessary

Process

First, an approved medical practitioner (AMP) must carry out an **3–38** examination of the patient and has three days thereafter to grant a short-term detention certificate. All of the above criteria must be met.

---

[33] Mental Health (Care and Treatment) (Scotland) Act 2003, Pt 6, s.44(1).

Second, the AMP must consult and obtain consent from an MHO before granting a short-term detention certificate. The MHO must interview the patient and ascertain the name and address of the patient's named person or, if this is not practical, record what steps were taken with a view to complying with this; and within a period of seven days from the initial consultation give a copy of this record to the AMP. In addition, the MHO duties listed for an emergency detention certificate apply. These include informing the patient of the availability of independent advocacy services and taking appropriate steps to ensure that the patient has the opportunity of making use of those services. The MHO must consent to the short-term detention or justify any refusal to consent. If the MHO refuses to give consent a short-term detention certificate cannot be granted and it is not acceptable for the doctor to use an emergency detention certificate instead.

Third, the AMP must consult the patient's named person and consider any views expressed about the proposed certificate, unless it is impractical to do so; and have regard for the patient's views and any advance statement.

Fourth, the certificate must state the AMP's reasons for believing the conditions for detention are met and must be signed by him. The certificate must be given to the hospital managers as soon as practicable after it is granted and before admission if the individual is not already a patient.

Fifth, within 21 days of the commencement of a short-term detention certificate, the MHO must prepare a social circumstances report (SCR)[34] and send copies to the patient's RMO and the Commission, unless he considers that this report would serve little or no practical purpose. In this case he must record the reasons for deciding this and send a copy to the patient's RMO and the Commission. It is proposed that the SCR[35] will include routine patient details and the reasons for the use of powers to detain; the views of the patient, and any carers or family members on this; the current state of the patient's mental and physical health; the patient's psychiatric, personal, family, criminal, substance misuse and social history; an assessment of risk to self and others; an opinion on the patient's ability to care for himself; information on the care provided prior to detention; any matters of concern that may suggest a duty to inquire[36]; the alternatives to detention considered; the care package established to deal with relevant factors; any ethnic, cultural and religious factors to be considered; and any relevant language or communication issues.

Finally, the hospital managers must, as soon as practicable after receiving the short-term detention certificate, inform the patient, the patient's named person, any guardian, and any welfare attorney of the certification; and within seven days of the commencement of the certificate notify the Tribunal and the Commission.

---

[34] Mental Health (Care and Treatment) (Scotland) Act 2003, s.231.

[35] Mental Health (Care and Treatment) (Scotland) Act 2003: Regulation Policy Proposals Consultation Document (31/3/04), Health Department, Scottish Executive.

[36] Mental Health (Care and Treatment) (Scotland) Act 2003, s.33.

Box 2: Short-Term Detention Process Summary

AMP	: Examine patient
	: Consider conditions for short term detention
	: Consult MHO
MHO	: Interview patient
AMP	: Obtain MHO consent
	: Complete short term detention certificate
Hospital Managers	: Inform patient, named person, any guardian, any welfare attorney as soon as possible
	: Inform Tribunal and Commission within 7 days
	: Inform patient of his rights
MHO	: Complete Social Circumstances Report in 21 days
AMP = Approved Medical Practitioner	MHO = Mental Health Officer

Powers

A short-term detention certificate gives the power to: **3–39**

(a) Remove the patient to hospital within three days of the commencement of the certificate.

(b) To detain the patient in hospital for a period of 28 days beginning with the day on which the patient was admitted and the certificate was given to the managers of the hospital, or, if the patient is already in hospital, the day on which the certificate was granted.

(c) To give the patient medical treatment in accordance with Part 16 of the Act.

The authority to detain can be suspended by the patient's RMO[37]. The RMO can grant a certificate specifying a period during which the short-term detention certificate shall not authorise the power to detain for an event or series of events and any associated travel. If the RMO considers it necessary in the interests of the patient or for the protection of any other person, the certificate may set out conditions including that the patient be kept in the charge of a person authorised in writing for the purpose by the RMO. This certificate can be revoked by the RMO in the interests of the patient or for the protection of any other person[38].

Any measures authorised by a compulsory treatment order cease to be authorised during the period in which a patient is subject to a short-term detention certificate.

Exclusions

The patient is excluded from short-term detention in hospital if the   **3–40** patient is detained in hospital under the authority of:

- A short-term detention certificate[39]

---

[37] Mental Health (Care and Treatment) (Scotland) Act 2003, s.53.
[38] *ibid.*, s.54.
[39] *ibid.*, s.44(1).

- An extension certificate[40]
- An extension of short-term detention pending determination by the Tribunal of an application for a compulsory treatment order[41]
- A compulsory treatment order—detention pending review or application for variation following non-compliance with a compulsory treatment order[42]; or an interim compulsory treatment order—detention pending further procedure following non-compliance with a compulsory treatment order[43]

Revocation

3–41   The RMO must consider from time to time whether the conditions for detention regarding the presence of a mental disorder, significantly impaired decision-making ability and significant risk continue to be met and whether it continues to be necessary for the patient to be detained in hospital by the use of a short-term detention certificate[44]. If this is not the case then the RMO should revoke the certificate and thereafter inform the patient, the patient's named person, any guardian, any welfare attorney and the MHO previously consulted; and within seven days of the certificate being revoked give notice to the Tribunal and the Commission. "From time to time" is not defined in the Act but realistically most clinicians consider such matters on each occasion a patient is interviewed and at each ward round or case review.

The Commission also has the power to revoke a short-term detention certificate or an extension certificate if it is not satisfied that conditions for detention as outlined above are met; and that it continues to be necessary for the detention in hospital of the patient to be authorised by the certificate[45]. The Commission must inform the patient, the patient's named person, any guardian, any welfare attorney, the managers of the hospital where the patient is detained, the MHO and the Tribunal of such a decision.

When a CTO or an interim CTO is made, any existing short-term detention certificate is revoked.

Appeal

3–42   Where a patient is in hospital under a short-term detention certificate, the patient or the patient's named person may apply to the Tribunal for revocation of the certificate[46]. The Tribunal must afford the patient, the patient's named person, any guardian, any welfare attorney, the AMP who granted the short-term detention certificate, the MHO, the patient's RMO, any *curator ad litem*, and any other person appearing to the Tribunal to have an interest in the application, the opportunity to make verbal or written representations and of leading, or producing evidence.

---

[40] Mental Health (Care and Treatment) (Scotland) Act 2003, s.47(1).
[41] *ibid.*, s.68.
[42] *ibid.*, s.114(2).
[43] *ibid.*, s.115(2).
[44] *ibid.*, s.49.
[45] *ibid.*, s.51.
[46] *ibid.*, s.50.

A tribunal must, if not satisfied that conditions for detention regarding the presence of a mental disorder, significantly impaired decision-making ability and significant risk are met; and that it continues to be necessary for the detention in hospital of the patient to be authorised by the certificate, revoke the short-term detention certificate, and thereby any subsequent extension certificate.

As with the Mental Health (Scotland) Act 1984, patients are likely to refer their cases to the Commission given that it also has the power to revoke a short-term detention certificate.

Example

A social worker contacted a consultant psychiatrist to express concern **3–43** about a client he had been asked to see who had taken refuge in a charitable boarding house. The 44-year-old woman was irritable and dishevelled, had no money and had travelled some 400 miles from her home area. At interview the woman had stated that she had come on a mission. She adamantly rejected any suggestion of seeking medical assistance and said that she was a "healer". The social worker feared that his client would flee from the area if he pursued this and was worried about her ability to care for herself. On the basis of this story it seemed likely that the woman had a mental disorder but would be unlikely to agree to voluntary treatment. The consultant therefore arranged to visit the boarding house in the company of an MHO. Two psychiatric nurses and an ambulance were also present to escort the patient should she require hospital care, and two police officers were located outside the building in case she tried to escape. At interview, the patient clearly fulfilled the conditions for short-term detention and the MHO consented to this. The patient would not give an address and it was therefore not possible to contact any relative or named person. She was admitted to hospital where it was later discovered that she had a diagnosis of bipolar disorder and was well known to psychiatric services in her home area. Her family had been extremely worried by her absence from home.

Table 3: Short-term detention certificate

Section	Conditions	Duration	Signatories/ Consent	Revocation	Appeal
44(1)	Mental disorder Significantly impaired ability to make decisions about treatment Necessary to detain to assess or give medical treatment Significant risk to health, safety or welfare; or safety of others Short-term detention certificate is necessary	28 days	Approved medical practitioner/ MHO	By RMO or the Mental Welfare Commission	To Mental Health Tribunal

Extension Certificate

3–44 The AMP can, within 24 hours of carrying out a medical examination, grant an extension certificate authorising the detention in hospital of the patient for a period of three days beginning with the day on which the short-term detention certificate ceases[47]. Its purpose is to allow time for the preparation of an application for a compulsory treatment order where there has been a change in the patient's mental health prior to the expiry of the short-term detention certificate.

Conditions

3–45 An AMP must consider that:

- It is likely that the patient has a mental disorder
- It is likely that the patient's ability to make decisions about the provision of medical treatment is significantly impaired because of that disorder
- It is necessary to detain the patient in hospital for the purpose of determining what medical treatment should be given to the patient; or giving medical treatment to the patient
- If the patient were not detained in hospital there would be a significant risk to his health, safety or welfare; or to the safety of any other person
- An application should be made for a compulsory treatment order because of a change in the mental health of the patient
- It is not reasonably practical to make an application, and no application has been made for a compulsory treatment order before the end of the short-term detention certificate

Process

3–46 First, the AMP must examine the patient, and consult and gain consent to the extension certificate by any MHO unless it is impracticable to do so.

Second, the AMP who grants an extension certificate must within 24 hours give the certificate to the managers of the hospital where the patient is being detained; and notify the patient, the patient's named person, the Tribunal, the Commission, any guardian, any welfare attorney, and the MHO of the granting of and grounds for granting the certificate and whether the consent of an MHO was obtained or, if not, why this was impracticable.

Powers

3–47 The extension certificate permits the detention in hospital of the patient for a period of three working days beginning with the expiry of the short-term detention certificate; and the giving to the patient of medical treatment in accordance with Part 16 of this Act. The extension period of three days excludes any day which is a Saturday, Sunday or a bank holiday.

---

[47] Mental Health (Care and Treatment) (Scotland) Act 2003, s.47(1).

Revocation

The certificate can be revoked by the RMO or the Commission as for **3–48** the short-term detention certificate.

Appeal

An appeal can be made to the Tribunal as for the short-term **3–49** detention certificate.

Table 4: Short-Term Detention—Extension Certificate

Section	Conditions	Duration	Signatories/ Consent	Revocation	Appeal
47(1)	Mental disorder Significantly impaired ability to make decisions about treatment Significant risk to health, safety or welfare; or safety of others Necessary to detain to assess or give medical treatment Application for CTO to be made because of a change in patient's mental health Not practical to apply for CTO before expiration of short-term detention certificate	3 working days (excludes Saturday, Sunday or Bank holiday)	AMP/ MHO	By RMO or the Mental Welfare Commission	To Mental Health Tribunal

Extension of short-term detention pending determination by the Tribunal of application for a compulsory treatment order

A short-term detention certificate or an extension certificate can be **3–50** extended[48] pending determination by the Tribunal of an application for a compulsory treatment order if an application has been made for a CTO before the expiry of the period of detention authorised. In these circumstances the patient may be detained in hospital for a period of five working days and given medical treatment, beginning with the expiry of the certificate authorising detention. The Tribunal must decide during

---

[48] Mental Health (Care and Treatment) (Scotland) Act 2003, s.68.

this period if an interim compulsory treatment order should be made, or determine the application.

Table 5: Extension of short-term detention pending determination of application by the Tribunal

Section	Conditions	Duration	Signatories/ Consent	Revocation	Appeal
68	Application for CTO made before expiry of short-term detention, pending determination by the Tribunal	5 working days	RMO	By RMO	Nil

Interim Compulsory Treatment Order

3–51   The Tribunal can make an interim compulsory treatment order (ICTO) pending its full determination of a compulsory treatment order[49], for example, if it needs further evidence.

Conditions

3–52   The Tribunal must consider that:

- The patient has a mental disorder
- Medical treatment would be likely to prevent the mental disorder worsening; or alleviate any of the symptoms, or effects, of the disorder; and that such treatment is available
- Without such medical treatment there would be a significant risk to the health, safety or welfare of the patient; or to the safety of others
- The mental disorder significantly impairs the patient's ability to make decisions about the provision of such medical treatment
- It is necessary to make an interim compulsory treatment order

Process

3–53   First, the Tribunal may make an ICTO for up to 28 days if the conditions for an ICTO are met pending a decision on a CTO. The Tribunal may NOT make an order that would authorise measures for a continuous period of more than 56 days.

Second, the Tribunal must allow oral or written representations and the leading or producing of evidence from those listed in the CTO.

Third, it is good practice to prepare and implement a care plan, as for a CTO, if time allows.

Powers

3–54   The Tribunal may specify measures in an ICTO as for a CTO for 28 days.

---

[49] Mental Health (Care and Treatment) (Scotland) Act 2003, s.65.

Review and Revocation

The patient's RMO must consider from time to time whether the **3–55** conditions for detention are met and whether it is necessary for the patient to be subject to an interim compulsory treatment order. If this is not the case the RMO must revoke the ICTO. The Commission may also revoke an ICTO for the same reasons. The RMO must inform the patient, the patient's named person, any guardian or welfare attorney, the MHO, the Tribunal and the Commission of the decision and send a statement of the reasons for that decision. The Commission must do the same and in addition send notification to the patient's RMO.

The ICTO is automatically revoked once a CTO is made.

Table 6: Interim Compulsory Treatment Order

Section	Conditions	Duration	Signatories/ Consent	Revocation	Appeal
65	Mental disorder Significantly impaired ability to make decisions about treatment Significant risk to health, safety or welfare; or safety of others Available treatments likely to prevent mental disorder from worsening or alleviate symptoms or effects Interim CTO is necessary pending full determination of CTO by tribunal	28 days (maximum total 56 days)	Application for CTO made/ Tribunal	By RMO or the Mental Welfare Commission	Nil

Compulsory Treatment Order

The compulsory treatment order (CTO) is designed to ensure that **3–56** tailor-made measures are applied to the care and treatment of patients who require a degree of compulsion to ensure that these measures are accepted[50].

Conditions

The medical practitioners and the Tribunal must consider that: **3–57**

---

[50] Mental Health (Care and Treatment) (Scotland) Act 2003, Pt 7, s.64(4).

- The patient has a mental disorder
- Medical treatment would be likely to prevent the mental disorder worsening; or alleviate any of the symptoms, or effects, of the disorder; and that such treatment is available
- Without such medical treatment there would be a significant risk to the health, safety or welfare of the patient; or to the safety of others
- The mental disorder significantly impairs the patient's ability to make decisions about the provision of such medical treatment
- The making of a compulsory treatment order is necessary

Process

3–58 First, two medical practitioners must carry out medical examinations of the patient[51]. Each must submit a mental health report to the MHO:

- Stating that he is satisfied that the conditions for a compulsory treatment order are met
- Giving his reasons for believing that the last four conditions above are met
- Specifying the type (or types) of mental disorder as defined in the Act that the patient has
- Describing the symptoms that the patient has of mental disorder and its affect
- Specifying the measures that should be authorised by the CTO
- Specifying the date(s) on which the medical examination was carried out
- Setting out any other relevant information

The reports must agree on at least one type of mental disorder and specify the same measures. One of the reports must state the views of the AMP regarding whether notice should be given to the patient of a CTO application and whether the patient is capable of arranging for a person to represent him. A medical practitioner may state the view that notice should not be given if it would be likely to cause significant harm to the patient or any other person. At least one medical examination must be carried out by an AMP. It is good practice for the patient's general practitioner to carry out the other but if this is not possible it can be done by another AMP. Each examination must be carried out separately but within five days of each other unless the patient is capable of consenting to the examination and consents to them being carried out at the same time; or if the patient is incapable of consenting to joint examination the patient's named person, any guardian or any welfare attorney consents to this.

The medical practitioners may recommend the following measures:

- Detention of the patient in hospital
- Medical treatment under Part 16 of the Act
- Imposition of a requirement on the patient to attend on and at specified times and places to receive medical treatment

---

[51] Mental Health (Care and Treatment) (Scotland) Act 2003, s.58.

- Imposition of a requirement on the patient to attend on and at specified times and places to receive community care services, relevant services or any treatment, care or service
- Imposition of a requirement on the patient to reside at a specified place
- Imposition of a requirement on the patient to allow the RMO, MHO or any person responsible for providing medical treatment, community care services, relevant services or any treatment, care or service to the patient who is authorised for the purposes by the RMO to visit the patient in their residence
- Imposition of a requirement on the patient to obtain the approval of the MHO to any proposed change of address, and
- Imposition of a requirement on the patient to inform the MHO of any change of address before the change takes effect

Second, the MHO must as soon as practicable after the duty to make the application arises, and before making the application, give notice that the application for a CTO is to be made to the patient, the patient's named person and the Commission. The patient need not be informed if one of the mental health reports states that the MHO need not give such notice, although the MHO may still do so if he considers it appropriate.

Third, before an MHO makes an application for a CTO, he must interview the patient unless impracticable, inform the patient of his rights in relation to the application and of the availability of independent advocacy services, and take appropriate steps to ensure that the patient has the opportunity of making use of those services. In addition, the MHO must prepare a report[52] stating:

- The patient's name and address
- The name and address of the patient's named person and primary carer
- Steps taken by the MHO to inform the patient of their rights in relation to the application
- The reasons why interview was impracticable if this was the case
- Details of the patient's personal circumstances
- The MHO's views on the mental health reports relating to the patient
- Details, if known, of any advance statement made by the patient, and
- Any other relevant information.

Fourth, the MHO making an application for a CTO must prepare a Proposed Care Plan[53] in conjunction with the medical practitioners who provided the mental health reports and after consulting, if practicable, any person who it is proposed would provide medical treatment, community care services, or other relevant services to the patient as described in the Proposed Care Plan.

---

[52] Mental Health (Care and Treatment) (Scotland) Act 2003, s.61(4).
[53] *ibid.*, s.62(2).

The Proposed Care Plan must specify:

- The patient's type(s) of mental disorder
- The needs of the patient for medical treatment as outlined in the mental health reports
- The assessed needs of the patient, either a child[54] or adult[55]
- The proposed medical treatment including the names of persons who are to give the treatment and the addresses at which the treatment is to be given
- The proposed community care services or relevant services to be provided to the patient in relation to each of the specified needs with the relevant names and service addresses
- Any other proposed treatment or care, or any other service not specified above
- The measures it is proposed that the CTO should authorise
- The details and objectives of the medical treatment; any community care services; any treatment, care or service to be provided to the patient as compulsory measures
- The name and address of any relevant hospital where detention is proposed
- The name of the hospital whose managers must have responsibility for appointing the patient's RMO where detention is not proposed

The proposed care plan must be signed by the MHO and should make clear which parts are provided with the patient's agreement and which are compulsory, and which of both are essential. The MHO needs to state:

- How the care plan complies with the principles of the Act
- The alternatives considered
- Contingency plans if the proposed options fail
- The degree to which the plan reflects the patient's wishes
- A list of those consulted and how much the plan reflects their views
- The risk assessment that was carried out

Fifth, the MHO must make an application to the Tribunal for a CTO within 14 days of the date of the second medical recommendation[56]. An application must specify measures sought in relation to the patient; any medical treatment, community care services, relevant services or other treatment, care or service specified in the proposed care plan; and where detention is not proposed, the name of the hospital responsible for appointing the patient's RMO. The application consists of the two mental health reports, the MHO report and the proposed care plan.

---

[54] Children (Scotland) Act 1995 (c.36), s.23(3).
[55] Social Work (Scotland) Act 1968 (c.49), s.12A(1)(a).
[56] Mental Health (Care and Treatment) (Scotland) Act 2003, s.63.

Sixth, the MHO must, within a period of 21 days following the making of a CTO, prepare a social circumstances report[57] and send copies to the patient's RMO and the Commission, unless the MHO thinks this would serve little, or no, practical purpose in which case he must record the reasons for this decision and send a copy to the patient's RMO and the Commission. The content of this is described under short-term detention.

Finally, the RMO must prepare a Care Plan[58] after a CTO has been made, setting out proposed or prescribed medical treatment for patients subject to a CTO, including community care services and other services and forms of treatment given to the patient, the objectives of such treatment, the compulsory measures granted by the Tribunal, recorded matters specified by the Tribunal and the date of the next CTO mandatory review. This must be placed in the patient's medical records.

Box 3: Compulsory Treatment Order Process Summary

AMP and GP	: Examine patient : Consider conditions for CTO : Complete Mental Health Report
MHO	: Notify patient, named person and Commission of CTO application : Interview patient : Prepare MHO report
MHO and AMP/GP	: Prepare Proposed Care Plan
MHO	: Apply to Tribunal
Tribunal	: Consider application
MHO	: Complete Social Circumstances Report in 21 days
RMO	: Complete Care Plan if CTO granted

AMP = Approved Medical Practitioner   GP = General Pracitioner
MHO = Mental Health Officer

Powers of the Tribunal[59]

First, the Tribunal must ensure that the patient, the patient's named **3–59** person, any guardian, any welfare attorney, the MHO, the medical practitioners who submitted the mental health reports, the patient's RMO, the patient's primary carer, any *curator ad litem* appointed by the Tribunal, and any other person appearing to have an interest in the application, have the opportunity of making written or oral representations, and of leading, or producing, evidence. The Tribunal can compel people to attend.

Second, the Tribunal, if satisfied that the conditions for a CTO are met, may make an order[60]:

---

[57] Mental Health (Care and Treatment) (Scotland) Act 2003, s.231.
[58] *ibid.*, s.76.
[59] *ibid.*, s.64.
[60] *ibid.*, s.64(4)(a).

- Authorising the measures specified in the order for a period of six months
- Specifying such medical treatment, community care services, relevant services, other treatment, care or service as the Tribunal considers appropriate
- Recording the type of mental disorder the patient has: mental illness, personality disorder or learning disability
- Specifying the name of the hospital the managers of which are responsible for appointing the patient's RMO if the order does not authorise detention of the patient in hospital

Alternatively, the Tribunal can refuse the application[61], or specify some of the measures set out in the application and add to others[62]. In the case of the latter, the Tribunal must afford all relevant persons the opportunity of giving their views.

Third, the Tribunal may authorise the following measures under a CTO[63]:

- The detention of the patient in a specified hospital for six months beginning on the day on which the CTO is made
- Giving medical treatment to the patient during this period in accordance with Part 16 of the Act
- The imposition of a requirement on a patient to:

  – attend for medical treatment, community care services, relevant services or any treatment, care or service on specified dates or directed intervals
  – reside at a specified address
  – allow the MHO, RMO or any person responsible for providing medical treatment or community care services to visit the patient at home
  – obtain approval of the MHO to any proposed change of address
  – inform the MHO of any change of address

Fourth, the Tribunal may record details of any such services required to enable a patient to comply with any measure specified.

Finally, a CTO specifying detention in hospital or residence at a specific place authorises the removal of the patient to that location within a seven-day period.

Review and Revocation of Compulsory Treatment Orders

3–60 The patient's RMO must during the two-month period prior to the ending of a CTO carry out a *first review* of that order[64]. The RMO must examine the patient or make arrangements for an AMP to carry out a medical examination, consider whether conditions one to four of the

---

[61] Mental Health (Care and Treatment) (Scotland) Act 2003, s.64(4)(b).
[62] *ibid.*, s.64(6).
[63] *ibid.*, s.66.
[64] *ibid.*, s.77.

CTO listed above apply and whether a CTO continues to be necessary. The RMO must consult with the MHO, persons who provide medical treatment, community care services or any other treatment, care or service set out in the care plan and any other appropriate person. It would be good practice to hold a case conference to do this. *Further mandatory reviews*[65] must be carried out during the two months before the end of a CTO extended by RMO determination under s.86; or two months before the end of a CTO extended or varied by virtue of an order by the Tribunal under s.103 of this Act.

If the RMO is not satisfied that conditions one to four for a CTO continue to apply, or that it is necessary for the patient to be subject to a CTO, then the RMO must make a determination revoking the CTO. Similarly the RMO must consider from time to time whether the conditions needed for a CTO are ongoing and may revoke or vary the order[66]. The Commission has powers to revoke a CTO for the same reasons[67]. As soon as practicable the RMO or Commission must give notice of any determination made and the reasons for it and send these to the patient, the patient's named person, any guardian and any welfare attorney, and within seven days to the MHO and the Tribunal; and to each other as appropriate.

After a first or further mandatory review of a CTO where the order was NOT revoked an RMO must consider, after consultation with the MHO and care providers, whether it will be necessary to extend the CTO; assess the needs of the patient for medical treatment; consider whether the CTO should be varied by modifying the measures, or any recorded matter (medical treatment or services), specified in it; and what modifications, if any, are appropriate[68].

Example

A 67-year-old woman is well known to her general practitioner as an **3–61** "eccentric". She comes regularly to the practice to receive medication for arthritis and to complain about her neighbours whom she claims are spying on her and breaking into her house. She has always rejected any suggestion of psychiatric assessment or psychotropic medication. This situation has been ongoing for 10 years but in recent months matters have got out of hand. She has developed a home-made security system with pots and pans, string and sticky tape. It takes her over three hours to assemble this every time she returns home and she has become more withdrawn and her self care is beginning to deteriorate. In addition, she intermittently shouts at her neighbours and the police have been called on one occasion. With the assistance of the practice nurse, she was seen at home by a psychiatrist. There was no evidence that she was cognitively impaired. A diagnosis of a delusional disorder: persecutory type was made but she rejected any offer of treatment. She fulfilled the conditions for a CTO and medical reports were completed by the consultant psychiatrist and her GP. She was seen by an MHO, informed that an

---

[65] Mental Health (Care and Treatment) (Scotland) Act 2003, s.78.
[66] *ibid.*, s.80.
[67] *ibid.*, s.81.
[68] *ibid.*, s.83(3).

application for a CTO would be made and given information on her rights. A care plan was prepared outlining the measures proposed for the CTO. The Tribunal authorised a CTO with measures to detain the patient in hospital for six months and to give medical treatment. Subsequently, the patient improved and no longer thought she needed a security system but continued to believe that her neighbours were spying on her. An application was made to extend and vary her CTO and conditions authorised to ensure that she took her medication, resided in her home, attended a day hospital and allowed access to her home by the MHO, RMO and community psychiatric nurse. In addition she had to inform the MHO of any change of address and to get MHO agreement to this.

Table 7: Compulsory Treatment Order

Section	Conditions	Duration	Signatories/ Consent	Revocation	Appeal
64(4)	Mental disorder Available treatment likely to prevent medical disorder from worsening or alleviate symptoms or effects Significant risk to health, safety or welfare; or safety of others without treatment Significantly impaired ability to make decisions about treatment CTO is necessary	6 months Renewable for 6 months and yearly thereafter	Two fully registered doctors (one AMP) Application by MHO must include proposed care plan/ Mental Health Tribunal approval	By RMO or the Mental Welfare Commission	To Tribunal

Suspension of Measures Authorised under a CTO or Interim CTO

3–62　　The RMO may suspend a detention in hospital requirement of a CTO or interim CTO[69] on a patient for up to 6 months or a maximum of 9 months in any 12-month period if there has been an earlier period of suspension. This suspension is the former leave of absence. Detention can be suspended by the RMO for an event or series of events including travel. If the RMO considers it necessary in the interests of the patient, or for the protection of any other person, the certificate may include conditions, for example that the patient must be kept in the charge of a person authorised in writing for the purpose by the RMO. The RMO must consult the patient, the patient's named person, the patient's General Practitioner and MHO if the RMO proposes to grant a

---

[69] Mental Health (Care and Treatment) (Scotland) Act 2003, s.127.

certificate for more than 28 days, whether continuous or in discrete periods. Any suspension of detention of more than 28 days must be notified to the Commission within 14 days.

Suspension of other measures[70]

An RMO can grant a certificate suspending CTO measures, other than detention, for a period of up to three months. The RMO must inform the patient, the patient's named person and the MHO of the measures he proposes to suspend, the proposed duration and the reasons for this. The RMO must similarly inform the Commission within 14 days.

Certificates granted to suspend detention or other CTO measures can be revoked if the RMO is satisfied that it is necessary in the interests of the patient or for the protection of any other person. The patient, the patient's named person, MHO, any person into whose charge the patient was given and the GP must be informed as soon as practicable of the revocation and the reasons for it. The Commission must be informed within 14 days giving reasons for the revocation of the certificate.

Extension and/or Variation of a Compulsory Treatment Order

CTOs can be extended and/or varied by a number of processes. The **3–63** Tribunal must allow the presentation of evidence as for an initial CTO application.

Extension of a CTO by RMO

An RMO can extend a CTO for 6 months after a first review or 12 **3–64** months after a subsequent review[71].

Conditions

An RMO can extend a CTO providing that: **3–65**

- It will continue to be necessary for the patient to be subject to a CTO after it was due to cease; and
- The order does not need varied by modifying the measures or any recorded matter specified in it.

Process

First, the RMO must consult with any appropriate person including **3–66** those involved in the care plan and inform the MHO in writing that he is intending to extend the CTO.

Second, the MHO must interview the patient unless impracticable; inform the patient of the RMO's proposal to extend the CTO; inform the patient of their rights and of the availability of independent advocacy services; take steps to ensure that patient has the opportunity of making use of those services; and inform the RMO of whether the MHO agrees,

---

[70] Mental Health (Care and Treatment) (Scotland) Act 2003, s.128.
[71] *ibid.*, s.86.

or disagrees stating why not, with the extension and of any other relevant matters.

Third, as soon as practicable and before the CTO ceases, the RMO must prepare a record stating the determination, the reasons for it, whether the MHO agrees or disagrees or has failed to comply with the duty imposed, the reasons for any disagreement with the MHO, and the patient's type of mental disorder. This must be submitted to the Tribunal and notice given to the patient (unless the RMO considers this inappropriate because of a risk of significant harm to the patient or others), the patient's named person, the MHO and the Commission. In addition, a statement must be sent to these people indicating whether the RMO is sending a copy of the record to the patient and if not, why not.

Powers

3–67   The measures specified in the CTO continue to be authorised for 6 or 12 months.

Tribunal's duty to review a determination to extend a CTO

The Tribunal must review cases which have been extended by the RMO[72] if there is a difference in type(s) of mental disorder stated in the record given to the Tribunal and recorded in the CTO; if the MHO disagrees with the determination or has failed to give the RMO a view; or if no decision has been made by the Tribunal in respect of a CTO in the last two years. The Tribunal may revoke the determination; revoke the determination and the CTO; confirm the determination; or confirm the determination and vary the CTO by modifying the measures authorised or any recorded matter[73]. Alternatively, it can make an interim order varying the CTO for up to 28 days.

Extension and Variation of a CTO by the Tribunal

3–68   At a first or further review the RMO must consider the need to extend and vary a CTO. If the measures authorised by the order require extension and variation, an application must be made to the Tribunal to do so[74].

Conditions

3–69   An RMO can apply to the Tribunal to extend and vary a CTO providing:

- That it will be necessary for the patient to be subject to a CTO after the day on which the order will cease to authorise the measures specified in it; but
- That the order should be varied by modifying the measures, or any recorded matter, specified in it.

---

[72] Mental Health (Care and Treatment) (Scotland) Act 2003, s.101.
[73] *ibid.*, s.102.
[74] *ibid.*, s.92.

Process

First, the RMO must inform the MHO that he is proposing to make **3–70** an application to the Tribunal to extend the CTO (for 6 months after the first review or 12 months thereafter), varying the measures or recorded matter in it and detailing the proposed modifications. It is good practice to do this at least two weeks before the CTO expires.

Second, the MHO must interview the patient unless impracticable and inform the patient of the RMO's proposal to make an application to the Tribunal extending and varying the CTO, of any proposed modifications, of their rights and of the availability of independent advocacy services, and ensure access to these. The MHO must inform the RMO if he agrees, or disagrees stating why not, with the proposed extension and variation of a CTO and prepare a report for the Tribunal.

Third, the RMO must consider the views of those interviewed for the review and the MHO and if satisfied that the conditions are met make an application to the Tribunal extending and varying the CTO.

Fourth, the RMO must give notice of this application as soon as practicable to the patient, the patient's named person, any guardian, any welfare attorney, the MHO and the Commission.

Lastly, an application is made by the RMO to the Tribunal for an order extending and varying a CTO. It must record the name and address of the patient and his named person; the proposed modification of measures or any recorded matter; the reasons for seeking that modification; and whether the MHO agrees, or disagrees, and if so the reasons why. The RMO must provide the Tribunal with a care plan update including an evaluation of its current working.

Powers of the Tribunal

The Tribunal may make an order[75] extending the CTO for 6 or 12 **3–71** months depending on total length of a continuous CTO and varying the measures or any recorded matter in the CTO, extending the CTO for that period, refusing the application, or refusing the application and revoking the CTO. Alternatively, the Tribunal can make an interim order extending, or extending and varying, a CTO for up to 28 days if it will be unable to determine the application to extend and vary a CTO before the CTO ceases to authorise its specified measures[76]; or make an interim order varying the CTO by modifying the measures or any recorded matter in it for up to 28 days[77]. These interim orders cannot be in force for a continuous period of more than 56 days.

Variation of a CTO

Process

An RMO must from time to time, as well as at a mandatory review, **3–72** consider whether a variation of the CTO measures is required. If required, he must assess the needs of the patient for medical treatment,

---

[75] Mental Health (Care and Treatment) (Scotland) Act 2003, s.103(1).
[76] *ibid.*, s.105.
[77] *ibid.*, 106.

consider what modification if any is appropriate and consult the MHO and other appropriate people. If satisfied that the CTO should be varied the RMO must make an application to the Tribunal[78] for an order varying the CTO. The process outlined above for the extension and variation of a CTO is then followed.

Powers of the Tribunal

3–73   Following an application to vary a CTO the Tribunal may vary the CTO by modifying the measures or any recorded matter specified in it; refuse the application; or refuse the application and revoke that order[79]. Alternatively, it can make an interim order[80] varying the CTO for up to 28 days pending a final determination, or a maximum of 56 days on all interim orders.

Recorded Matters

3–74   Recorded matters are any medical treatment, community care services, relevant services, and other treatment, care or service specified by the Tribunal in a CTO. If it appears to the RMO that any of the recorded matters in a CTO[81] are not being provided he must consult with the MHO and any other appropriate person and if satisfied make a reference to the Tribunal giving the patient's details, name and address of the patient's named person and the reason for making the reference. An MHO report and an RMO care plan update are required. The patient, the patient's named person, any guardian, any welfare attorney, the MHO and the Commission must be informed. The Tribunal may make an order[82] varying the measures and recorded matter in the CTO, revoking the CTO; or apply a 28-day interim order varying the CTO pending its decision[83].

Reference to the Tribunal by the Mental Welfare Commission

3–75   The Commission may refer a case to the Tribunal regarding any aspect of a CTO[84]. The Commission must give notice of this to the patient, the patient's named person, any guardian, any welfare attorney, the patient's RMO and MHO; including the reason for making the reference. The Tribunal may make an order[85] varying the measures and recorded matter in the CTO, revoking the CTO; or apply a 28-day interim order varying the CTO pending its decision[86].

Applications by a Patient for Revocation or Variation of a CTO

3–76   Patients or their named persons can apply for revocation or variation of a CTO.

---

[78] Mental Health (Care and Treatment) (Scotland) Act 2003, s.95.
[79] *ibid.*, s.103(4).
[80] *ibid.*, s.106.
[81] *ibid.*, s.96.
[82] *ibid.*, s.104(1).
[83] *ibid.*, s.106.
[84] *ibid.*, s.98.
[85] *ibid.*, s.104(1).
[86] *ibid.*, s.106.

Patient application for revocation of RMO determination extending a CTO

The patient or the patient's named person can make an application to **3–77** the Tribunal for an order[87] to revoke a s.86 RMO determination extending a CTO. One application to the Tribunal is permitted in each renewal of section period. The Tribunal may make an order[88] revoking the determination to which the application relates, revoking the determination and the CTO, confirming the determination, or confirming the determination and varying the CTO by modifying the measures or any recorded matter specified in it.

Patient application for revocation or variation of a CTO

The patient or the patient's named person can apply for the revoca- **3–78** tion or modification of measures or any recorded matter in a CTO[89]. An application cannot be made until three months after the CTO was made. Two applications are permitted during the initial CTO period and each period of renewal, although only one can follow an application to revoke a determination extending a CTO. The Tribunal may make an order[90] revoking the CTO, or varying the CTO by modifying the measures or any recorded matter; or refusing the application.

Non-Compliance with a CTO or Interim CTO

Breach of an Attendance Requirement

If a patient under a CTO or interim CTO with a requirement to **3–79** attend for treatment (attendance requirement) fails to do so, the RMO following consultation and agreement with the MHO, may take or authorise another person to take the patient into custody and to convey the patient to the agreed place of the attendance requirement or to any hospital[91]. The patient may be detained there for up to six hours commencing at the time of arrival, to give the patient medical treatment if it is authorised in the CTO or to determine whether the patient is capable of consenting to medical treatment and if so, whether the patient consents to receive any medical treatment.

Non-compliance generally with a CTO

When a patient subject to a CTO or an interim CTO fails to comply **3–80** with any measure authorised by the order the patient's RMO may take, or arrange for another person to take the patient into custody and convey the patient to a hospital[92]. The patient's MHO must be consulted and must consent. Such action can be taken if the RMO considers that reasonable steps have been taken to contact the patient following the patient's failure to comply with the measures; if contact has been made with the patient, he has been afforded a reasonable opportunity to

---

[87] Mental Health (Care and Treatment) (Scotland) Act 2003, s.99.
[88] *ibid.*, s.103.
[89] *ibid,* s.100.
[90] *ibid.*, s.103.
[91] *ibid.,* s.112.
[92] *ibid.*, s.113.

comply with the measures; it is reasonably likely that there would be a significant deterioration in the patient's mental health if he was to continue to fail to comply with the measure; and it is necessary as a matter of urgency to detain the patient in hospital. The patient may be detained in hospital until a medical examination has been carried out by the RMO or an AMP. This must be done as soon as "reasonably practicable". The power to detain the patient lasts 72 hours beginning with his arrival in hospital.

Compulsory Treatment Order: detention pending review or application for variation following non-compliance with a CTO

3–81   An RMO may grant a certificate authorising the continued detention in hospital of the patient for 28 days[93] if the following criteria are met:

- The patient is currently detained under s.113(5) of the Act because of non-compliance generally with the CTO
- A medical examination has been carried out
- The RMO is considering whether the compulsory measures in the CTO should be varied or is required to make an application to the Tribunal
- The RMO considers that without further detention in hospital it is likely that there will be a significant deterioration in the patient's mental health
- The RMO has consulted and obtained the consent of the patient's MHO
- The RMO has consulted the patient's named person, if practicable

The certificate must state the RMO's reasons for believing the conditions outlined have been met and be signed by the RMO. The RMO must revoke the certificate if he determines that the order should not be varied or is not satisfied that if the patient leaves hospital it is reasonably likely that there will be a significant deterioration in the patient's health.

Interim Compulsory Treatment Order: detention pending further procedure following non-compliance with a CTO

3–82   The same process is required to continue to detain a patient subject to an interim CTO in hospital for a further 28 days for non-compliance, except that the interim CTO must not expire during the 72-hour detention period and there is no requirement for the RMO to be considering variation of CTO measures[94]. The RMO must revoke this certificate if he is not satisfied that it is reasonable likely that there will be a significant deterioration in the patient's mental health if he leaves hospital.

For either of these options the hospital managers must inform the patient, the patient's named person, any guardian, and any welfare

---

[93] Mental Health (Care and Treatment) (Scotland) Act 2003, s.114(2).
[94] *ibid.*, s.115(2).

attorney as soon as practicable; and the Tribunal and Commission within seven days. Any revocation of the certificate must be notified to the same people. The patient has the right to apply to the Tribunal and the Tribunal can revoke the certificate if not reasonably satisfied that there will be a significant deterioration in the patient's mental health if he does not continue to be detained in hospital. Whilst the patient is detained in hospital under 72-hour detention for general non-compliance with a CTO, a 28-day detention certificate pending review or application for variation of a CTO, or an ICTO—detention pending further procedure, the measures authorised in the CTO or interim CTO cease, except measures authorising medical treatment.

Absconding

The Act sets out the powers available if a patient absconds.   3–83

Absconding by patients subject to a Compulsory Treatment Order[95]

A patient who is subject to a CTO can be taken into custody if: 3–84

- he absconds from any place where he is kept pending removal to hospital, during the removal to hospital or transfer to another hospital, or when detained in hospital
- he fails to comply with the conditions set out in a suspension of measures authorising detention or absconds from the charge of an authorised person
- he fails to comply with the requirement to reside at a specified place, or fails to obtain the approval of the MHO to any proposed change of address and changes address.

Absconding by other patients[96]

Any patient who absconds from hospital whilst being detained under 3–85 the following can be taken into custody:

- An interim compulsory treatment order authorising detention
- A short-term detention certificate
- A certificate authorising continued detention in hospital pending a review or application for variation of a CTO following non-compliance
- An extension of short-term detention pending determination of application for a CTO
- An emergency detention certificate
- A 72-hour detention for non-compliance generally with a CTO or interim CTO
- A nurse's power to detain pending medical examination
- In addition any patient subject to an interim CTO imposing a residence requirement who fails to comply with that, with the conditions set out in a suspension of detention, or who

---

[95] Mental Health (Care and Treatment) (Scotland) Act 2003, s.301.
[96] *ibid.*, s.302.

absconds from the charge of an authorised person can be taken into custody

Process

3–86   An MHO, a constable, a member of any hospital staff in which a patient can legally be detained, a person designated by the RMO or a person authorised under the Act to have charge of the patient, can return the patient to hospital or take the patient to any other place considered appropriate by the RMO in a period of three months from the date the patient absconded or the patient's conduct first gave rise to liability to be taken into custody, for those subject to a CTO or until the date of expiry of all other orders. This includes the power to use reasonable force.

A CTO ceases to have effect if the patient has an unauthorised absence of a period of 3 months. CTO measures continue to be authorised for 14 days to allow RMO review if a patient has an unauthorised absence for longer than 28 consecutive days but less than 3 months, is absent for less than 3 months but the CTO ends during this period or if the unauthorised absence ends within 14 days of the termination of the CTO.

A similar process exists for extending for 14 days a short-term detention certificate or a certificate of detention pending review or application for variation of a CTO, if the unauthorised leave ends within 13 days of the cessation of the certificate[97].

Entry, Removal and Detention Powers

3–87   Powers to allow the removal and medical examination of people known or thought to have a mental disorder, in specific premises or in a public place, can be necessary when an individual refuses to cooperate with mental health services or is behaving in a bizarre manner. A warrant to detain a patient for up to three hours for the purpose of carrying out a medical examination[98] can be issued by a sheriff or a justice of the peace but it does not authorise the patient's removal from the premises. This would require a warrant to remove to a place of safety.

Warrant to Enter Premises for Purposes of Taking a Patient

3–88   For patients already subject to the provisions of the Act, a sheriff or justice of the peace may grant a warrant[99] permitting an authorised person, any MHO appointed by the local authority for the area in which the premises are situated, and any constable of the local police force, to enter the premises specified if the authorised person is unable but requires to gain access. The police constable can use force to open lockfast places. An authorised person is someone permitted by the Act to take the patient to any place, or to take him into custody where he is

---

[97] Mental Health (Care and Treatment) (Scotland) Act 2003, s.308.
[98] *ibid.*, s.35.
[99] *ibid.*, s.292.

liable to be taken. A medical practitioner or any other authorised person may accompany the persons specified in the warrant to its execution. It is the authorised person who must make the application for the warrant and no statutory form is required.

Removal to a Place of Safety: Removal Order Conditions

A sheriff may make a removal order[1] on a person: **3–89**

- With a mental disorder
- Aged 16 years or over
- Likely to suffer significant harm if not removed to a place of safety and
- Who is subject, or exposed to ill-treatment, neglect or some other deficiency in care or treatment
- Suffering loss or damage, or at risk of suffering loss or damage, of his property because of mental disorder or
- Living alone or without care, and unable to look after him or his property or financial affairs

Powers

A removal order authorises an MHO, a police officer and any other **3–90** specified person, to enter the home, using force if necessary, of a mentally disordered person, and to remove and detain him in a specified place of safety for a period of up to 7 days, as set out in the order, within 72 hours of the order being granted.

Process

An MHO in the employ of the local authority area covering the **3–91** premises in question can apply for the order. There is no statutory form and oral evidence can be given. The sheriff must give the person subject to the application, and relevant others, the opportunity to make representations and of leading, or producing evidence unless such a delay would be likely to be prejudicial to the person concerned.

In an urgent situation where an application to the sheriff for a removal order is impracticable and any delay in obtaining a removal order would be harmful to the individual concerned, an application can be made to a justice of the peace for the commission area in which the premises are situated[2].

Recall or variation of a removal order

A person who is subject to a removal order, or any person claiming an **3–92** interest in the welfare of that person, may apply to the sheriff for an order to recall or vary the removal order[3]. A variation may specify a different place of safety, and authorise the person's removal to there within 72 hours and ongoing detention for the remainder of the period

---

[1] Mental Health (Care and Treatment) (Scotland) Act 2003, s.293.
[2] *ibid.*, s.294.
[3] *ibid.*, s.295.

specified in the removal order. The sheriff must allow representations, and the leading or producing of evidence in making such decisions. If a removal order is recalled the sheriff can order that the person is returned to the premises from which they were removed or be taken to some appropriate place chosen by that person.

Appeal

3–93   No appeal is permitted against the decision of a sheriff or a justice of the peace about removal orders, their recall or variation.

Removal to a Place of Safety from a Public Place

3–94   This is a power specifically for the police to obtain a medical examination of person in a public place thought to have a mental disorder. It is fully described in Chapter 5.

Nurse's Power to Detain Pending a Medical Examination

3–95   Under the Act, psychiatric nurses continue to have the power to detain patients for a short period prior to a medical examination[4]. This is used to prevent voluntary patients with a mental disorder believed to require ongoing treatment for their health, welfare or safety of themselves or others, from leaving a ward before a medical assessment is carried out.

Conditions

3–96   • It is not practicable to secure the immediate medical examination of the patient by a doctor
        • The patient has a mental disorder
        • It is necessary for the protection of the health, safety or welfare of the patient, or the safety of any other person, that the patient be immediately restrained from leaving the hospital
        • It is necessary to carry out a medical examination of the patient for the purpose of determining whether the granting of an emergency detention certificate or a short-term detention certificate is warranted

Powers

3–97   A patient may be detained in hospital for two hours for the purpose of enabling arrangements to be made for a medical examination of the patient to be carried out.

Process

3–98   First, a nurse of the prescribed class, usually a registered mental nurse, can detain a patient in hospital for up to two hours if he is being treated in hospital but not already subject to the provisions of this Act or the 1995 Act, excluding attendance for parole conditions.

---

[4] Mental Health (Care and Treatment) (Scotland) Act 2003, s.299.

Second, the detention expires at the end of two hours; or if the doctor arrives to carry out the examination in the second hour, one hour after his arrival.

Third, the nurse must as soon as possible after the holding period begins inform an MHO. The nurse must record in writing the fact of the patient's detention, the time it began and the reasons for believing an emergency or short-term detention certificate may be warranted. This record must be delivered to hospital managers as soon as practicable and a copy sent to the Commission within 14 days.

Appeal

There is no appeal against the use of the nurse's power to detain **3–99** pending a medical examination.

Example

A 27-year-old woman was admitted voluntarily to hospital two days **3–100** previously. She was brought to see psychiatric services by her husband who was concerned about her low mood, disturbed sleep, poor appetite and excessive weight loss since the birth of their first child four months earlier. In addition, she had difficulty seeing any future and had made negative statements that her husband and child would be better off without her. A diagnosis of postnatal depression was made and she was persuaded to enter hospital by her husband. At the time she stated her intention to leave hospital, there had been no improvement in her depressed presentation, she refused to wait to see a doctor or for her husband to visit, and the nurse in charge feared that the patient was planning to commit suicide. She was therefore detained using the nurse's holding power and the MHO alerted. The MHO immediately attended the ward and following a subsequent medical examination, the patient was detained under an emergency detention certificate.

Table 8: Nurse's Power to Detain Pending a Medical Examination

Section	Conditions	Duration	Signatories/ Consent	Revocation	Appeal
299	Mental disorder Necessary for protection of patient's health, safety or welfare; or safety of others to restrain from leaving hospital Not practicable to secure immediate medical examination Necessary to carry out a medical examination to determine if an emergency or short-term detention certificate is required	Two hours or one hour from the time of the doctor's arrival if it is in the second hour of detention	Registered Mental Nurse	Nil	Nil

MEDICAL TREATMENT

3–101   Patients subject to the provisions of the Mental Health Act are protected via an independent review process to ensure the necessity and appropriate nature of any proposed medical treatment if they do not, or cannot, consent to a proposed treatment. The designated medical practitioner[5] (DMP) has the primary role in this. This is a doctor who has the necessary qualifications and experience to give second opinions regarding medical treatment. The Commission is responsible for compiling and maintaining a list of DMPs and for the provision of training in this role. A DMP can interview and examine a patient in private at any reasonable time, and inspect his medical records. A doctor cannot fulfil both the role of DMP, and RMO or medical practitioner responsible for treating the patient, for the same patient. Either the RMO or the DMP must be a child specialist in any decision regarding medical treatment for a person under the age of 18 years.

The definition of medical treatment within the Act is wide and includes nursing care, psychological interventions, habilitation and rehabilitation as well as psychosurgery, ECT and medication. Psychosurgery, ECT, medicine and urgent medical treatment are considered separately under Part 16 of the Act. A s.47 certificate under the Adults with Incapacity Act (2000) permits medical treatment for a physical disorder or for a mental disorder where the patient is deemed incapable of reaching a decision about medical treatment. This certificate does not authorise neurosurgery, ECT, ongoing psychiatric treatment or urgent medical treatment. It does not include powers to detain and this is clearly the remit of the Mental Health Act.

Consent to Psychosurgery

3–102   A patient capable of consenting must consent to any surgical operation for destroying brain tissue or the functioning of brain tissue.[6] A DMP must certify in writing that the patient is capable of consenting to the treatment; that the patient consents in writing to the treatment; and that it is in the patient's best interest that the treatment should be given to alleviate, or prevent a deterioration in the patient's condition. Two lay people, appointed by the Commission, must certify in writing that the patient is capable of consenting to the treatment and that the patient consents in writing to the treatment. These individuals must have the opportunity to interview the patient in private. Treatment must stop if the patient withdraws consent to it at any time before its completion.

If the patient is incapable of consenting but does not resist or object, treatment can go ahead[7]. This is a major change in the legislation governing psychosurgery. First, a DMP must certify in writing that the patient is incapable of consenting to treatment, does not object to the treatment and that it is in the patient's best interest that the treatment should be given to alleviate, or prevent, a deterioration in the patient's

---

[5] Mental Health (Care and Treatment) (Scotland) Act 2003, s.233.
[6] *ibid.*, s.235.
[7] *ibid.*, s.236.

condition. Secondly, two lay people appointed by the Commission must certify in writing that the patient is incapable of consenting to the treatment and does not object to the treatment. Thirdly, the Court of Session must make an order declaring that the treatment may lawfully be given following an application by the patient's RMO or the Medical Practitioner primarily responsible for treating the patient. The Court of Session may make such an order if it is satisfied that it is in the patient's best interest that the treatment should be given to alleviate or prevent deterioration in the patient's condition and if the patient does not object to the treatment.

Electro Convulsive Therapy

Electro Convulsive Therapy (ECT)[8] can be given if the patient's RMO **3–103** or a DMP certifies in writing that the patient is capable of consenting to the treatment; the patient consents in writing to the treatment; the treatment is authorised by the Mental Health Act or the 1995 Act; and it is in the patient's best interests that the treatment should be given to alleviate or prevent deterioration in the patient's condition. The treatment must stop if the patient withdraws consent at any time.

If the patient is incapable of consenting[9], a DMP must certify in writing that the patient is incapable of understanding the nature, purpose and likely effects of ECT; that the ECT is authorised by the Mental Health Act or the 1995 Act; and that it is in the patient's best interest that the treatment should be given to alleviate, or prevent a deterioration in the patient's condition. If the patient resists or objects to the treatment, the DMP must certify to this and that it is necessary to give the treatment for the purposes of saving the patient's life; preventing serious deterioration in the patient's condition; or alleviating serious suffering on the part of the patient. ECT cannot be given, even on an urgent basis, to a patient with capacity to make a treatment decision who refuses.

Medicine

Any medicine, or medicine given for the purpose of reducing sex drive **3–104** (except surgical implantation of hormones), given as treatment for a mental disorder for more than two months since the patient became subject to the Act, must go through a consent or second opinion procedure[10]. This includes the provision, without consent and by artificial means, of nutrition to the patient. If the patient refuses consent or is incapable of consenting, medical treatment can be given if a DMP certifies to this in writing; and confirms that the treatment is authorised by this Act or the 1995 Act; and that it is in the patient's best interests that treatment should be given to alleviate, or prevent deterioration in the patient's condition. The DMP must consider the reason for a patient's refusal to consent if known and give reasons why treatment should be given. Where the patient is not in hospital this certification

---

[8] Mental Health (Care and Treatment) (Scotland) Act 2003, ss.237–238.
[9] *ibid.*, s.239.
[10] *ibid.*, s.240.

does not authorise the giving of medical treatment by force to the patient.

For other forms of medical treatment[11], if the patient is capable of consenting to the treatment and consents in writing, the medical treatment can be given to the patient under the direction of the patient's RMO. If the patient is capable of consenting to the treatment but does not consent or consents but not in writing, or is incapable of consenting, then the treatment can be given under the direction of the patient's RMO if the RMO determines that it is in the patient's best interests that the treatment be given and has considered the patient's reasons for not consenting; any views expressed by the patient or the patient's named person; any advance statement made by the patient; and the likelihood of the treatment alleviating, or preventing a deterioration in the patient's condition. An AMP who is not the patient's RMO must carry out this process for patients subject to an assessment order. The RMO or the AMP must record in writing the reasons for giving the treatment. Where the patient is not in hospital, this does not authorise the giving of medical treatment by force.

Copies of all certificates issued for psychosurgery, ECT or medication must be sent to the Commission within seven days. The person giving a certificate must consult the patient and the patient's named person and other people that are principally concerned with the patient's medical treatment unless it is impracticable to do so.

Urgent Medical Treatment

3–105   If a patient detained in hospital under the 2003 Act or the 1995 Act requires urgent medical treatment but does not consent or is incapable of consenting to the treatment, this may be given for the purposes of saving the patient's life, preventing serious deterioration in the patient's condition, alleviating serious suffering on the part of the patient, and preventing the patient from behaving violently or being a danger to himself or others[12]. This can be given if it is not likely to entail unfavourable, and irreversible, physical or psychological consequences except for the purposes of saving the patient's life; or if it does not entail significant physical hazard to the patient except if it involves saving the patient's life or preventing serious deterioration in the patient's condition. It does not authorise ECT if the patient is capable of consenting but refuses to do so. Within seven days the RMO must notify the Commission of the type of treatment given and its purpose, and give an update to the Commission when next applying or reporting to the Tribunal, on the treatment given and the patient's condition.

PATIENT REPRESENTATION

3–106   Optimising the opportunities for patient representation is a central aim of the Act. This includes the provision of information, assistance with communication, access to advocacy services and the creation of the

[11] Mental Health (Care and Treatment) (Scotland) Act 2003, s.242.
[12] *ibid.*, s.243.

new role of a patient's named person. The statutory involvement of patients and their representatives in decision making is to be welcomed greatly and it will be important to ensure that advocacy services extend their role to include those unable because of their mental disorder to request support and representation.

Named Person

The role of a patient's named person is to represent the interests of, **3–107** and support and intervene on behalf of the patient who is the subject of any procedures under the Mental Health Act[13]. The named person acts independently of the patient and has defined rights and powers described in each section of this chapter. The named person must be 16 years or over and can be nominated by the patient if he is at least 16 years of age. The patient must sign the nomination and this must be witnessed by a prescribed person. The witness must certify that the nominator understands the effect of nominating a person to be his named person and has not been subject to any undue influence in making the nomination. The patient can revoke the nomination of a named person or prevent someone taking this role, and either must be signed, witnessed and certified in the same fashion.

A nominated named person may decline the role by giving notice to the patient and the local authority area in which the nominator resides. The nomination is effective even if the nominator later becomes incapable by reason of mental disorder or inability to communicate because of physical disability. If no named person is nominated or the nominee declines to act, then this role will fall to the individual's primary carer or, if not 16 years of age, to another carer. If a patient has two or more carers, they may agree which is to be the named person. If the patient has no primary carer or the role is declined, then the patient's nearest relative shall be the named person. The meaning of "nearest relative"[14] is set out in Box 4.

Box 4: Meaning of Nearest Relative

Nearest relatives are defined by descending order of "relatedness":

Spouse—disregarded if permanently separated or deserted.
Common-law spouse or same sex partner living together for at least six months prior to admission to hospital
Child
Parent
Sibling
Grandparent
Grandchild
Aunt or uncle
Niece or nephew

---

[13] Mental Health (Care and Treatment) (Scotland) Act 2003, ss.250–253.
[14] *ibid.*, s.254.

Person living with the individual for five years, or had been until admission to hospital

Half-blood relationships are treated as whole-blood relationships for the purposes of this list. Step-children are treated as blood children. It excludes anyone under the age of 16 or not resident in the UK. If two or more people fall within the list at the same place, they can agree who should be the nearest relative or, if not, whole blood siblings will be preferred over half-blood siblings; and older over younger siblings.

For children the named person is the individual with parental rights and responsibilities; the local authority if there is a care order; or, in any other case, the child's primary carer. The parents must agree who is to be the named person or, if they do not agree, it is the one who provides, on a regular basis, all, or most, of the care for and support to the child.

An MHO must establish if the patient has a named person and who it is when using the 2003 or 1995 Acts[15]. If the person does not have a named person or it is not possible to establish this, the MHO must record what steps were taken and copy this to the Commission and the Tribunal. The MHO may apply to the Tribunal for an order to appoint a named person. If the MHO considers that it is inappropriate for an identified named person to have this role, the MHO can apply to the Tribunal for an order declaring that the acting named person be removed from this role or appointing another person specified in the order to be the patient's named person.

Similarly the patient, the RMO, any parent of a child patient, the hospital managers if the patient is in hospital, any welfare attorney, any guardian, any relative of the patient and any other person with an interest in the welfare of the patient may apply to the Tribunal to appoint or change a named person[16]. The Tribunal has the powers to appoint or change a named person[17].

Advocacy

3–108   Under the Act every person with a mental disorder has a right of access to independent advocacy regardless of whether they are subject to the provisions of the Act[18]. It is the duty of each local authority and health board, in collaboration, to secure independent advocacy services in their area and to take appropriate steps to ensure that these services can be used. Advocacy services provide support and representation to enable a person to have as much control of or capacity to influence, their care and welfare as appropriate; and protect and advance that person's interests where he is unable to state an opinion on any matter concerning his care or welfare.

Provision of Information to the Patient

3–109   Hospital managers[19] must take all reasonable steps to ensure that patients subject to mental health legislation understand:

---

[15] Mental Health (Care and Treatment) (Scotland) Act 2003, s.255.
[16] *ibid.*, s.256.
[17] *ibid.*, s.257.
[18] ibid., s.259.
[19] *ibid.*, s.260.

- Their detention or the effect of any order
- What this means to them
- The powers of the RMO and the Tribunal to revoke certificates or orders
- Their right of application, or appeal, to the Tribunal
- How to exercise any such right
- The powers available to the Tribunal on application or appeal
- The functions of the Commission relevant to their case, and
- How to obtain legal assistance as respects any such right

This information must be provided after an order has been made or a patient requests it.

Provision of Assistance to Patients with Communication Difficulties

Mechanical aids, human assistance or an interpretation service must **3–110** be provided as required, for any patient subject to the Act who has communication difficulties during any medical examination for the purpose of assessing the patient's mental disorder, for any review of detention or any Tribunal proceedings[20]. These steps must be recorded.

Advance Statements

An advance statement[21] sets out the way a person wishes to be treated, **3–111** or not treated, for mental disorder in the event of him becoming mentally disordered and his ability to make decisions about treatment becoming significantly impaired. It is good practice for individuals making advance statements to discuss the content with medical staff and to be advised of the powers under the Act regarding medical treatment for mental disorder. An advance statement must be made in writing, signed by the person making it and witnessed in writing to the effect that the person making the statement has the capacity to intend the wishes specified in it. The individual making the statement should keep a list of those with copies and it is advisable to place copies in general practice and hospital casenotes. An advance statement may be withdrawn by the person who made it if he has the capacity, using the same process. The Tribunal, and any person giving medical treatment authorised by the Act, must have regard to the wishes specified in any advance statement. If a decision is taken contrary to the patient's wishes, this must be recorded in writing and placed in the medical notes, stating the reasons why; and a copy given to the patient, the named person, any welfare attorney, any guardian and the Commission.

APPEALS

Appeals can be made against the decisions of the Tribunal to court, **3–112** and from lower to higher courts.

Grounds for Appeal

Grounds for appeal against a decision of the Tribunal[22] include: **3–113**

---

[20] Mental Health (Care and Treatment) (Scotland) Act 2003, s.261.
[21] *ibid.*, ss.275 and 276.
[22] *ibid.*, s.324(2).

- An error of law
- Procedural impropriety in the conduct of any hearing
- Unreasonable action by the Tribunal in the exercise of its discretion
- Lack of evidence for the decision from the facts found to be established by the Tribunal

Types of Appeal

3–114   Appeals can be made to the sheriff principal; to the Court of Session against a decision of a sheriff principal; or directly to the Court of Session in specified circumstances.

Appeals to the sheriff principal

3–115   Appeals to the sheriff principal can be made on the following Tribunal decisions[23]:

- To refuse to revoke a short-term detention certificate
- To make or refuse to make a CTO
- To make an interim CTO
- To make an order confirming the determination of a patient's RMO to extend a CTO
- To make an order on an application by the patient's RMO to extend and vary a CTO
- To make an order confirming an RMO's determination, with or without modifying the CTO, to extend a CTO following an application for revocation of this
- To make an order varying a CTO or refusing to revoke a CTO following an application for revocation of a CTO
- To make an order on an application by a patient's RMO to vary a CTO
- To make an order refusing an application to vary a CTO
- To make an order to vary a CTO
- To refuse to revoke a certificate granting continued detention in hospital pending a review or application for variation of a CTO or detention pending further procedure under an interim CTO
- To make or refuse to make an order preventing transfer or requiring that a transferred patient be returned
- Decisions regarding compulsion orders
- To make or refuse an order appointing a patient's named person
- To make or refuse an order removing or replacing a named person
- To make an order on a named person the Tribunal thinks fit
- To make or refuse to make an order regarding detention in conditions of excessive security on non-restricted patients
- To grant or refuse an application for an order requiring the managers to cease to detain a patient

---

[23] Mental Health (Care and Treatment) (Scotland) Act 2003, s.320.

Appeals to the Court of Session

Appeals to the Court of Session can be made against the decision of:

- The sheriff principal allowing or refusing an appeal[24]
- The Tribunal regarding mentally disordered offenders[25]

Process

First, the patient, the patient's named person, any guardian or any **3–116** welfare attorney may appeal in all cases. In addition the MHO and the patient's RMO may appeal to the sheriff principal against a decision by the Tribunal except if the patient is restricted, in which case Scottish Ministers may appeal. In an appeal about conditions of excessive security the Commission and the relevant Health Board may also appeal, or in the case of a decision granting or refusing an application for an order requiring managers of the hospital to cease to detain a patient, the managers of the hospital or the person who applied for the order may appeal. An appeal can be made to the sheriff principal in the sheriffdom where the patient lives or is in hospital. The sheriff principal may remit the appeal to the Court of Session if it raises an important or difficult question of law. Appeals directly to the Court of Session can also be made by Scottish Ministers. The Tribunal may be a party to an appeal against any decision of the sheriff principal.

Second, where Scottish Ministers appeal against any decision of the Tribunal regarding mentally disordered offenders, the patient continues to be detained and the compulsion order plus restriction order, hospital direction or transfer for treatment direction continues to have effect[26]. This lasts until the expiry of the time period for application to the House of Lords against the decision of the Court of Session or where such an appeal is made, until it is abandoned or finally determined.

Third, in allowing an appeal the Court (Sheriff Principal or Court of Session) sets aside the decision of the Tribunal; and can substitute its own decision or remit the case to the Tribunal for reconsideration. In the case of the latter, the Court may direct that the Tribunal be differently constituted from when it made the original decision and issue other directions about the consideration of the case.

OFFENCES

Specified offences have been extended under the new Act to protect **3–117** vulnerable individuals and to discourage the deliberate obstruction of the working of the Act. There are two forms of behaviour that can lead to specific charges: first, sexual acts with or ill-treatment of a mentally disordered person; and, secondly, interference with the functioning of the Act. Abuse of a person with a mental disorder by anyone should lead to charges but offences against the working of the Act must be used

---

[24] Mental Health (Care and Treatment) (Scotland) Act 2003, s.321.
[25] *ibid.*, s.322.
[26] *ibid.*, s.323.

sparingly for relatives or carers who try to support a patient in a misguided way, or who are bullied into obstruction or assisting a person to abscond. Conviction for the following offences on summary proceedings can lead to imprisonment of between 3 and 6 months and/or a fine; or a sentence of up to two years and/or a fine on indictment. The offence of obstruction is liable to summary proceedings alone.

Non-consensual Sexual Acts[27]

3–118 Sexual intercourse or sexual acts with an individual who does not consent or is incapable of consenting because of a mental disorder is an offence. Any consent is invalidated if a patient is placed in a state of fear; or subject to any threat, intimidation, deceit or persuasion. A patient cannot consent if unable to understand what the act is, form a decision about it or communicate such a decision. It is a legitimate defence to argue that a person charged could not reasonably have been expected to know that the patient had a mental disorder or was incapable of consenting to the sexual act.

Persons Providing Care Services: Sexual Offences[28]

3–119 A person providing care services to an individual with a mental disorder who engages in intercourse or a sexual act with him is guilty of an offence regardless of consent, unless it is their spouse or there was a pre-existing sexual relationship.

Ill-treatment and Wilful Neglect of Mentally Disordered Person[29]

3–120 It is an offence to ill-treat or wilfully neglect a patient if an individual is employed in a hospital or contracted to provide care services. This excludes volunteers.

Inducing and Assisting Absconding[30]

3–121 A person who knowingly induces or assists a patient to abscond or fail to comply with conditions imposed by the Act, or harbours a patient who has absconded is guilty of an offence. It is a defence to a charge of harbouring a patient, to argue that it did not obstruct the discharge of a function conferred or imposed by the Act and that it was intended to protect the interests of the patient.

Obstruction[31]

3–122 It is an offence to refuse access to premises or to a mentally disordered person; to refuse to allow an interview or examination of a mentally disordered person; to persist in being present when requested to withdraw from a private interview; to refuse to produce required documents or records; or to obstruct an authorised person exercising

---

[27] Mental Health (Care and Treatment) (Scotland) Act 2003, s.311.
[28] *ibid.*, s.313.
[29] *ibid.*, s.315.
[30] *ibid.*, s.316.
[31] *ibid.*, s.317.

functions under this Act unless the accused has a reasonable excuse for doing so. This offence excludes the mentally disordered person himself.

False Statements[32]

A person who knowingly makes a false entry or statement in an **3–123** application under the Act or related documents, or makes use of any such entry or statement knowing it to be false with intent to deceive is guilty of an offence. This excludes a nomination of a named person, a declaration in relation to a named person and an advance statement.

HOSPITAL POWERS TO ENSURE SAFETY

Powers are set out in the Act to ensure the safety of patients, staff, **3–124** visitors and other members of the public. For those working in clinical settings the primary use of this legislation is to avoid drugs of abuse being brought into a hospital setting. These have a profound effect on the mental health of patients. In addition, such legislation is commonly used to remove temporarily items from the property of patients that potentially could be used as weapons and to prevent nuisance telephone calls, often to the emergency services. The most draconian of these potential powers is the removal of body tissue, blood or other body fluid. This will most commonly be used to permit urinary drug screens. The safety of patients could, however, be interpreted very widely and taken to include routine blood tests on admission. The practicalities of establishing a working rapport with patients will make this unlikely.

Correspondence Restrictions[33]

Correspondence from a detained patient can be withheld from the **3–125** postal service if it is addressed to an individual who has requested in writing to the hospital managers, the RMO or to Scottish Ministers, that communications from that patient are withheld; or if the hospital managers consider that the letter is likely to cause distress to the person in question or any other person who is not on the staff of the hospital; or cause danger to any person. No mail can be withheld that is addressed to Ministers of the Crown or Scottish Ministers; members of Parliament (European, Westminster, Scottish or Northern Ireland Assembly); the Commission; the Parliamentary Commissioner for Administration; the Scottish Public Services Ombudsman; a local authority; any judge or clerk of court; the Tribunal; the managers of the hospital in which the patient is detained; a Health Board; a Special Health Board; a National Health Service Trust; any person providing the patient with independent advocacy services; the patient's legal adviser; or the European Court of Human Rights.

A postal packet can be withheld from a patient detained in hospital if it was not sent by one of those listed above, and in the opinion of the managers of the hospital, it is necessary to do so in the interests of the

---

[32] Mental Health (Care and Treatment) (Scotland) Act 2003, s.318.
[33] *ibid.*, s.281.

health or safety of the patient or for the protection of any other person. The managers of a hospital may inspect and open any postal packet to see if it should be withheld.

If a postal packet or any of its contents are withheld, the managers of the hospital must record this in writing and within seven days inform the Commission specifying the detained patient's name, the nature of the postal packet or contents withheld, and the reason for so doing. In addition, the detained patient and the sender must be informed of the decision to withhold a postal package and of their right to a review of this decision[34]. The Commission will review any such decision following an application by the detained patient or sender up to six months after they received notice of this. The Commission can direct that the item should not be withheld.

Use of Telephones[35]

3–126   Detained patients can have their right to use the telephone restricted or prohibited except to those people listed under correspondence, unless a person has requested the interception of telephone calls made by the patient or the telephone call would be unlawful.

Safety and Security in Hospital[36]

3–127   To ensure patient, visitor and staff safety in hospital regulations may authorise the search of a detained patient's person and property; removal of body tissue, blood or other body fluid; restrictions on belongings in hospital; restrictions on visitors; surveillance of visitors; and a search of visitors and their property.

TRANSFER OF PATIENTS

Transfer to another Hospital

3–128   Patients detained in hospital under a CTO may be transferred to another hospital if the managers of that hospital consent to the proposed transfer[37]. The patient, the patient's named person and the patient's primary carer should be given seven days notice of the proposed transfer unless it is necessary to transfer the patient urgently or the patient consents to the transfer in which case they should be informed as soon as practicable. The Commission must be informed of the transfer within seven days. If the proposed transfer does not take place within three months of the initial notice, the patient may be transferred if the agreement with the receiving hospital managers is still in place, and a further seven days notice is given to the patient, his named person and primary carer.

Patients or their named persons may appeal to the Tribunal against the proposed transfer from the day on which notice is given or the

---

[34] Mental Health (Care and Treatment) (Scotland) Act 2003, s.283.
[35] *ibid.*, s.284.
[36] *ibid.*, s.286.
[37] *ibid.*, s.124.

transfer occurs until 28 days after transfer.[38] If the named person is notified after transfer he has 28 days to appeal from the time of notification. If an appeal is lodged before the transfer has taken place then the patient must not be transferred unless the Tribunal makes an order transferring the patient pending the determination of the appeal. Following an appeal the Tribunal can make an order that the proposed transfer should not take place or that the patient be returned to the hospital from which he was transferred.

In the case of a proposed or actual transfer to the State Hospital, the patient or the patient's named person has from the period of notification until 12 weeks after transfer in which to appeal to the Mental Health Tribunal[39]. If the named person is notified after transfer there is a 12-week period to appeal from the time of notification. The appeal period was only four weeks under the 1984 Act. As before, if an appeal is lodged before transfer has taken place then the patient must not be transferred unless the Tribunal makes an order transferring the patient pending the determination of the appeal. The Tribunal must be satisfied that the patient requires to be detained in hospital under conditions of special security and that those conditions can be provided only in a state hospital.

Cross-border Transfer of Patients

Provisions exist: **3–129**

- To transfer a patient detained under this Act to a place outwith Scotland (or the UK)[40]
- To remove to Scotland a person subject to corresponding measures in England, Wales, Northern Ireland, the Isle of Man or the Channel Islands[41]

A warrant is issued by the patient's RMO if the patient wishes to be transferred and is subject to requirements other than detention under the Act, and the RMO is satisfied with the arrangements in place. The warrant can still be issued by the RMO if the patient is not capable of consenting to transfer but the patient's named person considers that it is in his best interests to go. The RMO must notify a patient's named person, MHO and the Commission. If the patient is detained in hospital, Scottish Ministers must consider the best interests of the patient, the arrangements proposed, the patient's wishes, and any risk to the safety of any person in deciding on transfer. The patient must be given at least seven days notice of the decision to remove him from Scotland for UK transfers and 28 days for places out with the UK. The patient has a right of appeal.

COMMENT

It is essential that the new Act is made to work to ensure that patients **3–130** who need the care and protection it provides receive it. This Act is more complex than the 1984 Act and it is difficult to read. Sadly, its language

---

[38] Mental Health (Care and Treatment) (Scotland) Act 2003, s.125.

[39] *ibid.*, s.126.

[40] *ibid.*, s.289.

[41] *ibid.*, s.290.

and layout do not assist its own principles of encouraging participation and communication although other jurisdictions have found it is possible to have more easily comprehensible legislation[42]. This, combined with the known deficiencies in knowledge of the 1984 Act[43], makes a strategy for educating mental health and legal professionals on the new legislation even more essential.

Mental Health Tribunals are new to Scotland and the practicalities of such as system, particularly staffing, have still to be resolved. This is no minor issue given the recruitment difficulties of Tribunals south of the border. The Tribunals must consider long-term patient care as paramount. Evidence will be heard from all sides however prolonged, adversarial contests between patients, their representatives, and mental health professionals must be avoided to prevent lasting damage to the doctor-patient relationship. RMOs must avoid the temptation to pass difficult decisions to the Tribunal that belong to them.

There are many good points to the Act including its statement of principles and the statutory basis to patient representation. New legislation does not itself advance medical knowledge or service provision for those with mental disorder, but it is hoped that the principle of reciprocity may encourage the latter.

---

[42] Mental Health Act 1986, State of Victoria, Anstat Pty Ltd, Melbourne, Australia.

[43] Humphreys M.S. (1994) *Junior psychiatrists and emergency detention in Scotland*, International Journal of Law and Psychiatry, 17(4), 421–429.

CHAPTER 41

ADULTS WITH INCAPACITY

INTRODUCTION

Scots law assumes that adults have the ability to make legal decisions. **4–01** Traditionally, a distinction has been drawn between decisions involving financial or business matters and decisions pertaining to personal welfare, such as consent to medical treatment. "Incapacity" is simply the term which refers to the lack of such an ability and is usually termed "incompetence" in the North American context[2]. Incapacity to make a specific legal decision may arise because of mental disorder and it is estimated that some 100,000 Scots may be incapable of making some financial or welfare decisions[3]. A person who is incapable of one sort of decision may not be incapable of other decisions; if a person is thought to be incapable of a specific decision it should never be assumed that that incapacity extends more widely. It would also be wrong to assume that an individual found to be incapable will remain incapable, especially if the cause of the incapacity is a remitting and relapsing mental disorder such as manic depression. However, many cases of incapacity arise either from a developmental disorder, causing generalised learning disability; or a degenerative disorder, such as dementia; in these cases it is unlikely that capacity will be regained, but there may be ways to first maximise decision-making ability.

Up until the Adults with Incapacity (Scotland) Act 2000 (AI(S)2000), Scots law was confusing: it provided no comprehensive framework which protected the interests of adults with incapacity and there were poor provisions for proper decision making on their behalf. Those with substantial funds might have had a *curator bonis* appointed, but such a proxy to manage financial matters was expensive. The practice of appointing (in advance by an adult with capacity) a proxy with enduring powers of attorney to manage future financial decisions if the adult became incapable has been preserved by the new Act. There was no such mechanism, however, for welfare decisions. Using ancient common law a small number of *tutors-dative* were appointed by the Court of Session to have partial parental rights over an "idiot or furious" adult to manage welfare decisions[4]. Using ancient statute law a *tutor-in-law* could be appointed to manage both welfare and financial matters of an incapable

---

[1] Chapter author: Dr J. Crichton, Ph.D.

[2] Grisso, P. and Appelbaum, P.S. (Ed.s) (1998) *Assessing competence to consent to treatment: A guide for physicians and other health professionals*, Ch.1.

[3] Scottish Executive (1999) *Making the right moves: Rights and protection for adults with incapacity*, p.4.

[4] Ward, A., *Revival of Tutors-dative*, 1987 S.L.T. 69–72.

adult but such a tutor was limited to the nearest male relative[5]. Both types of tutorage were very rarely used[6]. Most treatment decisions regarding incapable adults were justified using the defence of necessity[7] but that principle is far less developed in Scotland than in England and there has been legal debate regarding its scope in Scots law[8]. The AI(S)2000 was designed to replace these various curatorships with a comprehensive principled framework for decision making for incapable adults. However, as can be seen from the section on medical treatment, the Act is not fully comprehensive regarding emergency treatment and in such cases common law justifications continue to apply. It also does not extend to Testamentary Capacity or whether an adult can consent to marriage.

Adrian Ward, solicitor, has had a long-term interest in this area of law; his textbook *Adult Incapacity*[9], although principally aimed at the legal profession, provides more detailed examination on this topic.

OVERVIEW OF THE ADULTS WITH INCAPACITY (SCOTLAND) ACT 2000

Guiding Principles

4–02　　Section 1 of the Act provides that the principles summarised in Table 1 shall be followed in relation to any intervention in the affairs of an adult pursuant to or under the Act.

Table 1:

Principle 1—Beneficence
"Section 1 (2)
There shall be no intervention in the affairs of an adult unless the person responsible for authorising or effecting the intervention is satisfied that the intervention will benefit the adult and that such benefit cannot reasonably be achieved without the interventions."
Principle 2—Minimum intervention
"Section 1 (3)
Where it is determined that an intervention . . . is to be made, such intervention shall be the least restrictive option in relation to the freedom of the adult, consistent with the purpose of the intervention."

---

[5] Ward, A., *Tutors to adults: some developments*, 1992 S.L.T. 325–9.
[6] Crichton, J.H.M., 2000, *Mental incapacity in consent to treatment: the Scottish experience*, Journal of Forensic Psychiatry, Vol.11 457–464.
[7] *ibid.*
[8] Ferguson, W., 1986, *Necessity and Duress in Scots Law*, Criminal Law Review, 103–9.
[9] Ward, A.D., *Adult Incapacity* (W. Green, 2003).

Principle 3—Consideration of the wishes of the adult
Paragraph 4
"In determining if an intervention is to be made and, if so, what intervention is to be made, account should be taken of
(a) present and past wishes and feelings of the adult so far as they can be ascertained by any means of communication, whether human or by mechanical aid (whether or an interpretative nature or otherwise) appropriate to the adult"
Principle 4—Consultation with relevant others
Paragraph 4
"In determining if an intervention is to made and, if so, what intervention is to be made, account should be taken of—
(b) the views of the nearest relatives and the primary carer of the adult, in so far as it is reasonably practical to do so;
(c) the views of—(i) any guardian, continuing attorney or welfare attorney of the adult who has powers relating to the proposed intervention; and (ii) any person whom the Sheriff has directed to be consulted, in so far as it is reasonable and practical to do so; and
(d) the views of any other person appearing to the person responsible for authorising or affecting the intervention to have in interest in the welfare of the adult or in the proposed intervention, where these views have been made known to the person responsible, in so far as it is reasonable and practical to do so (11)."
Principle 5—Encouraging the adult to exercise residual capacity
Section 1 (5)
"Any guardian, continuing attorney, welfare attorney or manager of an establishment exercising functions under this Act or under any order of the Sheriff in relation to an adult shall, in so far as it is reasonably and practical to do so, encourage the adult to exercise whatever skills he has concerning his property, financial affairs or personal welfare, as the case may be, and to develop new such skills."

These establish the ethical context for all decisions made on behalf of incapable adults.

Beneficence

Beneficence is one of the oldest principles of medicine[10]. A decision **4–03** regarding an adult with incapacity must be for the benefit of that adult and no third party. If, for example, a financial decision on behalf of an

---

[10] Potts, S. & Crichton, J.H.M. (2004) *Legal and ethical aspects of psychiatry*; E.C. Johnston *et al, Companion to Psychiatric Studies* (7th ed., Churchill Livingstone, 2004), Ch.30.

incapable adult was to benefit a third party and not the adult, that decision would be legally challengeable.

Minimum Intervention

4–04 If the desired outcome of any intervention can be brought about without a restrictive measure, then that is preferable. The principle of least restriction comes from both mental health legislation[11] and principles regarding the management of mentally disordered offenders[12]. An adult with incapacity should not be detained in conditions more secure than their needs simply because of financial considerations. This has important implications on the use of locked-door policies in elderly residential homes with a high proportion of people who lack capacity for various decisions because of dementia. Some of the residents may require a locked door to prevent wandering and harm but some may not. Sometimes it is possible for there to be a conflict between the various principles: if it was in the best interests of an individual to be in a locked environment in all other respects, even though that restriction was not necessary, a careful balancing of the competing principles would be required.

Consideration of the Views of the Adult

4–05 Respect for autonomy is another ancient medical principle embodied in the Adults with Incapacity Act with regard to taking into account present and past wishes. In the development of the Adults with Incapacity Act there was immense controversy over the role of advance directives. These are statements of intention made whilst an adult has capacity regarding future decisions. An example might be the decision of a Jehovah's Witness not to accept blood products if, as a result of an accident, they were incapable and in need of transfusion. The Act allows that such declarations of intent must be taken into account when making a decision under the Act but they are not completely binding. Currently, such an advance directive from a Jehovah's Witness would be followed by Scottish doctors and the Act is not intended to change that practice. In other areas, however, there may be an advance in medical treatment between the time an advance directive was made and the need for an intervention. In such a circumstance the Act would allow doctors to carry out the treatment despite an advance directive, but the expectation would be that this would have to be carefully justified and would be legally challengeable.

This particular principle of the Act is not restricted to formal advance directives but might include other less formal statements of intention or reported wishes relayed by relatives or close friends. A problem in interpreting such wishes is that the capacity of the adult when such wishes were made may be difficult to confirm and there may be error in the reporting of wishes made by interested third parties. For all these

[11] Millan, Bruce (Chairman) (2001) *New Directions: Report on the review of the Mental Health (Care and Treatment) (Scotland) Act 2003*, Ch.3, s.13.

[12] Scottish Office, *Health, Social Work and related services for mentally disordered offenders in Scotland* (1999) NHS MEL (99) 5.

reasons, therefore, the views of past wishes must be considered with great importance but are not completely binding.

Consultation with Relevant Others

The Act establishes a new principle of consultation with relevant **4–06** others. Whereas it has been good practice to consult carers and relatives in the past, this has never been formalised as a statutory duty. There had been problems in the past with confusion about the disclosure of confidential information in the context of medical treatment decisions. One effect of this principle is to erode the principle of confidentiality. There may again be a conflict with the principle of beneficence or the past wishes of a patient if consultation with others necessitated a disclosure of confidential information, which might otherwise be harmful. For example, someone with temporary incapacity because of a remitting and relapsing mental disorder who might require treatment for a sexually transmitted disease. Again in such difficult cases a careful balancing of competing principles needs to be undertaken by whoever is authorising a particular intervention or treatment.

Encouraging the Adult to Exercise Residual Capacity

Even if an adult does not have capacity it may be possible to access **4–07** their residual capacity, *i.e.* their decision-making ability which whilst insufficient to make a legally valid decision might indicate a general preference. At its most basic level an adult with severe learning disability, incapable of making choices about basic diet, might still be able to indicate a preference for various foods or beverages if given a choice of different foods. Another example might be someone with a dementing illness who cannot remember a topic of conversation for more than a few minutes. That individual might be able to make a clear indication of preference whilst being unable to remember the topic and the discussion moments later.

ASSESSING CAPACITY

Section 1(6) of the Act defines "incapable" as meaning incapable of— **4–08**

"(a) acting; or
(b) making decisions; or
(c) communicating decisions; or
(d) understanding decisions; or
(e) retaining the memory of decisions, as mentioned in any provision of this Act[13], by reason of mental disorder or of inability to communicate because of physical disability; a person shall not fall within this definition by reason only of a lack or deficiency in the faculty of communication if that lack of deficiency can be made good by human or mechanical aid (whether or an interpretative nature or otherwise)".

---

[13] Scottish Executive (2002) *Adults with Incapacity (Scotland) Act 2000: Code of Practice for persons authorised to carry out medical treatment or research under Part V of the Act.*

Whereas this definition helps to interpret the meaning of incapacity in the Act it is less helpful for the medical practitioner in concluding whether someone is incapable or not. The first thing to draw from this definition is that the decision making in question is broadly based, relating to any sort of decision regarding any aspect of life for an adult. In assessing whether an individual has decision-making skills, in most cases it first has to be established whether a mental disorder is responsible for the deficiency in decision making.

It is a medical practitioner who must decide if an individual is incapable. In some cases this would involve a psychiatrist or a specialist in the psychiatry of the elderly or people with a learning disability. In most cases it will be the general practitioner who makes an assessment of capacity. Assessing capacity is a basic medical skill and all medical practitioners should be familiar with it. In certain parts of the Act a solicitor or advocate is also permitted to test that an adult understands the nature and extent of the powers he is granting in connection with financial property and personal welfare matters. This is an assessment to confirm capacity and not to confirm incapacity.

The meaning of "mental disorder" in the Act is the same as found in broader Mental Health legislation. Under that definition no person shall be treated as suffering from mental disorder by reason only of promiscuity or other immoral conduct, sexual deviancy or dependence on alcohol or drugs. The Mental Health (Scotland) Act 1984, as reformed by the Mental Health (Public Safety and Appeals) (Scotland) Act 1999, specifically added the definition of personality disorder to the meaning of mental illness and therefore also mental disorder. Personality disorder is now a category of mental disorder in the Mental Health (Treatment and Care) (Scotland) Act 2003. Also added was the exception that someone should not be considered mentally disordered simply because of "acting as no prudent person would act". An individual who was simply intoxicated by alcohol and drugs would not normally be thought to satisfy the legal definition of mental disorder unless some other condition was also present.

The only exception to the presence of mental disorder as being responsible for the incapacity is in the case of rare medical conditions where someone has the ability to make decisions but is physically unable to communicate the nature of those decisions. The Act makes it clear that all attempts should be made to facilitate communication and that someone should not be considered incapable if there was a remedy to facilitate communication. The Code of Practice for the Medical Treatment part of the Act is further guidance on how a medical practitioner may assess capacity. Section 1.6 of the code states:

"normally an assessment under Part 5 should seek to determine whether an adult:

- is capable of making and communicating their choice
- understands the nature of what is being asked and why
- has memory abilities that allow the retention of information
- is aware of any alternatives
- has knowledge of the risks and benefits involved

- is aware that such information is of personal relevance to them
- is aware of their right to, and how to, refuse, as well as the consequences of refusal . . .
- is expressing views consistent with their previously preferred moral, cultural, family, and experiential background"

This fuller guidance in the Code of Practice approaches a functional definition of incapacity but doctors may still need to refer to other resources to help such as guidance published by the BMA and Law Society[14]. In the English context the court adopted a functional test of capacity employed by a forensic psychiatrist, Professor Nigel Eastman, in *Re C*[15]. Incapacity was based on the ability to comprehend and retain the treatment choices being given; believe the information being given; weigh the pros and cons in the balance and arrive at a true choice. Such a decision is likely to be influential in the Scottish context and is mirrored in the fuller guidance given in the Code of Practice. There are also developments from the United States of America where Grisso and Applebalm (1999) have developed the MacArthur Competence Assessment Tool, which provides a structured interview and rating procedures to assess competence[16].

PARTS OF THE ACT AND CODES OF PRACTICE

The Act consists of seven parts listed in Table 2.   **4–09**

Table 2:

Part 1—General
General principles and fundamental definitions; publications and appeals to Sheriff and the court of session; the function of various statutory bodies and codes of practice *etc.*
Part 2—Continuing powers of attorney and welfare powers of attorney
Part 3—Accounts and funds
Part 4—Management of resident finances
Part 5—Medical treatment and research

---

[14] British Medical Association and The Law Society (1995) *Assessment of mental capacity: Guidance for doctors and lawyers*, British Medical Association, London.
[15] *Re C (Adult Mental Patient: Refusal of Medical Treatment)* [1994] 1 W.L.R. 290.
[16] Grisso and Appelbaum, *op. cit.*, Ch.6.

> *Part 6—Intervention orders and guardianship orders*
>
> *Part 7—Miscellaneous* (including defence of ill treatment and wilful neglect, publication to guardians appointed under Criminal Procedure (Scotland) Act 1995 etc)

Outline

4–10   Part 1 of the Act sets out the general principles and definitions of the Act. It also defines the powers of the Sheriff and Court of Session in relation to the Act and introduces the Public Guardian (see below). There are also new statutory duties for the Mental Welfare Commission and local authorities. Part 1 of the Act establishes the duty on Scottish Ministers to prepare codes of practice to give guidance on matters arising from the Act (see below). Part 2 of the Act concentrates on the provisions individuals with capacity can make for the possibility of their future incapacity. Part 3 deals with access by an individual, normally a carer or relative, to the funds of an adult with incapacity held by a fund holder *e.g.* a bank. Part 4 allows for the management of funds and property of residents by care establishments for residents who are unable to carry out this function for themselves. Part 5 introduces a statutory framework protecting the interests of patients unable to consent to medical treatment. It allows for the treatment of incapable adults and their participation in research without their consent. Part 6 introduces a flexible and accessible system for financial decisions and welfare decisions to be made for those who did not have the foresight to appoint an attorney. Where a one-off decision is required *e.g.* selling a property, then an intervention order can be sought from the Sheriff. Where a number of decisions are required in the future, a guardianship order can be sought instead.

Offences

4–11   The final part of the Act contains a miscellaneous section, which includes s.74: the offence of ill treatment and wilful neglect. Mirroring mental health legislation the Act creates an offence for any person exercising powers under the Act who ill-treats or wilfully neglects an incapable adult under the Act. On summary conviction for such an offence the disposal is imprisonment for a term not exceeding six months and/or a fine, on indictment the maximum term of imprisonment is increased to two years.

CODES OF PRACTICE

4–12   Section 13 of the Adults with Incapacity Act creates a duty upon Scottish Ministers to prepare Codes of Practice which contain guidance on the exercise of the Act. There is a statutory duty for Scottish Ministers to consult such bodies as appear to them to be concerned in the preparation of the codes and to lay copies of them before Parliament. Table 3 lists the eight Codes of Practice.

Table 3:

Codes of Practice for the Adults with Incapacity (Scotland) Act 2001

(a) local authorities and their chief social work officers and mental health officers
(b) continuing and welfare attorneys
(c) persons authorised under interventions orders
(d) guardians
(e) withdrawers
(f) managers of authorised establishments
(g) supervisory bodies
(g) persons authorised to carry out medical treatment or research under Part 5

Although the use of detailed codes of practice can be found in English mental health legislation, the Code of Practice for the Mental Health (Scotland) Act 1984 was modest in comparison to the eight codes prepared for this Act. The codes themselves give special guidance on their own status. The Act does not impose legal duty to comply with them but "the code is a statutory document and there may, therefore, in certain circumstances, be legal consequences arising from failure to observe the terms of the code"[17].

If, for example, a legal action for negligence was raised against a medical practitioner the relevant Code of Practice would be an important standard for the court to consider when assessing whether the action of that doctor has reached a necessary professional standard. It is hard to imagine in what circumstances the Codes of Practice would not be seen to have authority by the courts, unless it could be argued that there was a conflict with existing law or there was evidence that a body of professional opinion did not follow the advice in the Code for a sound reason. It would not be acceptable for somebody exercising powers under the Act to be simply unaware of the provisions of the Code of Practice. The Codes of Practice all include a section repeating the general principles which would inform not only the interpretation of the Act but also the Code. In the introduction to the Code of Practice for the Mental Health Act 1983 (in England and Wales) there was a financial exclusion allowing the code not to be followed if statutory bodies did not have the funds to do so. That exclusion was removed from later editions of the English and Welsh Code and does not appear in the Codes of Practice for the AI(S)2000.

ROLE OF THE PUBLIC GUARDIAN

Section 4 of the Adults with Incapacity (Scotland) Act creates a new **4–13** public official, the Public Guardian. The origins of this office can be found in the Accountant of Court who was responsible for the super-

---

[17] Scottish Executive (2002) *Code of Practice Pt V op. cit.*, s.1.25.

vision and audit of all cases where a *curator bonis* was appointed. It continues to be part of the Supreme Courts and is therefore part of the Scottish Court service. The Guardian is located in Falkirk and the office was opened in March 2001. Section 4 of the Act outlines the role of the Public Guardian, which is summarised in Table 4.

Table 4:

Section 4—Adults with Incapacity (Scotland) Act

Public Guardian and his functions—

1. To supervise any guardian or any other person who is authorised under an intervention order in the exercise of his functions relating to the property or financial affairs of the adult.
2. To establish and maintain registers of all documents relating to

   (i)   Continuing powers of attorney
   (ii) Welfare powers of attorney
   (iii) Authorisations to intermit funds
   (iv) Guardianship orders
   (v)   Intervention orders.

3. To investigate complaints relating to the property or financial affairs of an incompetent adult.
4. To investigate any circumstances made known to him in which the property or financial affairs of an adult seem to be at risk.
5. To provide advice for a guardian, continuing attorney, a withdrawer or a person authorised under an intervention order relating to performance of functions regarding property or financial affairs.
6. To consult the Mental Welfare Commission and any local authority where there is a common interest.

The decision to replace the term "accountant of court" to the term "Public Guardian" was deliberate and aimed to engender a more accessible image. The office of Public Guardian has a statutory duty to provide advice to people appointed under the Act to manage financial affairs. It provides telephone advice to anyone with an interest in finances or property of an adult with incapacity. The various codes of practice can be accessed via the Office of the Public Guardian website[18] and are available in CD format from the same office.

Role of the Mental Welfare Commission

4–14   The Adults with Incapacity Act extends the role of the Mental Welfare Commission and specifically extends its protective functions in respect to all adults with incapacity subject to an intervention or guardianship order in so far as that order relates to personal welfare. The historic

---

[18] *www.publicguardian-scotland.gov.uk.*

distinction between personal welfare and finance is thereby maintained in the division between the supervisory role of the Public Guardian and the Mental Welfare Commission. The Mental Welfare Commission also has a role to investigate complaints made through a local authority and has the power to investigate any circumstances known to it in which the personal welfare of an adult with incapacity appears to be at risk. There is also created a statutory duty to provide advice to welfare guardians, welfare attorneys and people authorised under intervention orders regarding their performance and function in relation to personal welfare. The Mental Welfare Commission has a special role regarding Part 5 of the Act and consent to treatment issues, which are discussed below.

Duties on Local Authorities

The Adults with Incapacity Act creates a duty on local authorities to **4–15** supervise guardians appointed with functions relating to personal welfare of an adult and to consult the Public Guardian and Mental Welfare Commission on cases where there appears to be a common interest. A local authority has the statutory duty to receive and investigate any complaints relating to the personal welfare of adults in relation to welfare attorneys, guardians or people authorised under intervention orders. It also has a statutory duty to provide advice to guardians, welfare attorneys or people authorised under intervention orders when requested to do so. There are particularly helpful training packages available for social workers and others involved in the duties of the local authority[19].

Continuing Powers of Attorney and Welfare Powers of Attorney

Part 2 of the Act preserves the ability of adults to anticipate the **4–16** possibility of their own incapacity by granting a power of attorney over financial affairs. Continuing attorneys are attorneys with financial powers, which continue when an individual becomes incapable. The Act extends this to allow people to appoint welfare attorneys who have authority over personal welfare decisions, which commence on the grantor's incapacity. It is clearly the intention of legislation that, as people in Scotland become more familiar with the workings of the Act, many will have the foresight to appoint continuing attorneys and welfare attorneys. A continuing or welfare power of attorney is only valid if expressed as a written document, which is signed by the grantor. That document must incorporate a clear statement expressing the grantor's wish that the power is a continuing one. The document must also incorporate a certificate by a solicitor, advocate or registered medical practitioner. The certificate required must certify that the professional has interviewed the grantor immediately before the grantor has signed

---

[19] There are four training packs and other guidance:
Pack 1: Workbook and guidance pack for social and health care staff.
Pack 2: Workbook and guidance pack for assessment and care management staff.
Pack 3: Workbook and guidance pack for mental health officers.
Trainer's guide to workbook and guidance Packs 1, 2 and 3.
Implementation guide for senior management.
Briefing papers for local authority elective members.

the document, is satisfied that at the time of granting the power the grantor understands its nature and extent and also does not believe that the grantor is acting under undue influence. Usually a solicitor will guide the capable adult through this process and in time such arrangements are likely to be as common as preparing a will. Information on how to go about the process is available from the Public Guardian.

There should be separate certificates for continuing powers of attorney and welfare powers of attorney. Continuing or welfare attorneys have no authority to act until the power of attorney has been registered with the Public Guardian. Before registering the Public Guardian will check that the attorney is prepared to act and there is a registration fee payable, which is currently £35. When the power of attorney is registered a copy of it, together with a certificate of registration, is returned to the sender with a copy to the grantor and, where the power of attorney so requires, to two specified individuals. If the power of attorney relates to welfare powers a copy of it is sent to the Mental Welfare Commission and the local authority. It is advisable when a power of attorney is prepared that the opportunity is taken to specify two individuals to get copies. These individuals could be the grantor's doctor, a solicitor, care provider or nearest relative.

The Public Guardian should be informed if an attorney dies and an attorney who wishes to resign shall give notice in writing of their intention to do so to the grantor, the Public Guardian, any guardian or primary carer and the local authority. Resignation will not take effect until 20 days after receipt of a letter of resignation by the Public Guardian.

At the time of preparing the document creating either a continuing or welfare power of attorney, there is the opportunity of appointing substitute attorneys, in the case of the death or resignation of the principal attorney. Once the Public Guardian has been made aware of the death or resignation of an attorney and there is evidence that the substitute attorney or a remaining joint attorney is willing to act, they will then become the continuing or welfare attorney. If the grantor and the continuing or welfare attorney are married then the power of attorney automatically comes to an end (unless the document confirming it provides otherwise) should they be granted a decree of separation, a degree of divorce or a declarator of nullity of the marriage. The powers of the attorney may be revoked by order of the Sheriff or end automatically with the appointment of a financial or welfare guardian. The power ends in the case of continuing attorneys, if the attorney becomes bankrupt. In any case if the adult recovers capacity he or she can revoke the power of attorney.

Accounts and Funds

4–17   Part 3 of the Adults with Incapacity Act provides for individuals (withdrawers) to obtain authority to access (or intromit) funds of an adult to meet that adult's living expenses. Prior to the Act, joint accounts were often automatically frozen if the incapacity of one account holder occurred. It is now clear that joint accounts, which are operable on either signature, should continue to be open if one of the account holders becomes incapable. The office of the Public Guardian has the authority to allow the intromission of funds for a period of normally three years. Table 5 summarises the purposes for which intromission of funds is possible.

Table 5:

Purposes of intromissions with funds
1. Utility bills—gas, electricity, phone, TV licence
2. Taxes—council tax
3. Food and household expenses
4. Clothing
5. Mortgages
6. Rent
7. Insurances
8. Care charges
9. Loan repayments
10. Club or other subscriptions
11. Holidays
12. Miscellaneous—for example the Public Guardian may authorise payments for small gifts to family members

At any time the Public Guardian may suspend or terminate the authority to intromit with funds and there is a power to appeal to the Sheriff by the withdrawer to challenge an order to terminate that authority. The authority would also end if there was put in place a superior order such as a financial guardian.

The Code of Practice[20] makes a distinction between the specified account, which is the adult's existing bank account, and a designated account, which is the new account set up by the withdrawer into which approved funds can be transferred from the fund holder's account. Prior to making an application for intromission with funds the applicant should follow the general principles of the Act: for example, assure themselves that the action will benefit the adult; that there is no less restrictive alternative; ascertain the adults wishes; consult with the nearest relative and primary carer; and consult with any welfare attorney or welfare guardian.

The application for authority must state the purpose for the intromission and contain details of what money is required and a three-year estimation of costs. The application must be countersigned by a pre-scribed person and received by the Public Guardian within 14 days of countersigning. A prescribed person would include a police officer, civil servant, MP, minister of religion, teacher, solicitor, *etc*. The Public Guardian can also authorise the fund holder to continue existing standing orders and direct debits but these need to be detailed at the application stage. Once received by the Public Guardian a copy of the application will be sent to the adult, nearest relative and primary carer. Interested individuals have 21 days to raise any objections to the

---

[20] Scottish Executive (2001) *Adults with Incapacity (Scotland) Act 2000: Code of Practice for continuing and welfare attorneys.*

application. The office of Public Guardian will either deal with any objections themselves or remit the matter to a Sheriff to deal with. If no objections are raised the Public Guardian can either grant the application, refuse it or remit the matter to a Sheriff.

Once an application has been granted a certificate will be issued giving details of the authority given and the period of time it is valid. The certificate will allow the withdrawer to set up a designated account and present it to a fund holder. Only one certificate can be enforced at any one time. A fresh application is required if the certificate requires changing, in which case the existing certificate would be recalled and replaced. It is, therefore, very important that the application is carefully prepared. Once granted the withdrawer must keep careful records of all financial matters, including everything where the cost is £20 or more. The records must be kept at least one year after the authority ends. Records should be kept for up to five years if there is any prospect of an enquiry by an interested party. The Public Guardian continues to have the duty of general oversight and operates a system of random selection of cases for examination which have been in place for over 12 months.

Transfer of Funds

4–18   The authority of the Public Guardian to authorise access to funds should not be confused with the ability to authorise the transfer of funds from one account to another. At the time of an application for access to funds, there is also an opportunity to ask for the transfer of funds, for example, from a low interest account to a high interest account.

Management of Residents' Funds

4–19   Part 4 of the AI(S)2000 places a statutory basis on the good practice which has evolved in the management of residents' funds in nursing homes[21] and replaces the incapax system for incapable patients in hospital, the latter detailed in the Crosby report[22]. The Act modified existing, widely used practices and harmonised them under a unified legislative framework. Although the guiding principles of the Act are crucial in the interpretation of Part 4 there are important differences with the rest of the legislation, particularly regarding the supervisory framework. Because of the antecedents of this part of the Act, Health Boards and the Care Commission (which now carries out many of the former functions of local authorities) have the role of supervising this part of the Act. Part 4 was the last part of the legislation to be implemented and was partially amended by the Regulation of Care (Scotland) Act 2001, which created the Care Commission. The Commission regulates care services against national standards, a function carried out before by local authorities and Health Boards.

Scope

4–20   This part of the AI(S)2000 enables managers of nursing homes and hospitals to apply for the authorisation to manage the funds of residents. Provisions of Part 4 do not apply if there is a superior provision in force,

---

[21] Scottish Executive, *Protection of the finances and other property of people incapable of managing their own affairs*, Circular no. CCD2/1999.
[22] Scottish Office (1985) *Report of the working party on the management of incapax patients funds.*

such as a continuing attorney or financial guardian. It is intended that only relatively small sums of money should be administered under Part 4 of the Act. The regulations that accompany the Act[23] set the limit of £5,000 in total assets; if a resident has more than £5,000 then an alternative mechanism for managing finances should be used, such as a financial guardian. There is some flexibility, however, if the total assets of a resident are just above the £5,000 limit and it is envisaged that in a short space of time the total assets will fall below that threshold. Table 6 summarises the locations where Part 4 might apply to residents who lack capacity, together with the relevant supervisory body.

Table 6:

Locations of where Part 4 of the AI(S)2000 applies with details of relevant supervisor body	
Location	**Supervising body**
1. Independent hospital/private psychiatric hospital	The Care Commission
2. A care home service	The Care Commission
3. Limited registration service	The Care Commission
4. Health Service Hospital	The local Health Board
5. State Hospital	State Hospital Board for Scotland

The Act uses the term "registered establishments" to refer to those locations supervised by the Care Commission. The remainder are referred to as "unregistered establishments" and are supervised by Health Boards; both, however, are referred to as "authorised establishments" by the Act. Care homes or independent services are not required to manage the funds of incapable residents and have the right to opt out of Part 4 of the Act; this will be documented under the terms of their registration. It is also possible for unregistered care providers, such as sheltered housing schemes, to register simply to enable them to utilise the provisions of Part 4 of the Act. The authority to manage residents' funds by an authorised establishment must be approved annually by the supervising body.

Applying for Authority to Manage a Resident's Funds

It is for the managers of an authorised establishment to seek authority **4–21** to manage the funds of a resident, by making an application to their supervising body. Managers must first consider that their management of financial matters, as set out in Table 7, is the most appropriate course of action and would benefit the resident. A medical practitioner must then

---

[23] SSIs: Adults with Incapacity (Scotland) Act 2000: Adults with Incapacity (Management of Residents' Finances) (Scotland) Regulations (SSI 2003/155).

assess the adult's capacity to make decisions in relation to those matters listed in Table 7 and issue a certificate accordingly. Such certification should be reviewed if there is any change of circumstances and in any case would expire and require renewal after three years. A certifying medical practitioner must not be related to the resident or any of the managers of the authorised establishment and must have no pecuniary interest in the authorised establishment. The managers have a duty to notify the resident and their nearest relative that it is their intention to arrange for a doctor to assess them under this part of the Act. There is, however, an exception to such notification—if the managers believe telling the resident was likely to pose a serious risk to health. In such a circumstance they may apply to the supervising body for dispensation not to inform the resident.

Table 7:

Matters which may be managed by an authorised establishment (s.37 AI(S)2000)
(a) Claiming, receiving, holding and spending any pension, benefit, allowance or other payment other than under the Social Security Contributions and Benefits Act 1992 (Chapter 4).
(b) Claiming, receiving, holding and spending any money to which a resident is entitled.
(c) Holding any other movable property (*e.g.* furniture, pictures, jewellery, bank accounts, shares but not land or property).
(d) Disposing of such movable property.

Once the medical certificate has been completed a notice of intention to manage the financial affairs of a resident should be sent with the medical certificate to the supervising body for authorisation. Again, subject to the possible exclusion of serious risk to health, this application should also be sent to the resident and to the nearest relative. The fee for the medical examination should be met from the estate of the resident and the Care Commission may charge a fee for processing the application. Health Boards, however, are not entitled to charge a fee. The application should provide the information set out in Table 8.

Table 8:

Information which should be contained in the notice of intention to manage the financial affairs of a resident
(a) Nature of incapacity and copy of certificate of incapacity.
(b) What alternative arrangements were explored.
(c) How the intervention will benefit the resident.
(d) The proposed duration of the intervention.
(e) Proposed timing and arrangements for review.
(f) Name and designation of authorised persons to manage the funds and their relationship to the resident (*e.g.* key worker).
(g) The identity of the fund holder and details of the account(s).

Only after a certificate of authority is granted from the supervising body can the managers of the authorised establishment start managing funds. The certificate will specify what accounts and funds are to be managed, will identify the "authorised persons" who can manage the money and specify the period of validity, which must be shorted than that of the medical certificate of incapacity.

Managing Funds

In any decision to use resident's funds the managers must only act for **4–22** the benefit of the resident and have proper regard to the sentimental value of any item. The regulations which accompany the AI(S)2000 put in place certain financial thresholds which have to be followed. Currently, if a resident does not have an interest bearing account and their assets exceed £500 the authorised manager should arrange for these assets to be placed in an interest bearing account. Part 4 of the Act enables the opening of such an account in the name of the resident to be managed by the authorised manager. Authorised managers may manage the financial affairs of residents whose total assets do not exceed £5,000[24] at any one time. When applying for a certificate of authority, therefore, a supervisory body should be given an indication of the scale of the assets it is proposed to manage. It is the duty of authorised managers to monitor any changes in the resident's accounts. If it is likely that the resident's total funds would exceed £5,000 for only a short time, the supervising body may allow the arrangements with the authorised establishment to stand. Alternatively, the supervising body may indicate that the local authority should seek a guardianship order, under which a level of delegated authority to the authorised establishment may be arranged. The authorised manager must seek further written authority if it is planned to dispose of a resident's valuables or any movable property whose value is likely to exceed £250[25]. The authorised manager is required to keep careful records of financial transactions and specifically to ensure that any transaction over £10[26] is signed for by a member of staff.

Authorised managers are required to prepare financial statements in **4–23** the course of managing residents' financial affairs and Table 9 summarises what information such financial statements should contain.

Table 9:

Information to be included in financial statements
(a) An opening balance.
(e) The date of all credits and debits.
(f) The amount of the transaction.
(g) A running balance.

---

[24] SSIs: Adults with Incapacity (Scotland) Act 2000: Adults with Incapacity (Management of Residents' Finances) (Scotland) Regulations (SSI 2003/155).

[25] *ibid.*

[26] *ibid.*

> (h) A closing balance.
> (i) A narrative which explains the source of credit—and purpose of the debit.
> (j) Any transaction over £10 signed by a member of staff.
> (k) Notes from the last review.

It is envisaged that managers of an authorised establishment should be imaginative in their use of a resident's funds to benefit the resident and the Code of Practice gives some suggestions for what funds may be used for, as summarised in Table 10.

Table 10:[27]

Possible uses of resident's money (Section 7.6.7 Code of Practice)
(a) Purchasing beneficial therapies, such as aromatherapy.
(b) Engaging a mobility assistant or supporter for a few hours a week to undertake befriending activities.
(c) Meeting mobility requirements over and above those provided for by the establishment or hospital.
(d) The leasing or hiring of vehicles or equipment for specific residents.
(e) The payment of reasonable expenses to selected volunteers undertaking activities on a one-to-one relationship with particular residents.
(f) The payment of accommodation charges and travel costs for relatives, staff and volunteers who accompany residents on holiday.

Appendix 5 of the Code of Practice[28] contains further examples of how funds may be used. The list is not exhaustive: for example, cigarettes are not included in the list but cigars and snuff are.

Ending Powers to Manage

4–24　　Should the circumstances be of the resident change, for example, if they regain capacity, then the supervising body should informed and the power to manage a resident's funds would be revoked. The authority to manage a resident's funds is also time limited and would expire at the end of a time specified in the certificate of authority from the supervising body. In the case where a resident moves out of an authorised establishment or ceases to be incapable the managers of the establishment may continue to manage the resident's affairs for up to three months until other arrangements can be made. The supervising body also has the authority to revoke the power to manage. This may be done, for example, in circumstances where the supervising authority is not

---

[27] *Adults with Incapacity (Scotland) Act 2000, Pt IV: Code of Practice for manager's authorised establishments.*
[28] *ibid.*

satisfied with the arrangements in the authorised establishment to manage residents' funds or the use to which patients' funds have been put. In such a case the supervising body is required to take over management of the residents' affairs within 14 days of revocation. It is also possible for an authorised establishment to cease to be authorised, either because of deficits discovered by the supervising body during an annual inspection or because the establishment opts out of managing patient funds. In either case the supervising body is required to manage the resident's affairs within 14 days of the revocation and make alternative arrangements to manage the resident's affairs within three months. If within that period an alternative arrangement cannot be made, it will fall upon the local authority to apply for an intervention or guardianship order under Part 6 of the Act.

The Role of Supervisory Bodies

Supervisory bodies are responsible for monitoring and reviewing the **4–25** manner in which the management of residents' finances are being conducted by authorised managers, as well as approving application forms as described above. For the Care Commission this work will be conducted in parallel to their other statutory duties regarding registration and inspection. There is a potential conflict of interest for an NHS board who fulfil both the role of supervisor and provider, in which case there needs to be clarity regarding the appropriate separation of functions within the Board. The supervisory bodies also have the power to conduct enquiries regarding any patients subject to this part for the Act. There is also a provision for both supervising bodies to deal with complaints. The key power of the supervising bodies is the authority to revoke the power to manage. In the case of the Care Commission managers of authorised establishments have recourse to an internal appeal and subsequent appeal to the Sheriff. The supervisory role of the Care Commission and NHS Boards is complex and a specific Code of Practice has been prepared to guide those authorities in their duties under the Act[29].

MEDICAL TREATMENT AND RESEARCH

Introduction

Up until the AI(S)2000 the legal authority to treat the medical **4–26** problems of incapable adults was far from clear. Although the Court of Session could be approached to empower a *tutor-dative* to give consent by proxy, this was only done in a handful of cases. Since 1994 the Mental Welfare Commission was informed of all such petitions and from 1994 to 1998 only 42 cases were reported to it[30]. The Scottish Law Commission commented in 1995: "as far as authority to give medical treatment to incapable adults is concerned, the law in Scotland is uncertain"[31].

---

[29] *Adults with Incapacity (Scotland) Act 2000, Pt IV: Code of Practice for supervisory bodies.*
[30] Personal correspondence with the Mental Welfare Commission.
[31] Scottish Law Commission (1995) *Report on Incapable Adults*, No.151, Cm 2962.

Medical practitioners continued to treat such patients, often following guidance from England where the common law of necessity is much more clearly established. The AI(S)2000 replaces this confusing situation by establishing a general authority to treat incapable adults in their best interest. This part of the Act, however, is not comprehensive and does not extend to emergency situations. The Act itself preserves previous common law justifications for treatment and therefore medical practitioners in Scotland still need to be aware of the common law principle of necessity within the Scottish context, which is described below.

The General Authority to Treat

4–27   Section 47 of the AI(S)2000 creates the category of a medical practitioner primarily responsible for the medical treatment of an adult (MPPR). The MPPR is granted by virtue of s.47, a general authority to treat, if he or she is of the opinion that an adult is incapable in relation to a decision about medical treatment and has certified such an individual as incapable. Such a general authority to treat also extends to any other person authorised by the MPPR for medical treatment. The definition of medical treatment is wide. In the Act it is defined as "any procedure or treatment designed to safeguard or promote physical or mental health". The Code of Practice[32] introduced the phrase "fundamental health care procedures", which could be used on a certificate and which would include basic nursing care, such as nutrition, hydration, hygiene, skin care, mobility, *etc.* The general authority to treat also includes dental care, but dentists must seek certification from a medical practitioner, usually the general practitioner, to authorise such treatment.

A pro forma is available to certificate adults under s.47. Such a certificate includes the statement:

> "I have today examined the above patient and consider he/she needs to undergo procedures to safeguard or promote physical or mental health in relation to the treatment plan below. I have assessed his/her capacity to consent to treatment in relation to each area of intervention. . . . I have consulted the following people over this treatment plan and over the patient's capacity. . . ."

Description of the intervention can be brief. The Code of Practice reminds practitioners that any intervention must be the least restrictive in relation to the patient's freedom in order to achieve the required benefit[33]. Most patients within a nursing home environment will require a broad scoped treatment plan. However, interventions that would normally require a separate signed consent of a patient would need an additional certificate of incapacity specifically regarding that treatment in addition to the treatment plan. Certificates issued pursuant to s.47 are valid for one year following the date of examination on which the certificate is based and are renewable.

---

[32] Scottish Executive (2002) *Code of Practice Pt V op. cit.* s.2.20.
[33] *ibid.*, s.2.47.

The MPPR

The identity of the MPPR is not defined in the Act. The Code of **4–28** Practice advises that this matter is essentially a practical one, commenting[34]:

> "who is primary responsible would depend on the circumstances in any particular situation. In the context of general practice it would normally be the adult's general practitioner, while in a hospital setting it will normally be the appropriate consultant."

In terms of out of hours hospital work the MPPR should be the doctor who is in attendance and to whom it is delegated to give treatment in the absence of the consultant[35]. Such a doctor should be a fully registered medical practitioner competent in terms of the intervention proposed[36]. The Code of Practice also reminds MPPRs that in their decisions, pursuant to s.47, the general principles of the Act apply. The Code of Practice also makes it clear that although generally treatment will involve some positive intervention in the patient's condition, a decision not to do something is still an intervention in terms of the Act. Therefore, do not resuscitate orders are subject to Part 5 of the Act[37].

MATTERS EXCLUDED FROM THE GENERAL AUTHORITY TO TREAT

Where there is a Proxy

General authority to treat does not apply when there is a continuing **4–29** welfare attorney, a guardian or a person authorised under an intervention order. In such a circumstance the MPPR must seek the consent from the appropriate proxy with the *caveat* that seeking such consent would be reasonable and practicable. The onus is on the medical practitioner to make reasonable enquiries regarding whether a proxy exists. If it is not reasonably practical to obtain the consent from a proxy, then the general authority to treat still applies.

Where the MPPR and the proxy agree about a treatment plan, any other interested party may appeal the decision to the Court of Session. Where the MPPR and the proxy disagree, a nominated medical practitioner (NMP) will be appointed on request by the Mental Welfare Commission. The NMP will be a medical practitioner with particular expertise in the proposed treatment. If the NMP concurs with the opinion of the MPPR, then medical treatment can proceed. If the NMP does not concur with the treatment decision of the MPPR, then an application can be made to the Court of Session for a determination whether proposed treatment should be given or not. If an appeal has been made to the Court of Session by an interested party, for example when the MPPR and NMP concur, then the treatment should not be

---

[34] Scottish Executive (2002) *Code of Practice Part V op. cit.* s.2.8.
[35] *ibid.*, s.2.9.
[36] *ibid.*
[37] *ibid.*, s.2.34.

given unless it can be justified by common law to preserve life or prevent serious deterioration. However, if there is an interdict preventing medical treatment, common law justifications to treat will not apply.

Special Treatments

4–30   The general authority to treat does not extend to any of the forms of treatment for which Part 10 of the Mental Health (Care and Treatment) (Scotland) Act 2003 applies and certain other controversial treatments listed in Table 11[38].

Table 11:

Schedule 1: Treatments excluded from the general authority to treat
Part 1—sterilisation. Where there is no serious malfunctional disease of the reproductive organs
—surgical implantation of hormones for the purpose of reducing sex drive
Part 2—Drug treatment for the purpose of reducing sex drive, other than surgical implantation of hormones —electro-convulsive therapy for mental disorder —abortion —any medical treatment considered likely by the MPPR to lead to sterilisation as an unavoidable result

The above Part 1 treatments may only be administered when the Court of Session is satisfied, on application by the MPPR, that the treatment will safeguard or promote the physical or mental health of the incapable adult, who does not oppose the treatment. Opposition to the treatment can be assessed by accessing the adult's residual capacity and may be demonstrated by any resistance to the treatment. For those treatments set out in Part 2 of Table 11 the MPPR must obtain a second opinion from a doctor appointed by the Mental Welfare Commission.

There are also additional safeguards in relation to treatment of mental disorder for adults aged 16 or 17[39]. No treatment for mental disorder pursuant to s.48 of the Act may be administered to an adult with incapacity who is 16 or 17 unless the MPPR has a qualification or special experience in child and adolescent psychiatry or has sought and obtained an opinion in writing from such an expert. If a second opinion is required in relation to Part 2 treatments of Table 11 for young adults, the certifying doctor appointed by the Mental Welfare Commission must also have appropriate expertise.

Notwithstanding the safeguards above, the AI(S)2000 preserves the common law justification of life saving treatment under the common law

---

[38] Scottish Executive (2002) *Adults with Incapacity (Scotland) Act 2000: Supplement to Code of Practice for persons authorised to carry out medical treatment or research under Pt V of the Act.*

[39] *ibid.*, ss.12–14.

of necessity for special treatments[40]. In such a situation the MPPR would have to be satisfied that the administration of the treatment was immediately necessary to preserve life or prevent a serious deterioration and that the necessary procedures, as outlined above, could not be reasonably followed because of the urgency of the situation. In such a circumstance, if unregulated treatment is carried out, the MPPR must inform the Mental Welfare Commission in writing within seven days and give details of the intervention and justification for doing so.

Use of Force and Psychiatric Hospital Admission

The general authority to treat does not extend to the use of force or **4–31** detention unless immediately necessary, and only for as long as is necessary in the circumstances, or placing an adult in hospital for the treatment of mental disorder against that adult's will. The Act, therefore, identifies that incapable adults who do not show dissent and are admitted to psychiatric hospital should be treated pursuant to Part 5 of the Act. If an incapable adult shows dissent, however, they should be detained pursuant to the relevant Section of the Mental Health (Care and Treatment) (Scotland) Act 2003. This follows the practice prior to the AI(S)2000 when non-dissenting incapable patients were admitted informally to hospital under the authority of common law and only if dissent was shown the powers under the Mental Health (Care and Treatment) (Scotland) Act 2003 used. In the English context this practice was examined in *R. v Bournewood Community and Mental Health NHS Trust Ex p.*[41].

Authority for Research

Section 51 of the Act enables researchers to conduct research on **4–32** incapable adults if research of a similar nature cannot be carried out on capable adults and that research is to obtain knowledge of the causes, diagnosis, treatment and care of the adult's incapacity. Such research is conditional on requirements laid out in Table 12 being satisfied.

Table 12:

Conditions which must be satisfied before research on incapable adults can be pursued
1. The research is likely to reveal real and direct benefit to the adult.
2. The adult does not indicate unwillingness to participate in the research.

[40] Scottish Executive (2002) *Adults with Incapacity (Scotland) Act 2000: Supplement to Code of Practice for persons authorised to carry out medical treatment or research under Pt V of the Act*, ss.15–17.

[41] [1999] 1 A.C. 458; Crichton, J.H.M. (1998) *The Bournewood Judgement and mental incapacity*, Journal of Forensic Psychiatry, Vol. 9, 513–7.

3. The research has been approved by the Ethics Committee.

4. The research entails no foreseeable risk or only a minimal foreseeable risk to the adult.

5. The research imposes no discomfort or only minimal discomfort on the adult.

6. Consent has been obtained from any guardian or welfare attorney who has the power to consent to the adult's participation and where there is no such proxy, from the adult's nearest relative.

7. If the research is not likely to produce real and direct benefit to the adult it may nevertheless be carried out if it will contribute to significant improvements in the scientific understanding of the adult's incapacity with the attainment of real and direct benefit to the adult or to other persons having the same incapacity.

Part 5 of the Act also authorises Scottish Ministers to make regulations in relation to the authorisation of research. That regulation specifies the composition of the Special Ethics Committee appointed by Scottish Ministers to consider applications under s.51 of the Act[42]. Researchers who wish to conduct research on incapable adults must not only approach their local Research Ethics Committee or, if necessary, the Multi Centre Research Ethics Committee, but also this specially constituted Ethics Committee. Local Research Ethics Committees are not authorised to approve research under s.51 of the Act.

The Common Law Justification of Necessity

4-33   In various places in Part 5 of the Act it is clear that previous common law justification for urgent treatment is preserved, for example, s.47 para. 2:

> "Without prejudice to any authority conferred by any other enactment or rule of law . . . The medical practitioner primarily responsible for the medical treatment of the adult shall have . . . authority to do what is reasonable in the circumstances in relation to the medical treatment to safeguard or promote the physical or mental health of adult."

The Code of Practice acknowledges that what may be considered an emergency treatment and what should only be done pursuant to Part 5 of the Act is not clear-cut. It states: "it would be contrary to good practice to risk prejudice to a patient's health through any delay in providing necessary treatment in order to give effect the procedures under Part 5 of the Act."[43] The Code then goes on to admit that the

---

[42] Adults with Incapacity (Ethics Committee) (Scotland) Regulations (SSI 2002/190).
[43] Scottish Executive (2002) *Code of Practice Pt V op. cit.*, s.2.4.

definition of an emergency will vary from speciality to speciality. The example is given of a patient found unconscious, through injury or illness, where medical treatment decisions must be taken and acted on within seconds or minutes if a fatality or severe damage is to be avoided. The example is also given of somebody who might require urgent life saving surgery, but that there may be a period during which rehydration and antibiotics are given prior to emergency surgery which would allow the MPPR time to consult and to complete the necessary forms. The intention of the draftsmen of the Code of Practice is, therefore, not to create unnecessary delay in appropriate treatment but to encourage the use of Part 5 of the Act whenever it is possible to do so. Decisions requiring seconds or minutes could be considered an emergency and decisions over many minutes or hours should follow Part 5 of the Act. It is for MPPR to decide which course of action is most appropriate and then potentially for the court to consider if such a course of action was reasonable.

The area of common law which would justify emergency treatment is the principle of necessity: there is a defence to a charge of committing a criminal act if the defendant was attempting to prevent a greater wrong occurring. Unfortunately, in Scotland, there is very little apt case law to guide the medical practitioner. In England there was a re-statement of the common law of necessity in relation to medical treatment in the late 1980s. In *F (Mental Patient Sterilisation) v West Berkshire Health Authority* [1989][44] doctors were allowed to treat an incapable adult in her best interests. Unfortunately there is considerable uncertainty about whether that ruling has any influence in a Scottish context[45]. The concept of necessity remains rather unclear in Scots Law[46]. A High Court ruling on a traffic violation[47] (*Moss v Howdle (1997)*) eroded the distinction between necessity and coercion. It would appear that necessity is an aspect of coercion, as[48] MacCall Smith and Sheldon (1997) put it "the coercion of circumstance". In this judgement the institutional writings of Hume were drawn on and necessity was held to be limited to those situations where there was "an immediate danger of death or great bodily harm". The Code of Practice makes detailed reference to the treatment of emergencies under the justification of necessity but it would be more reassuring to medical practitioners in Scotland if this area of law had been clarified by the AI(S)2000 as it was found to be deficient in the reviews of existing law as the Act was being prepared.

Intervention and Guardianship Orders

Introduction

Part 6 of the AI(S)2000 gives the power to Sheriff Courts to grant **4–34** intervention and guardianship orders, which replace the former system of *curators bonis* and guardianship provisions in the Mental Health

---

[44] *F v West Berkshire Health Authority* [1989] 2 W.L.R. 1025; [1989] All E.R. 545.
[45] Scottish Executive (1999) *Making the Right Moves op. cit.* para. 6.5.
[46] Ferguson, W. (1986) *Necessity and duress in Scots Law*, Criminal Law Review, 103–9.
[47] *Moss v Howdle* [1997] SCCR 215.
[48] McCall-Smith, R.A.A., and Sheldon, D., *Scots Criminal Law* (1997, Butterworths).

(Scotland) Act 1984. Intervention orders allow for single decisions on either financial or personal welfare matters. An example might be a sale of a house or a particular surgical procedure. Guardianship orders will grant the guardian either powers of financial guardianship, welfare guardianship or both with regards to an adult with incapacity. The guardian's powers would be similar to those of an attorney. The principle of least restriction would mean that where the desired outcome can be achieved via an intervention order, this would be preferred to a guardianship order. This part of the Act repealed the Curators Act 1585 and existing *curators bonis* automatically became financial guardians in April 2002.

Intervention orders

4–35   Anyone claiming an interest in the finance or welfare of an adult with incapacity can apply to the Sheriff Court for an intervention order. The local authority could apply for an order where it appears necessary and no-one else is applying. The purpose of such an order is to authorise one-off decisions, and it is not intended to impose continuous management. If continuous management is required, then a guardianship order should be sought. Reports are required to be laid before the court based on an examination of the adult, carried out not more than 30 days prior to the application. In all cases two medical reports are required, one of which must be from a medical practitioner approved as having special experience in diagnosis and treatment of mental disorder. The second medical practitioner will normally be the patient's general practitioner. In the cases where a welfare intervention is sought, an additional report is required by a mental health officer, if an adult is suffering from mental disorder, or from the chief social work officer if an adult is suffering from inability to communicate. That third report should express an opinion as to the appropriateness of the order and the suitability of the nominee. In financial cases, a third report should be submitted by a person with sufficient knowledge to report on the appropriateness of the order sought and the suitability of the nominee. The Code of Practice for persons authorised under intervention and guardianship orders gives a wealth of practical information[49].

Guardianship orders

4–36   Guardianship orders are also made by application to the Sheriff Court and are the most intrusive type of order found in the AI(S)2000. Guardians may either be financial or welfare guardians and their powers would be similar to continuing attorneys or welfare attorneys. They are intended to provide a proxy where continuous management of a person's finances or personal welfare is required. The Sheriff Court requires three reports for the order to be considered. The authors of those three reports are the same for intervention orders, *i.e.* one approved doctor, another doctor and a mental health officer or chief social work officer in welfare cases and an appropriate person for a financial guardianship

---

[49] Scottish Executive (2002) *Adults with Incapacity (Scotland) Act 2000 Code of Practice: Persons authorised under an intervention order and guardians.*

order. A period of appointment of a guardian would be for three years or any other such period, including an indefinite period. The court must, however, consider whether a lesser intervention, such as an intervention order, would be less intrusive and therefore more appropriate. It is possible to appoint two or more individuals as joint guardians or a guardian and a substitute. When making a guardianship order the court must consider the suitability of the guardian and satisfy itself that they are aware of the adult's circumstances and needs. The guardian must be accessible to the adult and the primary carer. The guardian must be able to carry out the function of a guardian and the Sheriff should consider any likely areas of conflict of interest of undue concentration of power (s.59).

If there is a requirement for accounting, a financial guardian is entitled to remuneration from the estate of the adult unless the court rules otherwise. A welfare guardian is not entitled to that remuneration unless there are special circumstances laid before the Sheriff.

Guardians are required to keep records of how they exercise their powers. The Code of Practice, for persons authorised under the intervention orders, reminds guardians that they have a duty of care to the adult on whose affairs they are managing and that guardians have a fiduciary duty; in other words they are placed in a position of trust by the Sheriff. Financial guardians would be expected to keep an inventory of assets and keep the adult's financial affairs under review[50]. Complaints about financial guardians can be made to the Public Guardian who has the power to investigate any complaint. The Public Guardian is also available to give advice to financial guardians as to the exercise of their powers.

The Code of Practice informs welfare guardians of the duty placed on them and reminds welfare guardians that they should be contactable and inform the Public Guardian of any changes of address. The welfare guardian should hold regular review meetings to discuss the welfare of the adult. In certain circumstances, the powers of the welfare guardian can be delegated to others; for example, a guardian may delegate to a carer decisions regarding regular hairdressing or chiropody. The Code of Practice has a checklist of questions, which a welfare guardian should ask when reviewing the adult's circumstances[51], such as does the adult appear well and happy, accommodation needs, clothing needs, meaningful daytime activity *etc*. Welfare guardians are also required to keep proper records and appropriately liase with anyone who has financial powers over the adult. The local authority must supervise a welfare guardian and that supervision will take the form of regular meetings, reporting arrangements and visits both with and without warning to the guardian and the adult. Although the local authority should be the first point of contact and the supervisor for a welfare guardian, the Mental Welfare Commission has an overarching role and has the power to investigate complaints regarding welfare guardians.

Guardianship orders can be renewed, replaced, terminated or transferred on application to the Sheriff. Section 71 of the Act allows a

---

[50] Scottish Executive (2002) *Adults with Incapacity (Scotland) Act 2000 Code of Practice: Persons authorised under an intervention order and guardians*, ss.4.16–23.

[51] *ibid.*, s.5.25.

Sheriff, on the application of any person claiming an interest, the power to replace or remove a guardian. In circumstances where the grounds for the appointment of a guardian are no longer fulfilled, the guardianship order can be terminated. There is a particular procedure for a guardian who wishes to resign found in s.57 of the Act. The intention to resign should be notified to the Public Guardian, the local authority and, where appropriate, the Mental Welfare Commission and as much notice as possible should be given. At the time of the application of a guardian it would be good practice to appoint an additional guardian who would be available to act during periods of unavailability of the primary guardian. If a welfare guardian is temporarily unavailable, for example, because of hospitalisation, and there is no-one else willing to act who can become an additional guardian, the local authority can apply for an interim welfare guardianship order while the situation is resolved.

PSYCHIATRIC SYSTEMS AND SERVICES FOR MENTALLY DISORDERED OFFENDERS

A range of services is required to ensure that mentally disordered offenders can access psychiatric assessment and treatment at all stages and settings of the criminal justice process. The definition of, services for, and issues arising from, mentally disordered offenders involved with the police, courts, prisons and parole board are described here. Psychiatric facilities for mentally disordered offenders are described in Chapter One. Risk assessment and management are of major importance to both the mental health and criminal justice services in ensuring public safety. The methods utilised for risk assessment by both mental health and criminal justice services are outlined and the risk management of mentally disordered offenders is discussed.

MENTALLY DISORDERED OFFENDERS

The Scottish Office policy on *Health, Social Work and Related Services for Mentally Disordered Offenders in Scotland*[2] sets out expectations and methods of working for the care and treatment of this group. It describes mentally disordered offenders as those who are: **5–01**

> "considered to suffer from a mental disorder as defined in the Mental Health (Scotland) Act 1984, whether or not they are, or may be, managed under its provisions and come to the attention of the criminal justice system."

The policy uses mental disorder specifically to refer to people with mental illness or learning disability. It sets out guiding principles for the care of mentally disordered offenders. They

> "should be cared for:
> - with regard to quality of care and proper attention to the needs of individuals as far as possible in the community rather that in institutional settings
> - under conditions of no greater security that is justified by the degree of danger they present to themselves or to others
> - in such a way as to maximise rehabilitation and their chance of sustaining an independent life

---

[1] Chapter author: Dr L.D.G. Thomson, M.D. Michelle Davidson, formerly of the Division of Psychiatry, University of Edinburgh contributed to the section on risk.
[2] Scottish Office (1998) *Health and Social Work and Related Services for Mentally Disordered Offenders in Scotland*, LTS08903.

- as near as possible to their own homes or families if they have them."

Mentally disordered offenders can be moved, or diverted, from the criminal justice system to mental health services at any stage of the criminal justice process. See Box 1. The specific details of civil mental health legislation, psychiatric defences and legislation for mentally disordered offenders that sanction this are dealt with in Chapters 3, 6 and 7 respectively. Transfer to a psychiatric hospital does not prevent the criminal justice process from progressing either in tandem with an individual's assessment and treatment or at a later date. An individual can be returned to the criminal justice system at any stage, unless a final disposal has been made solely to psychiatric services. Clearly, involvement of mental health services with people in the criminal justice system is dependent on the recognition of mental health problems. Training of all staff, police officers, procurators fiscal, criminal justice social workers, and prison officers is therefore essential.

Box 1: Criminal Justice and Mental Health Systems: Diversion Pathway

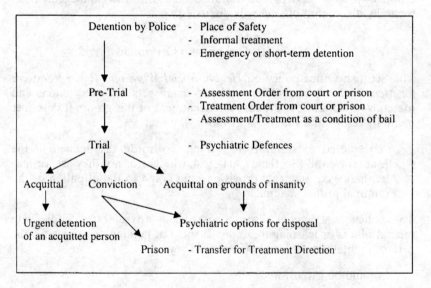

POLICE

5–02   The primary duty of the police is to prevent crime and to detect offenders. The police, however, deal regularly with people with mental disorders sometimes following an offence or because they are lost, vulnerable or confused. Many of these interactions are carried out on an informal basis, for example returning an elderly person with dementia to family. The police therefore require training in the recognition and management of people with mental disorders, and in accessing appropriate psychiatric services for people in their care. Such training was recommended by the Mental Welfare Commission following its inquiry into the death of P.C. Lewis Fulton[3]. Constable Fulton was killed at work when trying to assist an individual with schizophrenia. Basic training for all officers should cover the signs and symptoms of common mental disorders; advice on the management of people with a mental disorder; legal powers available to the police to assist in the management of people with mental disorders; information on local psychiatric services; and the role of appropriate adults.

Place of Safety

Many police officers quickly gain experience of dealing with people with mental disorders. It is not the job of the police to make diagnoses, but to have a high index of suspicion that bizarre behaviour may be due to mental disorder. In such cases a psychiatric opinion is required. The Act makes provision for this allowing an individual to be removed from a public place to a place of safety[4] for the purpose of a medical examination. **5–03**

Conditions

A constable may remove an individual to a place of safety if he reasonably suspects that: **5–04**

- a person in a public place has a mental disorder,
- is in immediate need of care or treatment,
- and that it would be in his interests, or necessary for the protection of any other person, to remove him to a place of safety

A public place is defined as a location to which the public has access and includes common parts of a building containing two or more homes.

Powers

The individual can be detained in a place of safety for a maximum of 24 hours after the time of removal from a public place. **5–05**

Process

During the period of detention in a place of safety, arrangements must be made for a medical examination and any necessary follow-up. If the person absconds, the constable may at any time during the 24-hour period take the person into custody and remove them to a place of safety. **5–06**

A place of safety can be a hospital, premises used for the purpose of providing a care home service, or any other suitable place (other than a police station) the occupier of which is willing temporarily to receive mentally disordered persons. If no place of safety is immediately

---

[3] Mental Welfare Commission (1996) Annual Report 1995–96, 13–15.
[4] Mental Health (Care and Treatment) (Scotland) Act 2003, s.297.

available, a constable may remove an individual to a police station. It is important for local psychiatric and police services formally to agree on a place of safety. Most commonly it is a psychiatric unit catering for emergency referrals or an accident and emergency department. The latter is particularly useful in cases of suspected self harm or substance abuse where an assessment of an individual's physical health is also required.

The constable must as soon as is practicable inform the local authority, and the person's nearest relative and carer, of the name and address of the person concerned, the date and time of his removal from a public place, the circumstances giving rise to this, the address of the place of safety, and the reason for the use of a police station if this occurred. Within 14 days the constable must inform the Commission of the above. A place of safety order existed under the 1984 Act (s.118) but no paperwork was required. This is the first time that its use will be formally reported and statistics will be available. It is hoped that police officers will not be discouraged from using this important power by the new bureaucracy.

Appeal

5–07   There is no right of appeal against removal to a place of safety.

Example

5–08   The police were contacted by members of the public concerned by the behaviour of a middle-aged, unkempt looking man in a town centre. On approach the man appeared to be gesticulating and shouting at some-thing unidentifiable to the officers. He did not smell of alcohol and he was very aroused. He agreed to go with the officers to get away from "them—they follow me everywhere". He was taken to the locally agreed place of safety at an accident and emergency department and seen by a psychiatrist. He believed that the devil was trying to kill him and had hallucinations of little devils looking like pit-bull terriers with horns that followed and threatened him. He refused voluntary admission to hospital and was detained under an emergency detention certificate.

Table 1: Removal to a Place of Safety from a Public Place—Police

Section	Conditions	Duration	Signatories/ Consent	Revocation	Appeal
297	• Police officer suspects mental disorder in a person in a public place • In immediate need of care and treatment • In patient's interest, or for the protection of others to remove him to a place of safety	24 hours	Police Officer	Nil	Nil

Alternatively, if a person has been arrested and taken to police cells, he can be assessed in that setting by a forensic medical examiner or duty psychiatrist depending on local arrangements.

Psychiatric Services to Police Stations

Psychiatric services to police stations vary throughout the country. In 5–09
most areas a forensic medical examiner (formally known as a police surgeon and usually a general practitioner) is initially summoned to the police station to assess an individual thought by police officers to have mental health problems. In some areas the forensic medical examiner can call a psychiatrist if further assessment is required but in others the forensic medical examiner must decide whether admission to hospital or further psychiatric follow-up is required. The following issues should be considered for a mentally disordered person in police custody:

Fitness to remain in custody

The custody officer may call a doctor if concerned whether an 5–10
individual is fit to remain in police custody. Such decisions are purely medical and there are no legal criteria to guide this. Major physical or mental illness causing an immediate and serious risk to health and safety may make an individual unfit to remain in custody and transfer to hospital would usually be required.

Assessment and treatment needs

An individual may be fit to remain in custody but have clear needs for 5–11
further assessment and/or treatment of a mental disorder. The doctor should advise on this. This can include advice to the police on medication or observation regarding risk of self harm whilst in custody, advice to the patient or recommendations for diversion to psychiatric care. Inpatient psychiatric care can be arranged on a voluntary basis or via emergency or short-term detention under the Mental Health (Care and Treatment) (Scotland) Act 2003. Such immediate diversion should only be carried out in cases involving less serious offences unless issues of fitness to remain in custody arise. For alleged offences of a serious nature or where the requirement for transfer to hospital is not immediate, a psychiatric report should be provided to the procurator fiscal recommending transfer to hospital under an assessment or treatment order. The initial court appearance will be on the first working day after an individual is charged. This psychiatric report can be handwritten and brief given the short timescale. Alternatively, oral evidence can be given. The police report to the procurator fiscal will note the presence of any mental disorder and any psychiatric recommendations.

Fitness to be interviewed

In carrying out any interview a police officer must consider whether an 5–12
individual is fit for interview. A suspect can be interviewed in three ways:

- Voluntary Interview: the interviewee can leave at any time.
- Interview of a detained person: a person can be detained for up to six hours by the police under ss.14 and 15 of the Criminal

Procedure (Scotland) Act 1995 if he is suspected of having committed a criminal offence. He usually has the right to inform a solicitor, and a friend or relative (unless thought to be involved in the crime) of his detention.

- Interview of a person arrested or charged: a person who is arrested will be cautioned and formally charged as soon as practicable. He can contact a solicitor, and friend or relative as before. He may be released on police bail or detained and appear in court on the next working day. He can see a solicitor before going to court. The police report to the procurator fiscal must provide details of any physical or mental disorder, and any use of an appropriate adult. It is the procurator fiscal's duty to inform the court of the presence of any mental disorder.

A person may be unfit for interview due to physical or mental ill-health. If the presence of a mental disorder is suspected, the officer must consider whether an individual requires to be assessed by a forensic medical examiner or a psychiatrist regarding his fitness to be interviewed. Medical or legal criteria regarding fitness for interview do not currently exist. Factors to be considered[5] include:

- Does the detainee understand the police caution after it has been fully explained to him?
- Is the detainee fully orientated in time, place and person and does he recognise the key persons present during the police interview.
- Is the detainee likely to give answers which could be seriously misconstrued by the court? For example is he able to understand the consequences of his answers. In some cases detainees may admit to anything in order to fill his immediate needs, such as the ending of the interview.

Need for an appropriate adult

5–13   If the detainee is found fit to be interviewed but does have a mental disorder, then an appropriate adult should be present during the interview. Alternatively, fitness to be interviewed may never have been in question but the presence of a mental disorder indicates the need for an appropriate adult.

APPROPRIATE ADULTS

5–14   It is recognised that police interviews of an adult with a mental disorder may be difficult because of potential problems with communication, lack of comprehension, delusional thinking, limited insight, emotional distress and suggestibility[6]. Most people with mental disorders are

---

[5] Gudjonsson, G., Hayes, G. and Rowlands, P. (2000) *Fitness to be Interviewed and Psychological Vulnerability: The views of doctors, lawyers and police officers*, The Journal of Forensic Psychiatry, 11, 1, 75–92.

[6] Gudjonsson, G and MacKeith, J. (1994) *Learning Disability and the Police and Criminal Evidence Act 1984: Protection during investigative interviewing a video-recorded false confession to double murder*, Journal of Forensic Psychiatry, 5 (1), 35–48.

able to provide reliable evidence but it is essential that the rights and obligations set out in statute and common law apply equally to people with mental disorder in contact with the police. This is the primary aim of appropriate adult schemes. Such schemes were developed in England following inquiries into high profile cases of miscarriages of justice primarily involving people with learning disability[7].

The Scottish Office guidance of April 1998[8] encouraged the establishment of appropriate adult schemes throughout Scotland. These schemes have no statutory basis, unlike their counterparts in England and Wales. It is for the court to decide whether the absence of an appropriate adult at interview brings into question the admissibility of the statements made by the interviewee. This has occurred on two occasions to date[9]. The appropriate adult schemes in Scotland were evaluated in 2002. There were 16 appropriate adult schemes covering the whole of Scotland[10]. There were over 400 appropriate adults and 70 per cent were social workers. Many police officers were aware of appropriate adult schemes but this was not the case for forensic medical examiners or the legal profession. Amongst those who were familiar with appropriate adult schemes there were some common misconceptions and a lack of clarity about their operation and management. There was evidence of a general under-utilisation of schemes across Scotland suggesting that not all those who required an appropriate adult were obtaining this service. Recording practices and monitoring varied greatly between schemes, with only 10 of the 16 schemes recording data on the use of appropriate adults. There was widespread support amongst appropriate adults and scheme co-ordinators for schemes to be placed on a statutory basis in Scotland. Almost all appropriate adults had received training relating to this role; however training amongst other professional groups was rare. Recommendations to improve the working of these schemes have been accepted by the Scottish Executive.

Definition of an Appropriate Adult

The role of the appropriate adult is to ensure that a person with a **5–15** mental disorder is not disadvantaged during a police interview because of their disorder. Appropriate adults can be used for a victim, witness, suspect or accused; and provide support and assist communication between that individual and the police.

Appropriate adults are people who:

- Understand mental disorder
- Are experienced and/or trained in dealing with people with mental disorders
- Are able to communicate with people with mental disorders

---

[7] Price, C. and Caplan, J., *The Confait Confessions* (Marion Boyars, 1977).

[8] Scottish Office (1998) *Interviewing People who are Mentally Disordered: "Appropriate Adult" Schemes*, Home Department and HM Inspectorate of Constabulary.

[9] *HMA v Vincent James Milligan* (2003) Judgment of Sheriff A.L. Stewart Q.C., 19/3/2003, Ref. DNO 2510128; *LB v HMA*, 2003 J.C. 94.

[10] Thomson L.D.G., Galt V. and Darjee R. (2004) *An Evaluation of Appropriate Adult Schemes in Scotland*, Scottish Executive Research Findings No. 78.

- Understand that whilst they may have professional qualifications and experience relevant to their appointment as an appropriate adult that they are NOT acting in their professional role
- Are NOT police officers or employees of the police force
- Are NOT relatives or friends of the interviewee although they may be present in addition to an appropriate adult
- Are NOT carers or former carers, or someone in a long-term professional relationship with the interviewee
- Can act for a victim/witness or a suspect/accused in the same case but not for both.

Use of an Appropriate Adult

5–16   An appropriate adult is required if a police officer suspects that a person being interviewed has a mental disorder. The following may assist the officer in making this decision:

- External information from a carer, general practitioner, mental health team or social worker.
- Information from the interviewee about a mental disorder; medication; attendance at an outpatient department, day centre or hospital; special education; or sheltered employment. This can be obtained by use of a standard question checklist.
- Presentation at interview; for example bizarre statements, incoherent speech (not solely due to drug or alcohol use), failure to understand or answer questions, unusual behaviour, excessive anxiety or agitation.

A police officer may call a forensic medical examiner and/or a psychiatrist to determine physical or mental fitness to be interviewed before an appropriate adult is contacted. The decision to call an appropriate adult is, however, the responsibility of the police officer. Transfer of an individual from a police station to a hospital does not automatically preclude interview in that setting and an appropriate adult should be in attendance there.

Role and Responsibilities of an Appropriate Adult

5–17   The appropriate adult may be involved at a number of stages of the criminal justice process. Their role at each stage is described below:
Pre-interview:

- To be introduced to the interviewee.
- To confirm the emotional and physical state of the interviewee as observed by the police.
- To clarify whether there is any sensory impairment that would hinder communication such as hearing impairment.
- To note the role the interviewee is alleged to have played in the events leading to interview.
- To discuss with officers how the interview can be suspended or terminated if there are concerns about the interviewee.

At interview:

- To provide support and reassurance to the interviewee.
- To ensure the interviewee understands the purpose of the interview.
- To ensure the interviewee understands the questions being put and the implications of his answers.
- To facilitate communication between the interviewee and the police officer.
- To ensure proper interview procedures are followed.
- To ensure the interviewee knows who is present and the role of each individual.
- To ensure a suspect with a mental disorder is not disadvantaged by that disorder and that he fully understands his rights and the stages of the process as explained by the police. For example, to ensure that the interviewee understands the role of a solicitor and is aware that that he has the right to have a solicitor informed of his arrest.
- To sign any document or statement signed by the interviewee and to indicate if he considers it is inaccurate.
- To advise police if the interviewee's statements appear to the appropriate adult to be unreliable.
- To advise police if the interviewee is becoming distressed and requires a break, and medical or other assistance, in a manner agreed in advance.
- To make notes if desired, on the conduct but not content of the interview. Any concerns can then appear in the police report and will be available to the procurator fiscal and defence lawyer.
- To ensure that any intimate search or medical examination only takes place in front of the appropriate adult (of the same sex) if the interviewee agrees.

Post-interview:

- To review the content of the interview with the police officers who conducted it.
- To identify any problem areas. The appropriate adult can make notes and would be able to refer to these in court at a later date.
- To provide the police with a statement about his involvement in proceedings.
- To ensure the police have informed the interviewee post-interview of support and services available, and to convey information to relatives or carers.

At precognition:

A precognition involves the preliminary examination of a witness and is used by the defence and prosecution to prepare a case for court. The appropriate adult may:

- Be precognosed as a witness to the police interview.
- Act as an appropriate adult during a precognition.

At Court:

- To visit court with the interviewee prior to a trial.
- To attend court to support and reassure the interviewee.
- To be a witness regarding the reliability of the interview process.

Other circumstances that may involve the use of an appropriate adult:

- Fingerprinting.
- Photographs.
- Search of premises.
- Identification parades.
- Intimate body searches.
- Medical examinations.
- E-fit interviews.

An appropriate adult should **not**:

- Act as a quasi-lawyer and tell the person whether or how to answer questions.
- Object to questions being asked except if this is to aid communication.
- Tell the police that a line of questioning is unfair.
- Prompt an identification of a suspect by a victim.

COURTS

5–18   In most parts of the country a mental health service is provided to the courts. This is usually a system to respond to requests for psychiatric reports from procurators fiscal, defence lawyers and sheriff clerks. In three areas there are formal court liaison schemes. Tayside has a non-acute liaison scheme whereby an individual can be sent for psychiatric assessment by the procurator fiscal if he agrees to plead guilty. Fewer than 12 patients per year are assessed in this way. Glasgow and Forth Valley operate acute court liaison schemes, in other words there is a psychiatric nurse or psychiatrist present in court on each day it sits assessing patients immediately following a request by a procurator fiscal. Between 1994 and 1998 referrals to the Glasgow Sheriff Court Forensic Psychiatry Liaison Service increased by 250 per cent from 118 to 294 per year but the proportion admitted fell from 46 per cent to 15 per cent (54 to 44 patients) and the proportion that was actively psychotic declined from 32 per cent to 17 per cent[11]. This evidence suggests that the remit of the scheme widened as it became more established although this may not be an appropriate use of mental health services.

Different options are available to courts for diversion of mentally disordered offenders to mental health services at varying stages of the

---

[11] White, T., Ramsay, L., Morrison, R. (2002) *Audit of the forensic psychiatry liaison service to Glasgow Sheriff Court 1994 to 1998*, Medicine Science and the Law 42(1), 64–70.

criminal justice process. Procurators fiscal can decide that it is not in the public interest to proceed with a case but this decision should only be taken, in part because of the presence of a mental disorder, for minor charges. It is a procurator fiscal's duty to bring the known presence of a mental disorder in an accused person to the attention of the court.

Pre-trial

After being charged an individual will appear at a pre-trial hearing(s). **5–19** He may be remanded on bail, remanded in custody or remanded to hospital. Options for recommendations for psychiatric assessment and treatment are set out in Box 2. Full details of the relevant legislation are contained in Chapter 7.

Box 2: Psychiatric Recommendations Pre-Trial

Informal treatment
Compulsory treatment under civil mental health legislation
Assessment or treatment as a condition of bail
Assessment order   s.52 B–J Criminal Procedure (Scotland) Act 1995
Treatment order   s.52 K–S Criminal Procedure (Scotland) Act 1995

Trial

At trial the relevant psychiatric issues to be considered include: **5–20**

- fitness to plead
- insanity at the time of the offence
- diminished responsibility
- automatism

Psychiatric defences are described in Chapter 6.

Post-trial

Options for disposal to the psychiatric system after trial are outlined in **5–21** full in Chapter 7. These are summarised in Box 3. Treatment can be offered on an informal basis and sentencing can be deferred.

Box 3: Psychiatric Disposal Post-Trial

Post-trial but pre-sentence	Criminal Procedure (Scotland) Act 1995
Assessment Order	s.52 B–J
Treatment Order	s.52 K–S
Remand for inquiry into mental condition	s.200
Interim compulsion order	s.53
Final disposal	
Compulsion Order	s.57A
Restriction Order	s.59
Hospital Direction	s.59A
Guardianship Order	s.58(1A)
Intervention Order for an incapable adult	s.60B
Probation for treatment of mental disorder	s.230

Drug Courts

5–22   The establishment of drug courts in Scotland is a specific example of the criminal justice system responding to a mental health and major social issue. This type of court was piloted in Glasgow and Fife and recognises the association between substance abuse and crime[12]. The aim of the court is to reduce drug abuse and associated offending by offering treatment-based disposals. The court deals with less serious offences committed by adults over the age of 20 with a recognised pattern of drug misuse and related offending. Potential candidates are identified by the prosecution service from the police report. The custody court can refer suitable cases to the drug court if the individual pleads guilty. The case is adjourned for four weeks to obtain a social enquiry report, a drug action plan and results of drug testing. All disposals for summary proceedings are available to the drug court and it can defer sentence or impose drug treatment and testing orders (DTTOs), probation orders with a condition of drug treatment or concurrent DTTOs and conditional probation orders. Cases are reviewed monthly and can be breached if the person is non-compliant. To date these courts deal with small numbers and adequate staffing (addiction workers and social workers) of the supervision and treatment teams is problematic.

PRISONS

5–23   The daily prison population in Scotland is over 6,000, having increased by over a quarter during the 1990s. Approximately one-fifth of these prisoners are on remand, one-tenth are young offenders and three per cent are women. The prison service policy for mentally disordered offenders is set out in Positive Mental Health[13] in conjunction with the Scottish Executive's policy on mentally disordered offenders[14].

Prevalence of Mental Disorders in Prison

5–24   The need for mental health services in prisons is well recognised. The evidence supporting this is outlined in Table 2. The prison service aims to provide psychiatric services within prison equivalent to those available to people in the community although it is acknowledged that the need within prisons for mental health services is much greater than in the community. Some people in prison do not have a formal mental disorder but are considered vulnerable because of isolation, loss of contact with their family, and self-harming or erratic behaviour. Support for these prisoners is often provided by mental health and social work staff working in conjunction with prison officers.

---

[12] McIvor G., Eley S., Malloch M. and Yates R. (2003) *Establishing Drug Courts in Scotland: Early Experiences of the pilot Drug Courts in Glasgow and Fife*, Crime and Criminal Justice Research Programme, Research Findings 71/2003, Scottish Executive.

[13] Scottish Prison Service (2002) Positive Mental Health, Edinburgh.

[14] Scottish Office (1998) *Health and Social Work and Related Services for Mentally Disordered Offenders in Scotland*, Edinburgh, LTS08903.

Table 2: Prison Studies of Psychiatric Morbidity in the United Kingdom

Authors	Study Cohort	Measures	Results
Gunn *et al* (1991)[15]	1769 male convicted prisoners	CIS	2% psychosis[1] 6% neurotic disorder[1] 23% drug/alcohol abuse[2]
Cooke (1994)[16]	247 male remand and convicted prisoners	SADS-L	7.3% major psychological disorders[1] 32% neurotic disorder[1] 38% alcohol dependence[2] 20.6% drug abuse/dependence[2]
Davidson *et al* (1995)[17]	389 male remand prisoners	CIS	2.3% psychosis[1] 24.8% neurotic disorder[1] 22% alcohol abuse/dependence[2] 73% drug abuse/dependence[2]
Brooke *et al* (1996)[18]	750 male remand prisoners	SADS-L	5% psychosis[1] 26% neurotic disorder[1] 38% drug/alcohol misuse[2]
Birmingham *et al* (1996)[19]	548 male remand prisoners	SADS-L	4% psychosis[1] 22% minor psychological disorder[1] 32% alcohol abuse/dependence[2] 33% drug misuse/dependence[2]
Singleton *et al* (1998)[20]	1250 male remand prisoners	CIS-R SCAN	10% psychosis[1] 59% neurotic disorder[1] 58% alcohol abuse[3] 51% drug dependence[3]
Singleton *et al* (1998)[21]	1121 male convicted prisoners	CIS-R SCAN	7% psychosis[1] 40% neurotic disorder[1] 63% alcohol abuse[3] 43% drug dependence[3]

Key   [1] Point prevalence   [2] Lifetime diagnosis   [3] Present in past year

[15] Gunn, J., Maden, A., Swinton, M., (1991) *Treatment needs of prisoners with psychiatric disorders*, British Medical Journal, 303, 338–341.

[16] Cooke, D. (1994) *Psychological disturbance amongst prisoners*, Scottish Prison Service, Occasional Papers, Report No. 3/1994.

[17] Davidson, M., Humphreys, M.S., Joynstone, E.C., Cunningham Owens, D.G. (1995) *Prevalence of psychiatric morbidity among remand prisoners in Scotland*, British Journal of Psychiatry, 167, 545–548.

[18] Brooke, D., Taylor, C., Gunn, J., Maden, A. (1996) *Point prevalence of mental disorder in unconvicted male prisoners in England and Wales*, British Medical Journal, 313, 1524–7.

[19] Birmingham, L., Mason, D., Grubin, D. (1996) *Prevalence of mental disorder in remand prisoners: a consecutive case study*, British Medical Journal, 313, 1521–4.

[20] Singleton, N., Meltzer, H., Gatward, R. (1998) *Psychiatric morbidity among prisoners in England and Wales*, The Office for National Statistics, The Stationery Office, London.

Authors	Study Cohort	Measures	Results
Bartlett *et al* (2000)[22]	119 male receptions in one week to HMP Barlinnie	CIS-R SCAN	5% psychosis[1] 30% depression/anxiety disorder[1] 79% drug abuse[2]

Key [1] Point prevalence [2] Lifetime diagnosis [3] Present in past year

Mental Health Services in Prison

5–25   All prisoners are assessed on reception to prison for physical and mental health problems. Ideally, these assessments are informed by any existing social enquiry or psychiatric reports but these are usually not available at this time. A risk and needs assessment is carried out for longer stay prisoners. Most penal establishments in Scotland have visiting psychiatrists. In some prisons, mental health teams have been formed consisting of a psychiatrist(s), registered mental nurses, community psychiatric nurses, medical officers, a social worker(s), chaplains, and at times forensic psychologists, staff from external agencies and occupational therapists. A review meeting is held weekly to discuss cases and, where required, to agree care plans for patients. The role of the psychiatrist is to assess, diagnose, treat and review patients, and to provide advice and support to other members of the mental health team. Access to a psychiatrist by prisoners is generally more direct than in the community. Referral systems vary but prisoners can be referred by the prison medical officer, nursing staff, prison officers or social workers, or can self-refer. Some prisons operate a screening system whereby referrals are seen initially by nursing staff and then by a psychiatrist if required. People with anxiety, mild to moderate depression, substance misuse, and adjustment problems are typically treated within prison.

As in the community, some prisoners with a mental disorder will require treatment in hospital and others will require treatment in their own setting. Powers exist within the Mental Health (Care and Treatment) (Scotland) Act 2003 to transfer prisoners on remand under an assessment order (s.52B–J) or treatment order (s.52K–S), and convicted prisoners under a transfer for treatment direction (s.136). These powers are summarised in Table 3 and described fully in Chapter 7. Prisoners can be transferred to psychiatric hospital without the use of mental health legislation by means of a Governor's warrant but this necessitates the presence of police officers on the ward to accompany the patient and is undesirable. Each year in Scotland approximately 65 remand and sentenced prisoners are transferred to a psychiatric hospital under mental health legislation. These prisoners typically suffer from a psychotic illness, a major depressive episode, or, less frequently, learning disability. An increasing number of reports to the Mental Welfare

[21] Singleton, N., Meltzer, H., Gatward, R. (1998) *Psychiatric morbidity among prisoners in England and Wales*, The Office for National Statistics, The Stationery Office, London.

[22] Bartlett, K., Thomson, L.D.G., Johnstone, E.C. (2001), *Mentally Disordered Offenders: an evaluation of the "Open Doors" Programme at HM Prison, Barlinnie*, Scottish Prison Service, Occasional Paper Series, No. 2/2001.

Commission suggest that at times finding a hospital bed for these patients has been difficult. In an ideal world, visiting psychiatrists would have direct access to beds. This is a model that works well for local prisons where there is a direct link to a local psychiatric hospital. Transfer to a psychiatric hospital becomes more complicated however, when an individual normally resides in a health board area outwith the location of the prison and has been in prison for less than six months.

Table 3: Transfer from Prison to Psychiatric Hospital

Order	Section	Conditions	Duration	Evidence/ Decision	Revocation/ Variation
Assessment Order —assessment in hospital pre-trial or pre-sentencing	s.52B–J	Making the order is necessary to assess: Mental Disorder If treatment is likely to alleviate symptoms or prevent deterioration, and is available Risk to health, safety or welfare of patient; or safety of others Bed available in 7 days	28 days (7-day extension)	1 registered doctor— oral or written Court	RMO applies to court
Treatment Order —treatment in hospital pre-trial or pre-sentencing	s.52K–S	Mental Disorder Treatment likely to alleviate symptoms or prevent deterioration is available Risk to health, safety or welfare of patient; or safety of others Bed available in 7 days	Not specified. Remand timescales apply : 40 days summary : 140 days solemn proceedings	2 registered doctors (1 approved) —oral or written Court	RMO applies to court
Transfer for Treatment Direction —treatment in hospital of sentenced prisoners	s.136	Mental Disorder Treatment likely to alleviate symptoms or prevent deterioration is available Risk to health, safety or welfare of patient; or safety of others Making the order is necessary Bed available in 7 days	Length of Prison Sentence	2 registered doctors (1 approved) —written Scottish Ministers	Scottish Ministers, Tribunal, Liberation, Parole Board, Life Licence

Some establishments have beds in a prison health centre. These are not exclusively used by patients with mental disorder and their use is not an alternative to transfer to a psychiatric hospital. Some, for example HM Prison Perth, have a day programme for prisoners with mental health problems or those deemed vulnerable. Prisoners can attend support and activity groups in the health centre. HM Prison Barlinnie in Glasgow established the "Open Doors" programme to assist mentally disordered offenders[23]. This is Scotland's largest prison housing up to 1300 prisoners. The programme was set up in 1991 by the social work department in response to the growing awareness of mental health problems in prisoners. The main aim of the programme is to promote

---

[23] Bartlett, K., Thomson, L.D.G., Johnstone, E.C. (2001), *Mentally Disordered Offenders: an evaluation of the "Open Doors" Programme at HM Prison, Barlinnie*, Scottish Prison Service, Occasional Paper Series, No. 2/2001.

positive mental health within the prison. The key to success with all such projects is the sharing of information and a multidisciplinary approach.

Specific programmes exist within prisons to tackle issues such as alcohol abuse, violent behaviour and sexual offending. Drug abuse is recognised as a serious problem in this population and drug free areas, mandatory drug testing and maintenance prescribing have been introduced.

Suicide in Prison

5–26   There were 14 suicides in Scottish prisons in 2001 and this was 67 per cent higher than the rate in prisons in England and Wales. Suicide in prisons has been calculated to be eight times the national rate for young men[24].

Risk factors have been identified from studies of prison suicides but these factors are common in the prison population as a whole[25]. These include a previous history of self harm and psychiatric morbidity. The majority of suicides are known to occur less than three months after incarceration and half of the deaths are of untried prisoners. Of those who kill themselves within one week of coming into prison, two-thirds have an established history of drug and/or alcohol dependence.

Most prison suicides are unpredictable but this emphasises the need for good prison mental health services, formal assessment and risk management strategies.

Act to Care Strategy

5–27   Act to Care is the suicide risk management strategy of the Scottish Prison Service launched in June 1998. All prisoners are assessed on reception into prison for risk of self harm. Information may also be available from the police (special risk prisoner form) or criminal justice social workers at this time.

Any member of staff who has concerns about the safety of a prisoner can complete an Act form at any time. This is a formally recorded system that triggers a decision making and review process. A prisoner's risk of self harm is assessed as high, medium or low. Decisions are taken regarding the needs of the individual, his location in prison and involvement with activities. The Act system allows for a degree of flexibility, for example not all high-risk prisoners are placed in anti-ligature cells. A prisoner placed on an Act form is assessed by a nurse, doctor (if required) and hall manager. A case conference is called within 24 hours of the Act form being completed. Subsequent case conferences take place up to a maximum of every 72 hours. When the final case conference is held and the decision to remove the prisoner from the Act strategy is taken, through care arrangements will be made if required. All new officers receive training on the Act strategy and each year all

---

[24] Royal College of Psychiatrists (2002) *Suicide in prisons* CR99, Royal College of Psychiatrists, London.

[25] Bogue J. and Power K. (1995) *Suicide in Scottish prisons 1976–93*, The Journal of Forensic Psychiatry, 6(3), 537–540; Dooley, E. (1990) *Prison suicide in England and Wales, 1972–87*, British Journal of Psychiatry, 156, 40–45.

residential and operational officers have a mandatory Act Strategy awareness booster session. The strategy is co-ordinated in each prison by a suicide risk management co-ordinator.

Listeners' Scheme

Listeners' Schemes have been established in some Scottish Prisons. **5–28** These are organised by the Samaritans with the support of the Scottish Prison Service. Prisoners are trained by the Samaritans to be listeners and will see fellow prisoners on a confidential basis as requested.

Through Care

Through care, linking care within prison to care in the community, is **5–29** important, particularly for mentally disordered offenders. Prior to release, prisoners should have a risk and needs assessment carried out by social workers and appropriate arrangements put in place. Similarly, those with recognised health needs should have arrangements made via the health centre with relevant services. Ideally, the care programme approach would be used for those with major mental disorders.

PAROLE AND LIFE LICENCE

In terms of the Prisons (Scotland) Act 1989 and the Prisoners and **5–30** Criminal Proceedings (Scotland) Act 1993, both as amended, early conditional release of all long-term prisoners on parole and of life sentence prisoners on life licence is a matter to be decided by the Parole Board for Scotland. All prisoners serving four years or more are long-term prisoners, and they are eligible to be considered for parole after serving one-half of their sentence. They must be released on licence after serving two-thirds of their sentence. Life sentenced prisoners must serve the "punishment part" of their sentence before they can be considered for release on life licence. The punishment part is fixed by the trial judge at the time of sentencing.

The procedure for considering determinate sentence cases is primarily a paper-based one. A dossier of reports on the prisoner is prepared about six months before the qualifying date, unless the prisoner chooses to self reject from the process. Everyone in the prison who has had dealings with the prisoner is invited to contribute. The prisoner is invited to sign a medical disclosure form to allow the medical officer to report on any relevant medical issues, and psychiatric reports are usually only sought when there has been specific psychiatric input during the sentence. The Board is assessing the risk that the person would pose if released at the qualifying time, and methods of managing this risk. Accordingly, reports should concentrate on these factors. The prisoner is given a copy of all reports, unless the author considers and the chair of the Board agrees, that this would be harmful to the prisoner or to third party interests. In these cases the author of the report must provide the gist of that report to the prisoner.

The determinate sentenced prisoner is also invited to make written representations to the Board, and may consult his lawyer in this process. The prisoner is offered an interview with a member of the Board, again in the presence of a lawyer if wished, the function of the interview being to ensure that the prisoner has presented all that he wishes to the Board. After writing a report on this interview, which is put into the dossier, the interviewing member can take no further part in that particular case. This process is equally relevant for those prisoners transferred to a psychiatric hospital.

The Board meets in groups of five to make decisions on release. They may decide to release on the qualifying date or at a date in the future or to have another review earlier than the annual anniversary of the qualifying date, which is the automatic date if the prisoner has more than 14 months of the sentence left to serve. Board decisions are now binding on Ministers. The Board also sets down the conditions attaching to any release. Standard conditions require the prisoner to report to a named local authority social worker and to be of good behaviour and keep the peace. Additional conditions may require the released person to undertake alcohol or drug counselling, or to co-operate with mental health input. Breaches of conditions are reported to the Justice Department, which may refer the case back to the Board. On such a referral, the Board may chose to note the report, issue a warning letter, amend the conditions of the licence or recall the person to custody. If a person is recalled, he is given the opportunity to make written representations against recall and has an interview with a board member. This may result in immediate re-release. If not, the person resumes serving the sentence, but is now liable to be detained until the sentence end date (though he will be reviewed for parole on the annual anniversary of recall).

Life sentenced prisoners are subject to a different procedure. A similar dossier of reports is constructed on them, but this dossier is presented to a tribunal of three members of the board before whom the prisoner, and legal representative if wished, appear in person. Scottish Ministers also appear to represent the public interest. The tribunal, which must be chaired by someone qualified to be a judge, hears any evidence either side presents and has the power, rarely used, to call for evidence itself. It is entirely possible in all cases, and usual in cases where a life sentence prisoner has been transferred to a psychiatric hospital, for a psychiatrist to be called to give evidence to the tribunal. Proceedings are less formal than in court, with no wigs or gowns and no oath administered. However, all witnesses are open to questioning by the prisoner, any legal representative, Scottish Ministers' representatives and the tribunal members themselves. The same preparation as for appearance in court is thus required. Tribunals meet in the prison or hospital in which the person is detained.

Tribunals always give their decision in writing and within 14 days of the hearing. The only order the Tribunal can make is for the release of the prisoner. If the tribunal decides not to order release, it is invited to advise Ministers on what steps should be taken to address the risk which the person is perceived as posing. This advice is not legally binding. The sole factor which the tribunal takes into account is the level of risk and the possibility of this being managed in the community.

On release, life sentence prisoners remain on licence for life. The Tribunal lays down the terms of the licence and any breaches are reported to the Justice Department, which may forward these reports to the Board. The Board, or, in an emergency, Scottish Ministers, can order recall of the prisoner, but the case must then be referred to a new Tribunal which decides whether to confirm the recall or order immediate re-release.

Under Sch.2 of the Prisoners and Criminal Proceedings (Scotland) Act 1993, membership of the Board must include a Lord Commissioner of Justiciary (a High Court Judge), a registered medical practitioner who is a psychiatrist, a social worker and a criminologist. The practice has usually been to have two psychiatrists. Appointments are made by Scottish Ministers, after public advertisement and interview. Members serve for a maximum period of six years.

RISK

Throughout the 1990s the concept of risk, that is the likelihood of an **5–31** adverse event or outcome, became part of clinical practice. It superseded dangerousness in the psychiatric lexicon because it allowed practitioners to develop a systematic and dynamic approach to problems and possible adverse outcomes. Significant risks for people with mental disorders include those of relapse, non-compliance, substance misuse, self harm or violence. It is the last that is of primary concern here. A Risk Management Authority (see Chapter 2) has been established in Scotland, *inter alia* to promote further research into risk assessment and management. It will develop criteria for accrediting both assessment techniques and assessors for the new court disposal of an Order for Lifelong Restriction of Liberty[26]. The Authority, which has among its six initial members a psychiatrist, two clinical psychologists and a retired social worker, may well promote significant developments in risk assessments and a clearer understanding of responses to risk within the Scottish criminal justice system and, perhaps, more generally in Scotland.

RISK ASSESSMENT

Clinical Risk Assessment

The assessment of risk of harm to others is essential to ensure public **5–32** safety. Traditionally risk assessments have been carried out by criminal justice, social work and health service professionals in an unstructured manner, perhaps guided by the research literature. Essential factors to be assessed include a patient's history of previous acts of aggression or self harm, cultural background of violence, social instability, substance misuse, poor compliance with treatment and follow-up, and precipitants of changes in mental state or pattern of behaviour before previous episodes of illness or violence. Specific factors to be assessed on mental state examination include the presence of strong emotions like hostility, anger, suspiciousness and irritability; the uttering of specific threats; command hallucinations; and evidence of threat/control override symptoms (persecutory delusions and delusions of being controlled by an

---

[26] Criminal Procedure (Scotland) Act 1995, s.210F.

outside force). The severity, specificity, volatility and temporal relationship with violence of each identified risk factor must be considered[27].
Clinical risk assessments have been criticised due to lack of reliability,
validity and transparency[28] and consequently a number of risk assessment
tools have been developed. See Table 4 for examples.

Actuarial Risk Assessment

5–33   It has been argued that actuarial methods are more accurate than
professional judgement for risk assessment[29]. These are statistical
approaches based on multivariate analysis of a number of factors and
samples of individuals (forensic patients or prisoners) to determine
which variables predict further violence or offending. Variables found to
be predictive of recidivism are given weightings and combined to give a
score. From this score, a probability can be calculated of an individual
committing a further act of violence. However, actuarial approaches to
risk assessment have been criticised as the factors identified are invaria-
bly historical, may be inaccurate, contain subjective components, under
use clinical data and judgement, and are static[30]. Further, there is
evidence that dynamic factors such as current mental state are relevant
to aggressive acts[31].

Structured Clinical Risk Assessment

5–34   A new approach to risk assessment was developed for mentally
disordered offenders, because of the problems with actuarial methods,
that combines actuarial risk assessment with assessment of clinical and
risk factors in a structured way. This can lead to a score from which a
determination of the level of an individual's risk can be made and this is
useful in research. In clinical practice, however, it is the identification of
the risk factor itself that is important in order to develop management
strategies. The proponents of actuarial methods dismiss this structured
clinical risk assessment approach stating that the addition of clinical
factors decreases the accuracy of the historical factors which are the
major and overriding determinants of recidivism.
      Within the criminal justice system a number of risk assessment tools
are used and the debate on actuarial, professional or structured assessment of risk is equally relevant. Some instruments combine risk and
needs assessments, based on the premise that to reduce needs will
decrease risk.

---

[27] Royal College of Psychiatrists (1996) *Assessment and clinical management of risk of
harm to other people*, CR52, Royal College of Psychiatrists, London.
[28] Monahan, J. (1984) *The prediction of violent behaviour: toward a second generation of
theory and policy*, American Journal of Psychiatry, 141: 10–15.
[29] Harris, G.T. and Rice, M.E. (1997) *Risk appraisal and management of violent
behaviour*, Psychiatric Services, 48(9): 1168–76.
[30] Grubin, D. (1997) *Predictors of risk and serious sex offenders*, British Journal of
Psychiatry, 170, supplement 32:17–21.
[31] Thomson, L.D.G., Bogue, J.P., Humphreys, M.S. and Johnstone, E.C. (1997) *The
State Hospital Survey: a description of psychiatric patients in conditions of special security in
Scotland*, Journal of Forensic Psychiatry, 8(2), 263–284.

Violence Risk Appraisal Guide (VRAG)

The clinical application of the actuarial approach to risk assessment is **5–35** exemplified by the Violence Risk Appraisal Guide (VRAG)[32]. The factors assessed in the VRAG with their different weightings are set out in Box 4. The range of total scores is divided into nine equal categories known as bins, with the percentage probability of violent recidivism at seven- and nine-year follow-up given for each. Somewhat counter-intuitively, it can be seen that having schizophrenia, injuring a victim or having a female victim are said to be negatively associated with a risk of future violence. This can be partly explained by examining the origins of the instrument. It was developed by multivariate analysis of factors collected from a sample of male forensic patients in a high security psychiatric facility in Canada. The sample had two major diagnostic categories: psychopathy and schizophrenia. Schizophrenia was a "protective factor" against risk of violence in comparison to psychopathy. The VRAG has been validated in a number of samples in North America and in prisoners in Scotland.

Box 4: Violence Risk Appraisal Guide

History of alcohol problems (.13)
Diagnosis of Schizophrenia (-.17)
Diagnosis of Personality Disorder (.26)
Psychopathy (PCL-R) (.34)
Elementary school maladjustment (.31)
Separation from biological parents before 16 years of age (.25)
Age at index event (young .26)
Non-violent offence history (.20)
Victim injury at index offence (-.16)
Female victim at index event (-.11)
Failure on prior conditional release (.24)
Marital status (single .18)

Table 4: Risk Assessment Instruments

Instrument	Assessment	Type	Target population
Violence Risk Appraisal Guide (VRAG)	Risk of violence	Actuarial	Mentally disordered male offenders

---

[32] Quinsey V.L., Harris G.T., Rice M.E. and Cormier C.A., (1998) *Violent offenders, appraising and managing risk*, American Psychological Association, Washington, DC.

Instrument	Assessment	Type	Target population
Historical Clinical Risk-20 (HCR-20)	Risk of violence	Structured Clinical	Any population with high proportion of people with violent histories, and a suggestion of mental illness or personality disorder
Iterative Classification Trees (ICTs)	Risk of violence	Actuarially determined algorithms	Civil psychiatric patients in community settings
Violence Risk Scale (VRS)	Risk of violence	Structured professional	Violent offenders
Spousal Assault Risk Assessment Guide (SARA)	Risk of spousal assault	Structured Clinical	Any individual (male or female) who is accused of assaulting their intimate current or former partner
Offender Group Reconviction Scale (OGRS)	Risk of reconviction during 2 years after release from prison or community sentence	Actuarial	Offenders being released from prison, or serving a community sentence
Risk Assessment Guidance Framework (RAGF)	Criminogenic needs, risk of reconviction and risk of harm to others	Structured Clinical	Offenders receiving a criminal justice social work assessment
Level of Service Inventory-Revised (LSI-R)	Risk of recidivism and needs	Structured Clinical/ Needs Assessment	Offenders in prison or on probation
Risk of Reconviction (ROR)	Risk of reconviction during 2 years after release from prison	Actuarial	Male offenders released from prison, (approximation given for females)—parole decisions
Offender Assessment System (OASys)	Risk of violence	Structured professional	Offenders in prison or probation system
Sexual Offender Risk Appraisal Guide (SORAG)	Risk of violence	Actuarial	Mentally disordered male, sexual offenders
Sexual Violence Risk-20 (SVR-20)	Risk of sexual violence	Structured Clinical	Individuals who have committed, or are alleged to have committed, a sexual offence

Instrument	Assessment	Type	Target population
Risk of Sexual Violence Protocol (RSVP)	Risk of sexual violence	Structured Clinical	Individuals who have committed, or are alleged to have committed, a sexual offence
Sex Offender Needs Assessment Rating (SONAR)	Change in risk of sexual violence	Actuarial	Sexual offenders
Rapid Risk Assessment for Sexual Offence Recidivism (RRASOR)	Risk of sexual violence	Actuarial	Adult (18+) male sexual offenders (at least one sex offence conviction)
Structured Anchored Clinical Judgement (SACJ)	Risk of sexual violence	Actuarial	Sexual offenders (3rd part can only be completed for those offenders who have entered treatment programmes)
Static-99	Risk of sexual violence	Actuarial	Adult (18+) male sexual offenders (at least one sex offence conviction)
Risk Matrix 2000	Risk of sexual and non-sexual violence	Actuarial	Adult (18+) male sexual offenders (at least one sex offence conviction)

Historical Clinical Risk-20 (HCR-20)

The predominant structured clinical risk assessment tool is the HCR-20[33]. It was developed from an extensive literature review of factors related to violence and from expert opinion. Related factors were combined and the HCR-20 is made up of 20 items: 10 historical, 5 clinical and 5 risk management. See Box 5.

Box 5: HCR-20

Historical (Past)	**Clinical (Present)**	**Risk Management (Future)**
H1. Previous violence	C1. Lack of insight	R1. Plans lack feasibility
H2. Young age at first violent incident	C2. Negative attitudes	R2. Exposure to destabilisers

---

[33] Webster, C.D., Douglas K.S., Eaves, D. and Hart S., (1997) *HCR-20, Historical/Clinical/risk-20, A structure clinical assessment guide*, Mental Health, Law and Policy Institute, Simon Fraser University, Vancouver.

Historical (Past)	Clinical (Present)	Risk Management (Future)
H3. Relationship instability	C3. Active symptoms of major illness	R3. Lack of personal support
H4. Employment problems	C4. Impulsivity	R4. Noncompliance with remediation attempts
H5. Substance use problems	C5. Unresponsive to treatment	R5. Stress
H6. Major mental illness		
H7. Psychopathy		
H8. Early maladjustment		
H9. Personality disorder		
H10. Prior supervision failure		

Each of the 20 items is coded on a 3-point scale, according to the certainty that the risk factors are present. The final or summary risk rating is determined by professional judgment and expressed as low, moderate or high. For research purposes the HCR-20 can be treated as an actuarial scale, simply summing the number of risk factors present, ranging from 0 to 20.

Iterative Classification Tree (ICT)

5–37　　　The Iterative Classification Tree[34] is an actuarial risk assessment tool that allows many different combinations of risk factors to be considered to classify a person as at high, average or low risk of committing future violence. The ICT was developed from the MacArthur Violence Risk Assessment Study which involved a sample of 939 civil psychiatric patients between the ages of 18 to 40 years who were released from hospital. 134 risk factors were studied. A statistical procedure was used to determine which combination of these risk factors was most reliably associated with violence in the community during the first 20 weeks after discharge. Two cut-off scores were applied: cases with a predicted probability of violence greater than twice the base prevalence rate (> 37 per cent) were categorised as "high risk", and cases with a predicted probability of violence less than half the base prevalence rate (< 9 per cent) were categorised as "low risk". As a result, 49.2 per cent remained unclassified as either high or low risk. These unclassified cases were then pooled and reanalysed until no further groups could be classified as either high or low risk. The resulting classification tree was named the Iterative Classification Tree (ICT), with the remaining unclassified cases being defined as average risk cases. This procedure was carried out twice, once with the full set of 134 risk factors to produce the "empirically optimal" ICT, and once with a reduced list of 106 risk factors deemed to be commonly available or easily scored in clinical practice, in order to produce the 'clinically feasible' ICT.

The clinically feasible ICT contains 12 contingent risk factors about which information is easily obtainable in the context of a brief hospitalization. See Box 6.

---

[34] Monahan, J., Steadman, H.J., Silver, E. et al. (2001) *Rethinking risk assessment: The MacArthur study of mental disorder and violence*, Oxford University Press, New York.

Box 6: Iterative Classification Tree

Seriousness of Arrest (none, property/minor/drugs, robbery/rape/assault/murder)
Motor Impulsiveness (low/high)
Father used drugs: Self-report (weekly/daily, less often)
Recent Violent Fantasies (yes, no)
Major Disorder without substance abuse (yes, no)
Legal status (voluntary, involuntary)
Schizophrenia (yes, no)
Anger reaction (low, high)
Employed in two months prior to admission to hospital (yes, no)
Recent Violence in two months before hospital admission: Self-report (yes, no)
Loss of Consciousness due to head injury: Self-report using the Silver-Caton Head injury Questionnaire (yes, no)
Parents fought: Self-report when the patient was growing up. (yes, no)

Based on a sequence established by the classification tree, a first question is asked of all persons being assessed. Depending on the answer to that question, one or another second question is posed, and so on, until each subject is designated to a risk category. A table is provided which gives the percentage of people expected to be violent in each risk group. Software has been developed for this process.

Violence Risk Scale (VRS)

The Violence Risk Scale[35] is designed to assess risk of violent **5–38** recidivism for incarcerated offenders. It was developed in Canada with detainees being released into the community on various types of conditional discharge, or at the end of a sentence or hospital order. It contains 6 static and 20 dynamic factors identified from the risk assessment literature, and includes a measure of change in response to treatment. See Box 7.

Box 7: Violence Risk Scale

Static Factors	Dynamic Factors
Current age	Violent lifestyle
Age at first conviction	Criminal personality
Number of young offender convictions	Criminal attitudes
Violence throughout lifespan	Work ethic
Prior release failures or escapes	Criminal peers
Stability of family upbringing	Interpersonal aggression
	Emotional control
	Violence during institutionalisation
	Weapon use

[35] Wong, S. and Gordon A. (2000) *Violence Risk Scale*, Saskatoon: Regional Psychiatric Centre.

> Insight into violence
> Mental disorder
> Substance abuse
> Stability of relationships with significant others
> Community support
> Released into high risk situations
> Violence cycle
> Impulsivity
> Cognitive distortion
> Compliance with community supervision
> Security level of anticipated release institution

The VRS is completed at interview and by using third party information. The static factors indicate the extent of the identified problems whereas the dynamic factors are rated on their presence but also on an individual's preparedness and motivation to change. Each factor is scored from zero to three. The total number of static and dynamic factors indicate an individual's current risk level.

The Spousal Assault Risk Assessment Guide (SARA)

5–39   The Spousal Assault Risk Assessment Guide (SARA)[36] is a 20-item structured clinical risk assessment tool for the evaluation of risk of spousal assault, defined as "actual, attempted or threatened physical harm perpetrated by a man or a woman against someone whom s/he has had an intimate, sexual relationship". It also considers risk of harm to other family members such as children.

The SARA was developed through a comprehensive review of empirical and clinical literature regarding risk for violence in general, and spousal abuse more specifically. Factors that were shown to be associated with violent recidivism in known spousal abusers, and to discriminate between those who do and do not abuse their spouses were identified. The SARA contains 20 items, both static and dynamic. See Box 8.

Box 8: Spousal Assault Risk Assessment Guide

Criminal history	**Index Offence**
Past assault of family members	Severe and/or sexual assault
Past assault of strangers or acquaintances	Use of weapons and/or credible threats of harm
Past violation of conditional release or community supervision	Violation of 'no-contact' order
Psychosocial adjustment	
Recent relationship problems	
Recent employment problems	
Victim of and/or witness to family violence as a child or adolescent	
Recent substance abuse/dependence	
Recent suicidal/homicidal ideation/intent	

---

[36] Kropp, P.R., Hart, S.D. (2000) *The spousal assault risk assessment (SARA) guide: reliability and validity in adult male offenders*, Law and Human Behaviour 24(1), 101–118.

Recent psychotic and/or manic symptoms
Personality disorder with anger, impulsivity or behavioural instability
Spousal Assault History
Past physical assault
Past sexual assault/sexual jealousy
Past use of weapons and/or credible threats of death
Recent escalation in frequency or severity of assault
Past violation of 'no contact' orders
Extreme minimization or denial of spousal assault
Attitudes that support or condone spousal assault

There are specific criteria for defining and coding the presence of individual items and these are scored on a three-point scale: absent, subthreshold or present. If there is insufficient information to code a particular item it may be omitted. "Critical items" (that is those that are considered to be particularly relevant in a specific case and which lead the evaluator to decide that the individual is at high risk for spousal violence) are coded as either absent or present. On the basis of the presence (or absence) of individual and critical items, final risk ratings are made using clinical judgment, and coded on a three-point scale: low, moderate, and high. In addition, raters should assess whether there is an imminent risk of harm to "others" such as an individual's children or a new partner of an ex-spouse, and potential victims must be identified.

The SARA suggests specific management strategies for identified items. For example, recent relationship problems would indicate a need for group or individual interpersonal treatment, or crisis counselling; and recent suicidal or homicidal ideation/intent and psychotic symptoms suggest a need for inpatient care.

The Offender Group Reconviction Scale (OGRS)

The Offender Group Reconviction Scale (OGRS)[37] is an actuarial **5–40** scale that predicts, from a limited number of criminal history and demographic factors, the probability that an offender will be reconvicted within two years of release from prison or from the start of a community penalty for any standard list offence. The original OGRS was developed by the Home Office using logistic regression on a sample of 14,000 offenders discharged from prison or sentenced to a community penalty in 1990. It was developed to examine the effectiveness of probation services. The OGRS is used by probation officers and social workers, particularly in writing pre-sentence reports, to help aid decisions about appropriate sentences for individuals. A revised version of OGRS[38] was developed using data from over 30,000 offenders discharged from prison or sentenced to community penalty in 1995. It utilises offender's age at time of sentence, gender, current offence group, age at current conviction, age at first conviction, the Copas rate variable (the rate at which offenders are convicted), history of burglary, and history of breach of

[37] Copas, J.B., Marshall P. (1998) *The offender group reconviction scale: a statistical reconviction score for use by probation officers*, Applied Statistics 47(1), 159–171.
[38] Taylor R. (1999) *Predicting reconvictions for sexual and violent offences using the revised offender group reconviction scale*, London: Home Office.

sanctions. It can also be used to predict recidivism in violent or sexual offenders for those with a previous conviction of this type. The assessment is computerised and risk of re-offending is described in percentage terms. The OGRS score does not reflect an estimate of risk for a particular individual, but the average rate of reconviction expected for a group of offenders who match the individual on the set of covariates in the scale. Therefore, the main use of the OGRS is as a benchmark against which to measure subjective assessments of risk of reconviction.

The Risk Assessment Guidance Framework (RAGF)

5–41   The risk assessment guidance framework[39] is a set of structured clinical guidelines for assessing risk of general reconviction, criminogenic needs (social and personal needs that relate to offending), and risk of harm to others. It was designed to be used by criminal justice social workers in their every day work with offenders, but can be used by anyone who is involved in risk management such as police officers or those working with young offenders.

This tool combines actuarial measures (OGRS factors) and professional judgement. It consists of five risk assessment forms including a summary sheet.

RA1 provides a framework for assessing risk of re-offending, and consists of actuarial factors, specifically those from the OGRS (age at first conviction, number of custodial sentences under age 21, number of criminal convictions, offence seriousness). On the basis of the RA1 factors, the evaluator decides whether the individual is at high, medium or low risk for re-offending.

RA2 provides a framework for assessing criminogenic needs, and comprises a checklist of dynamic factors that can be influenced to minimize risk of re-offending:

- Financial problems
- Employment difficulties
- Limited education/work/social skills
- Poor relationships and/or social isolation
- Negative peer influence
- Alcohol and/or drug misuse
- Mental health problems
- Antisocial attitudes to the law and law enforcement

The rater is asked to indicate which needs are priorities; how these might be addressed; whether there are resources available to address these; whether the offender is motivated to address them; and whether the offender has previously complied with court orders.

This form can be used on its own as a needs assessment tool, but must be used in conjunction with RA1 to assess risk of reoffending. The assessment of need can modify the RA1.

RA3 is a brief framework for assessing risk of harm to others, and consists of eight questions:

---

[39] Social Work Services Inspectorate (2000) *Management and assessment of risk in social work services.*

- Has the offender already caused significant harm (serious physical injury or lasting psychological harm)?
- Is the number of offences, the frequency or the harm escalating?
- Does the offender commit different types of offences?
- Is there a risk to children or other vulnerable groups?
- Are there aspects of the offender's life that might increase risk *e.g.* alcohol abuse or mental health problems?
- Does he comply with court orders?
- Is the offender at risk of being harmed and what impact might this have on his behaviour?
- Is the offender motivated to reoffend/avoid reoffending?

RA3 is completed by giving yes/no answers to the questions, and the rater decides whether the individual is at high, medium or low risk of seriously harming others.

RA4 is a more comprehensive form for assessing risk of serious harm to others and should be used for those individuals assessed as high risk in RA3, and/or those who have committed one or more of a number of offences listed in the manual (*e.g.* murder, sexual offences, serious violent offences, other offences that give cause for concern). In RA4 professional opinion is used to give appropriate weight to each of the factors considered to be relevant. It does not contain specific questions or points like the other forms, but has several open sections designed to prompt consideration of relevant factors:

- Description and detail of current offence(s) (*e.g.* what, where, when, who, bizarre aspects, triggers)
- Analysis of current and previous offences (*e.g.* sadistic elements, random or targeted victim, unnecessary violence, aggravating factors)
- Analysis of offending patterns (*e.g.* similar to previous offences, serial or single offender, escalation of seriousness)
- Offender's current attitude to offending (*e.g.* denial, blaming, indifference)
- Attitudes to others (*e.g.* empathy, hatred, family relationships, jealousy)
- Mental health issues (*e.g.* diagnosed, stress, delusions, fantasies)
- Substance misuse (*e.g.* presence or absence, significant in offence?)

In making the overall judgment of risk of harm to others, the manual suggests that evaluators consider general risk of reoffending (assessed in RA1), risk of specific serious offences being repeated based on analysis of offending patterns, and likely frequency of serious offences being committed. The evaluator is asked to state the specific behaviour of concern, the circumstances in which it might occur, likely victims and likely consequences. In addition, RA4 also asks the evaluator to indicate what action should be undertaken to reduce risk, who needs to be informed of the risk, who should take the main responsibility in risk management, and what happens next.

The summary sheet allows the offender's level of risk to be quickly assessed by all those who need to know. It provides a simple matrix indicating the overall level of risk that the offender poses to the public in terms of high, medium and low risk. A risk management plan should be developed for those deemed to be high risk.

The Level of Service Inventory Revised (LSI-R)

5–42   The Level of Service Inventory (LSI-R)[40] is a structured clinical risk/ needs assessment instrument designed to aid decisions about risk of general recidivism, and contains both static and dynamic risk factors. It is a tool for systematically gathering information on risk and needs that should be considered when making decisions about offender treatment planning, and assigning levels of freedom and supervision. It is used by prison and probation officers to assess adult male and female offenders serving institutional or community sentences. However, the LSI-R has also been validated in samples of probationers, male and female young offenders, and mentally disordered offenders. The LSI-R was developed in Canada from three main sources: literature on recidivism, professional opinion of probation officers, and a broad social learning perspective on criminality.

The LSI-R comprises 54 items grouped into 10 subcomponents which reflect the major risk factors for recidivism identified by theory and research. The subcomponents are listed in Box 9 with the number of items in each subcomponent.

Box 9: LSI-R

Criminal history (10)	Education/Employment (10)
Financial (2)	Family/Marital (4)
Accommodation (3)	Leisure/Recreation (2)
Companions (5)	Alcohol/Drug Problems (9)
Emotional/Personal (5)	Attitudes/Orientation (4)

Each of the 54 items is answered with either a "Yes or No", or a "0-3" rating. For numerically rated items, 0 = a very unsatisfactory situation with a very clear and strong need for improvement; 1 = a relatively unsatisfactory situation with a need for improvement; 2 = a relatively satisfactory situation with some room for improvement evident; 3 = a satisfactory situation with no need for improvement evident. The manual provides guidelines on how to score each item, and gives examples of individuals who would score high and low on the numerically rated items.

The total LSI-R score is determined by summing the number of items scored either yes, 0, or no, 1. This score is then plotted on either a male or female profile sheet and automatically converted to percentiles based on normative groups (male and female inmates of Canadian penal institutions) indicating risk of recidivism. The profile form also provides cut-off scores that indicate the level of risk for various situations such as

---

[40] Andrews, D.A. and Bonta, J. (1995) *The level of service inventory—revised manual*, Multi-Health Systems Inc, Toronto.

making decisions about institutional classification, probation, parole, and halfway house placement.

Problem areas are identified using the subcomponent scores and the profile of these is examined. The rater is encouraged to note particularly salient aspects of an individual case not covered by the 54 LSI-R items, which may undermine the objective recommendation of the instrument. Thus professional judgement can be used to over-ride the LSI-R score. If more than five items cannot be scored due to lack of information, the LSI-R should not be used as its validity may be compromised.

The LSI-R contains dynamic risk factors, and therefore can be used to identify treatment targets, and changes in total LSI-R scores can be used to indicate effective risk management or impending difficulties.

The Risk of Reconviction Scale (ROR)

The Parole Board in Scotland does not employ an actuarial risk **5–43** assessment tool but such instruments have been developed. The ROR[41] is an actuarial scale that gives the percentage probability of reconviction for any offence, and for any serious offence (one likely to lead to re-imprisonment), in a given number of months after release, up to a maximum of two years. The ROR was developed through statistical analysis of the background characteristics of over 1200 prisoners who were released in 1987. Box 10 contains the six identified factors that predicted reconviction.

Box 10: ROR

Age at conviction
Number of youth custody sentences
Number of adult custodial sentences
Number of previous convictions
Offence type
Gender

Each of the six variables is weighted with offence type being divided into six categories with their own weightings. The numerical value for each variable (*e.g.* 21 for age at first conviction if the offender was 21 when convicted), excluding offence type and sex, is multiplied by the relevant weight, with the resulting totals then being summed, and added to 100 to give the ROR score. Tables are provided which give the percentage probability of reconviction for any offence and for any serious offence at monthly intervals ranging from 1 to 24 months after release.

The ROR does not produce an individual prediction, but represents the proportion of the sample that was reconvicted who matched the individual being assessed on the six variables. Other factors known to the Parole Board but not included in the ROR will be relevant. Only males

---

[41] Copas, J.B., Marshall, P., Tarling, R. (1996) *Predicting reoffending for discretionary conditional release*, Home Office, London.

were included in the development sample, but an approximate prediction score is given for women, based on the relationship between female
and male offending amongst those released from prison in 1987.
However, this score is less accurate. In addition, the individuals in the
sample on which the ROR was based were released under old parole
arrangements or at the completion of their sentence, and newer arrangements may make the ROR inaccurate.

Offender Assessment System (OASys)

5–44   The Offender Assessment System (OASys)[42] is a joint prison and
probation computerised system developed by the Home Office based on
factors identified in the research literature related to risk of reconviction.
OASys assesses how likely offenders are to re-offend and to cause
serious harm to themselves or others. It identifies whether an offender
has particular needs, for example addictions, literacy problems or
housing, that contributed to the offending. It assists probation and
prison staff to identify ways in which they can work with and supervise
the offender more effectively. It is used for offenders aged 18 and over,
with the Youth Justice Board's ASSET system being used for those
under the age of 18.

OASys is intended to be used by prison and probation service
personnel, to assess:

- offenders subject to court ordered pre-sentence reports
- offenders on community orders
- offenders on licence from prison
- hostel residents who are subject to an order, licence, or on bail
- young offenders serving one month or more in custody, and
  adults serving 12 months or more in custody

Assessment using OASys is ongoing throughout the sentence. OASys
is intended to guide an assessor's judgement by providing a comprehensive and evidence-based framework.

OASys is made up of five principal forms. The offending related
factors form is available in two versions: OASys One and the longer,
more frequently used, OASys Two. Other forms are entitled Risk of
Harm, Summary, Supervision and Sentence Planning and Self Assessment Questionnaire.

OASys One or Two forms consist of 14 main sections shown in Box
11. The first, unnumbered section—the Case ID—contains demographic,
administrative and sentencing information. The first 12 numbered sections examine factors related to likelihood of reconviction. Links to risk
of serious harm, risks to the individual, other risks, and offending
behaviour are highlighted at the end of each section. Section 13 is
concerned with practical issues affecting suitability for interventions.

---

[42] Home Office (2002) Offender Assessment System (OASys), *www.crimereduction.
gov.uk*.

Box 11: Offender Assessment System

> Offending Information
> Analysis of Offences
> Accommodation
> Education, Training and Employability
> Financial Management and Income
> Relationships
> Lifestyle and Associates
> Drug Misuse
> Alcohol Misuse
> Emotional Wellbeing
> Thinking and Behaviour
> Attitudes
> Health and Other Considerations

The Risk of Harm form consists of a screening for all offenders, followed by a full analysis, risk summary and risk management plan for those who require it. Risk of harm to the public, known adults, staff, children, prisoners, the individual (suicide, self-harm, coping in custody or hostel setting, vulnerability), and other risks (escape/abscond, control issues, breach of trust) are addressed.

Levels of risk of harm are expressed as follows:

- Low: no significant, current indicators of risk of harm.
- Medium: identifiable indicators of risk of serious harm. Potential to cause harm but unlikely to do so unless there is a change in circumstances.
- High: Identifiable indicators of risk of serious harm. Potential event could happen at any time and impact would be serious.
- Very high: imminent risk of serious harm. Potential event is more likely than not to happen imminently. The impact would be serious.

Vital information from the Risk of Harm and OASys One/Two forms are combined on the Summary form.

The Supervision and Sentence Planning form details the activities which will be undertaken in order to reduce the offender's risk of harm and likelihood of reconviction. As the sentence continues, review plans record new objectives and progress against existing objectives.

OASys also includes an optional Self Assessment Questionnaire in which the offender can record his own views. This gives insight into the issues the offender considers important, and also provides evidence of the offender's thinking style.

Sex Offender Risk Appraisal Guide (SORAG)

The SORAG[43] is an actuarial scale that assesses risk of violent **5–45** recidivism. It is intended for use with mentally disordered male sexual offenders. The SORAG was developed from retrospective studies that

---

[43] Quinsey, V.L., Harris, G.T., Rice, M.E., and Cormier, C.A. (1998) *Violent offenders, appraising and managing risk*, American Psychological Association, Washington, DC.

examined characteristics discriminating sexual offenders from non-offenders and offenders who committed nonsexual crimes at Oakridge maximum security hospital in Ontario. The SORAG is scored in the same way as the VRAG, with each item score being summed to give a total score. The SORAG contains 14 static variables listed in Box 12.

Box 12: Sex Offender Risk Appraisal Guide

Lived with biological parents to age 16
Elementary school maladjustment
History of alcohol problems
Marital status
Criminal history score for nonviolent offences (from the Cormier-Lang system)
Criminal history score for violent offences (from the Cormier-Lang system)
Number of previous convictions for sexual offences
History of sex offences only against girls under 14
Failure on prior conditional release
Age at index offence
Meets DSM-III criteria for any personality disorder
Meets DSM-III criteria for schizophrenia
Phallometric test results
Psychopathy checklist score

Sexual Violence Risk-20 (SVR-20)

5–46   The SVR-20[44] is a structured clinical risk assessment scheme for evaluating risk of sexual violence, defined as "actual, attempted or threatened sexual contact with a person who is non-consenting or unable to give consent". It was developed primarily for use in criminal and civil forensic contexts, and should be used in cases where the individual being assessed has committed, or is alleged to have committed, an act of sexual violence. The SVR-20 was developed through consultation with academics and mental health professionals, and a comprehensive review of the literature concerning risk factors for sexual offence recidivism. Redundant factors were then eliminated, and related factors combined, producing the 20 items that comprise the SVR-20.

The 20 risk factors in the SVR-20 are divided into three sections, as listed in Box 13. In addition, there is a section marked "other considerations" which allows the rater to consider factors that may be highly important in an individual case, but not common enough to be considered in every case. However, the authors are very clear that the inclusion of factors not empirically supported by the literature in risk judgments is not advised, and should be backed up with compelling evidence.

---

[44] Boer, D.P., Hart, S.D., Kropp, P.R., Webster, C.D. (1997) *Sexual Violence Risk-20 (SVR-20)*, Professional Guidelines for Assessing Violence, The Mental Health, Law and Policy Institute, Simon Fraser University, Vancouver.

Box 13: SVR-20

Psychosocial adjustment	Sexual Offences
Sexual Deviation	High density Sex Offences
Victim of child abuse	Multiple sex offence types
Psychopathy	Physical harm to victim(s) in sex offences
Major mental illness	Uses weapons or threats of death in sex offences
Substance abuse problems	Escalation in frequency or severity of sex offences
Suicidal/homicidal ideation	Extreme minimization or denial of sex offences
Relationship problems	Attitudes that support or condone sex offences
Employment problems	**Future Plans**
Past nonsexual violent offences	Lacks realistic plans
Past non-violent offences	Negative attitude toward intervention
Past supervision failure	

Each of the 20 items is coded on a three-point scale, according to the certainty that the risk factors are present or have been present in the past. For those items coded as definitely present, a second three-point scale is used to indicate whether there has been any recent change in the status of that factor, typically in the last year. The final or summary risk rating is determined by professional judgment and expressed in terms of low, moderate and high. For research purposes the SVR-20 can be treated as an actuarial scale, simply summing the number of risk factors present, ranging from 0 to 20, ignoring any case-specific risk factors that were coded under "other considerations".

Risk for Sexual Violence Protocol (RSVP)

The Risk for Sexual Violence Protocol[45] is a structured clinical **5–47** instrument based on previous works, including the SVR-20. It contains 22 static and dynamic variables divided into 5 sections: social, psychological, and sexual adjustment, as well as management and "other" considerations under which the rater can add items thought to be particularly relevant in an individual case. See Box 14.

Box 14: Risk of Sexual Violence Protocol

Problems with intimate relationships	Sexual deviance
Problems with non-intimate relationships	Chronicity of sexual offending
Problems with employment	Diversity of sexual offending
Problems resulting from child abuse	Escalation of sexual offending
Nonsexual criminality	Physical coercion
Major mental illness	Psychological coercion
Psychopathic personality disorder	Extreme minimisation or denial
Problems with substance use	Attitudes that support or condone sexual offending

[45] Hart, S.D., Kropp, P.R., Laws, D.R., Klaver, J. & Watt, K.A. (2003) *The Risk for Sexual Violence Protocol (RSVP)*, Burnaby, BC: Simon Fraser University, Mental Health, Law and Policy Institute.

Violent/Suicidal ideation	Problems with planning
Problems with self-awareness	Problems with treatment
Problems with stress or coping	Problems with supervision

Each risk factor is coded as present in the past, currently present, or as a management concern (*i.e.* present and relevant) in the future. Ratings are made on a three-point scale: 'N' = no, '?' = possibly or partially, and 'Y' = yes. Summary risk rating is decided by professional clinical judgment based on the factors in the scale, and indicates risk of sexual violence as well as risk of general violence, expressed in 'Low', 'Moderate' and 'High' terms.

The Sex Offender Needs Assessment Rating (SONAR)

5–48   The SONAR[46] is an actuarial risk assessment tool designed to evaluate change in risk of sexual violence. It is intended for use with sexual offenders. It was developed from identified risk factors for sexual recidivism in a group of non-incestuous, hands-on sexual offenders on community supervision in Canada, half of whom were already known to have re-offended.

The SONAR contains nine dynamic factors: five relatively stable items expected to persist for months or years and assumed to be related to long-term recidivism potential, and four acute factors which may last for only days or hours, intended to be useful in identifying when individuals are most likely to reoffend. See Box 15.

Box 15: Sex Offender Needs Assessment Rating

Stable items	**Acute items**
Intimacy deficits	Substance abuse
Negative social influences	Negative mood
Attitudes tolerant of sexual offending	Anger
Sexual self-regulation	Victim access
General self-regulation	

Stable factors are assessed over the year preceding the risk assessment, and are scored on a 3-point scale from 0 to 2, depending on specific criteria given for each item. The acute factors are scored from -1 to 1, depending on whether they have deteriorated, stayed the same, or improved over the last month. The sum of the four acute item scores is then subtracted from the sum of the stable item scores to give the total score. A table is provided which translates total scores into five risk categories from low to high, giving the proportion of individuals with these scores expected to reoffend given a base rate of 50 per cent. The authors urge caution in the interpretation of their validity results, as an artificial base rate of recidivism of 50 per cent was used in the development sample, which may have inflated the results.

---

[46] Hanson, R.K. and Harris, A.J.R. (2001) *A structured approach to evaluating change among sexual offenders*, Sexual Abuse: a journal of research and treatment 13(2):105–122.

The Rapid Risk Assessment for Sexual Offence Recidivism (RRASOR)

The Rapid Risk Assessment for Sex Offence Recidivism (RRASOR)[47]   **5–49**
is a brief actuarial scale, intended to provide a quick and easily scored
screening instrument for predicting sexual offence recidivism. See Box
16. It is intended to be applicable in a wide variety of settings, for use
with adult (*i.e.* over 18) males who have already been convicted of at
least one sexual offence. It was developed in Canada by meta-analysis of
seven follow-up studies of sex offenders in both correctional and forensic
psychiatric settings.

Box 16: Rapid Risk Assessment for Sexual Offence Recidivism

Prior sex offences
Age at release
Victim Gender
Relationship to victim

Scoring instructions are given for each item, and item scores are
simply summed, to give a total score of 0 to 6. A table provides the
percentage recidivism at 5 and 10 years for each total score (except 6 as
no offenders in the samples achieved this score). The RRASOR is quick
and easy to score and should be used as a screening measure to put
offenders into relative risk levels, which can then be adjusted according
to other relevant information, such as deviant sexual preferences and
treatment compliance.

The Structured Anchored Clinical Judgment (SACJ)

The Structured Anchored Clinical Judgement (SACJ)[48] Scale is a   **5–50**
three-stage actuarial scale developed within the national prison Sex
Offender Treatment Plan (SOTP), and is intended to be a relatively brief
screening instrument for predicting sexual offence recidivism. The SACJ
can be completed even if some of the data is missing—only the factors in
the first stage and the first half of the second stage are necessary, and are
collectively referred to as SACJ-Min.

The SACJ is used with sex offenders in prison and by police
departments. The SACJ is based on variables identified in the literature
as being predictive of sexual violence recidivism, and was developed
through exploratory statistical analysis of several UK data sets. The
SACJ has three stages, dealing with official convictions, aggravating
factors, and progress in prison or treatment programs respectively. See
Box 17.

---

[47] Hanson, R.K. (1997) *The development of a brief actuarial risk scale for sexual offence
recidivism* (User Report 97-04), Department of the Solicitor General of Canada, Ottawa.

[48] Hanson, R.K. Thornton, D. (2000) *Improving risk assessments for sex offenders: a
comparison of three actuarial scales*, Law and Human Behaviour, 24(1), 119–136.

Box 17: Structured Anchored Clinical Judgement

Stage 1 items
Current sex offence
Past conviction for a sex offence
Non-sexual violent offence in current conviction
Past conviction for non-sexual violence
More than 3 past convictions of any sort

Stage 2 items
Any stranger victims
Any male victims
Never married
Convictions for non-contact sex offences (*e.g.* exhibitionism, obscene
   phone calls)
Substance abuse
Placement in residential care as a child
Deviant sexual arousal
Psychopathy

Stage 3 does not contain any specific items, but relates to whether
the offender is making improvement or not.

One point is scored for each of the first stage items that apply to the individual, and a table converts the total score into either low, medium or high. If two or more of the Stage Two factors are present, then the offender is reclassified by increasing the initial risk level by one category (*i.e.* low to medium or medium to high). Stage three is based on progress in prison, and the risk level is increased by one category if the offender fails to complete a treatment program, deteriorates while in treatment, or has displayed behaviour that is potentially relevant to sex offending in the past five years in prison (*e.g.* shows continuing interest in pictures of children). Conversely, if he successfully completes an offending program, shows significant improvement on relevant risk factors (*e.g.* no longer shows interest in children and develops appropriate victim empathy), *and* there is acceptable performance on these risk factors (*e.g.* can devise ways of reducing his exposure to situations that may lead to offending), the risk category is decreased one level.

Static-99

5–51   The Static 99[49] is an actuarial scale for assessing long-term risk of sexual recidivism. It is intended for use in males of at least 18 years who have committed at least one sexual offence. It was derived from the RRASOR and the SACJ. Exploratory analysis revealed that when both RRASOR and SACJ-min scores were put into a regression equation, they contributed unique variance, suggesting they were assessing related but different concepts. The Static-99 contains 10 static variables. See Box 18.

---

[49] Hanson, R.K. and Thornton, D. (2000) *Improving risk assessments for sex offenders: a comparison of three actuarial scales*, Law and Human Behaviour, 24(1), 119–136.

Box 18: Static-99

Prior sex offences
More than three prior sentencing dates
Any convictions for non-contact sex offences
Index non-sexual violence
Prior non-sexual violence
Any unrelated victims
Any stranger victims
Any male victims
Young (<25 years)
Single

A guideline is provided for scoring each item and these are summed. The total score is then interpreted using a table which divides the total scores into low, medium-low, medium-high, and high-risk categories.

The Static-99 was found to be a slightly better predictor of both sex offence recidivism and any violent recidivism than either the RRASOR or SACJ-min, which performed equally.

Risk Matrix 2000 (RM2000)

The Static-99 has lead to the development of the Risk Matrix 2000[50]. **5–52** It is an actuarial risk classification process for males 18 years and over who have been convicted of a sexual offence. At least one sexual offence must have been convicted after the age of 16.

RM2000 consists of 3 scales: RM2000/S is a prediction scale for sexual offending; RM2000/V is a prediction scale for non-sexual offending by sex offenders; and RM2000/C is a combination of both and predicts sexual or violent offending. See Box 19.

Box 19: Risk Matrix 2000

RM2000/S	RM2000/V	RM2000/C
Age at commencement of risk	Age	RM2000/S
Court appearances: sex offending charges/other charges	Court appearances: violent offences charges	RM2000/V
Criminal appearances in court	Burglary	
Sex offences against a male		
Sex offences against a stranger		
Single		
Non-contact sex offence		

Each item is described and instructions are provided for scoring each scale. RM2000/S and V scales are rated from I low to IV very high risk.

---

[50] Thornton, D., Mann, R., Webster, S., Blud, L., Travers, R., Friendship, C. and Erickson, M. (2003) *Distinguishing and combining risks for sexual and violent recidivism*. In R. Prentky, E. Janus and M. Seto (Eds.) *Understanding and managing sexually coercive behaviour*. Annals of the Academy of Sciences.

RM2000/C is scored from 0 low/low to 6 very high/very high with intervening categories such as 5 high/very high risk. Tables give the risk of recidivism within the different categories. For example, RM2000/S category IV has a long-term sexual reconviction rate of 60 per cent although these rates reflect the reconviction rates of the area where the research was carried out.

CLINICAL MANAGEMENT OF RISK

5–53 The purpose of risk assessment is to identify specific risks to be managed. The relevant professional must act to reduce and manage the risk effectively and to ensure that a management plan is set in place that increases safety and reduces risk. Risk management decisions must be taken regarding:

- Location/level of security
- Need for detention under mental health legislation
- Use of a restriction order
- Level of observation
- Medication
- Identified therapeutic needs *e.g.* for anger management or substance abuse education and relapse prevention programmes
- Response to aggression
- Social requirements—accommodation, employment, education, recreation
- Support and education for carers
- Information sharing
- Care plan
- Agreed response to deterioration or crisis
- Lines of communication
- Implementation of the Care Programme Approach
- Review of critical incidents

In hospital mental health legislation, medication and varying levels of observation are employed to decrease risk. In the community the Care Programme Approach is often utilised. This is a structured system of risk management involving an assessment of health and social care needs, the development of a care plan, the appointment of a co-ordinator, and planned case reviews. Crisis planning and good communication are essential. At times a clear and specific risk of violence to another may be identified. In such cases confidentiality can, and must, be breached. The General Medical Council has provided guidelines permitting doctors to breach confidentiality in such circumstances[51].

---

[51] General Medical Council (2000) Confidentiality: Protecting and Providing Information. GMC, London.

CHAPTER 61

PSYCHIATRIC DEFENCES

INTRODUCTION

The law recognizes that mental disorder may affect an individual's **6–01** responsibility for committing an offence and ability to participate in his or her trial. This chapter will describe the psychiatric defences which are available where mental disorder is present at the time when an accused commits an offence: *insanity at the time of the offence* and *diminished responsibility*. *Automatism* has an uncertain legal status in Scotland and will be considered under insanity at the time of the offence. *Insanity in bar of trial* will also be described in this chapter. Technically this is not a psychiatric defence as it relates to the capacity of an accused to participate in the trial rather than responsibility for his or her actions. However, it is conveniently described here due to its historical roots, its terminology and the similarity in procedure to insanity at the time of the offence.

Insanity both in bar of trial and at the time of an offence have been recognized under Scots law for many centuries[2]. These are ancient procedures which have their origins in times when approaches to offending and mental disorder were very different to the present day: imprisonment was rare; execution, torture and other forms of corporal punishment were common; and psychiatry did not exist. The current criteria for these legal concepts can be traced back to the 18th century. They were responsible for the emergence of forensic psychiatry, as in the early 19th century procedures and institutions were introduced to deal with the "criminal lunatics" who were defined by them[3]. Diminished responsibility has a shorter history, but still dates back to the 19th century.

With the abolition of execution under the Murder (Abolition of Death Penalty) Act 1965 and the introduction of a variety of procedures to deal with mentally disordered offenders who had been convicted of an offence (without having had to be judged insane first) under the Mental Health (Scotland) Act 1960, the use of insanity procedures has gradually diminished so as to account for a tiny minority of mentally disordered offenders. The inflexibility of automatic confinement at the State Hospital on a restriction order in solemn cases also made an insanity

---

[1] Chapter author: Dr Rajan Darjee MPhil.
[2] Walker, N. (1968) *Crime and Insanity in England. Volume One: the Historical Perspective*, Edinburgh: Edinburgh University Press.
[3] Baird, J. (1984) *The Transfer of Scottish Prisoners: a Historical and Descriptive Study of Convicted Prisoners Transferred to Psychiatric Hospitals,* MD Thesis, Edinburgh: University of Edinburgh.

defence a relatively unappealing option except where the charges were very serious. However, the recent introduction of flexibility in disposal of insanity cases by the Criminal Justice (Scotland) Act 1995 has potentially increased their appeal in more minor offences. In several jurisdictions outwith the United Kingdom, an insanity defence or inability to stand trial are the only ways in which a mentally disordered offender may be diverted from the criminal justice system if they are facing serious charges.

INSANITY IN BAR OF TRIAL

Background

6–02   It is an accepted legal principle that it is unfair to try accused persons whose mental disorder prevents them from mounting a proper defence. Such accused are described as unfit to plead or insane in bar of trial. Before the Criminal Justice (Scotland) Act 1995 the disposals in such cases were extremely limited: in solemn cases a mandatory hospital order with restrictions on discharge to the State Hospital (or an alternative hospital if there were special reasons); and in summary cases a mandatory hospital order, with or without restrictions, to any hospital. Historically, the criteria for fitness to plead were vague, medical evidence was accepted without question, the presence of psychosis was automatically seen as fulfilling the criteria and fitness to plead was confused with aspects of criminal responsibility[4]. Therefore insanity in bar of trial was the means by which the majority of mentally disordered offenders were formally detained in Scotland until the 1970s, and findings of unfitness to plead were more frequent in Scotland than in England and Wales until the 1980s[5]. Recently, psychiatrists and courts have paid more attention to detail. Fresh proceedings against persons who had recovered their fitness to plead were possible but rare in practice. Dissatisfaction with the mandatory disposal and the possibility of indefinite detention for an offence that an accused person had not actually been found to have committed led, belatedly, to changes in the procedures for the disposal of such cases[6]. Therefore the Criminal Justice (Scotland) Act 1995 (amending relevant provisions under the Criminal Procedure (Scotland) Act 1975) introduced an examination of facts and flexibility in disposal. These procedures are now set out in the Criminal Procedure (Scotland) Act 1995 as amended by the Mental Health (Care and Treatment) (Scotland) Act 2003 and the Criminal Justice (Scotland) Act 2003.

---

[4] Chiswick , D. (1990) Criminal responsibility in Scotland. In *Principles and Practice of Forensic Psychiatry* (Ed.s R. Bluglass and P. Bowden), pp. 313–318. Edinburgh: Churchill Livingstone.
[5] Chiswick, D. (1978) Insanity in Bar of Trial in Scotland: a State Hospital Study. *British Journal of Psychiatry* 132: 598-601.
[6] Home Office and Department of Health and Social Security (1975) *Report of the Committee on Mentally Abnormal Offenders.* Cmnd 6244. London: HMSO.
Scottish Home and Health Department and Crown Office (1982) *Criminal procedure in Scotland (Second Report).* Cmnd 6218. Edinburgh: HMSO.

Criteria

There is no statutory definition of insanity in bar of trial. The leading **6–03** case is *HMA v Wilson*[7]:

> "a mental alienation of some kind which prevents the accused giving the instruction which a sane man would give for his defence or from following the evidence as a sane man would follow it and instructing his counsel as the case goes, along any point that arises"

Similar criteria were set out more recently in *Stewart v HMA*[8]:

> "The question for [the trial judge] was whether the appellant, by reason of his material handicap, would be unable to instruct his legal representatives as to his defence or to follow what went on at his trial. Without such ability he could not receive a fair trial."

A requirement of a previous judgement (*HMA v Brown*[9]) that the accused be able to tell the truth and remember events accurately has been overturned. The test excludes amnesia for the circumstances of the alleged offence in itself (*Russell v HMA*[10]), and inability to give instruction due to physical defects, such as deaf mutism, is probably excluded (*HMA v Wilson*[11]). It should be noted that, unlike England and Wales[12], fitness to plead does not encompass the ability to challenge a juror as this is not part of the court process in Scotland.

PROCEDURE

Determination of Fitness to Plead

The issue may be raised by the prosecutor, defence or judge. It is **6–04** usually dealt with at a preliminary hearing (a "mental health proof") where a determination is made by the trial judge on the basis of written or oral evidence from two doctors[13].

Examination of Facts

When the court has determined that an individual is insane in bar of **6–05** trial, it records the finding, discharges the trial diet and orders an examination of facts (EOF)[14]. While awaiting the EOF the accused may be remanded on bail, in custody or committed to hospital (a temporary

---

[7] *HMA v Wilson*, 1942 J.C. 75.
[8] *Stewart v HMA (No. 1)*, 1997 J.C. 183.
[9] *HMA v Brown* (1907) 5 Adam 312.
[10] *Russell v HMA* (1946) J.C. 37.
[11] *HMA v Wilson* (1942) J.C. 75.
[12] *R. v Pritchard* (1836) 7 Car. & P. 303 and *R. v Friend* [1997] 1 W.L.R. 1433.
[13] Criminal Procedure (Scotland) Act 1995, s. 54.
[14] *ibid.*, s.55.

compulsion order[15]). At the EOF the court determines beyond reasonable doubt whether the accused committed the act charged and whether on the balance of probabilities there are grounds for acquittal. The accused does not have to attend the examination of facts. If the facts are not found the accused is acquitted and there are no further proceedings.

If the facts are found then the court must consider whether there are grounds for an acquittal on the ground of insanity (see below)[16]. The disposals available in the latter case are identical to those available if the facts are found without such an acquittal.

Disposal

6–06　　The disposals available are set out in s.57 of the Criminal Procedure (Scotland) Act 1995:

1. a compulsion order[17]
2. a compulsion order with a restriction order[18]
3. an interim compulsion order[19]
4. guardianship or an intervention order (under the Adults with Incapacity (Scotland) Act 2000)[20]
5. a supervision and treatment order[21]
6. a discharge with no order[22]

There is, therefore, a flexible set of disposals that may be tailored to the individual's mental health and risk. Previously, where the charge was murder the mandatory disposal was a hospital order (the predecessor of the compulsion order) and restriction order, but this is no longer the case as of June 2003, following the Criminal Justice (Scotland) Act 2003. Under s.57(3) of the Criminal Procedure (Scotland) Act 1995, as amended, there will be a mandatory compulsion order with a restriction order where although insane, following assessment on an interim compulsion order, the court determines the individual poses a high risk according to the criteria set out in s.210E of the Criminal Procedure (Scotland) Act 1995 (these are the same risk criteria that would lead to an "order for lifelong restriction" in non-insane offenders; see Chapter 7). The introduction of the interim compulsion order following a finding of insanity and the mandatory imposition of a restriction order in high-risk cases will begin with the commencement of the "order for lifelong restriction" and the Risk Management Authority, probably in 2005 (see Chapter 7).

The compulsion order[23] and restriction order[24] are identical to analogous disposals for convicted mentally disordered offenders[25] as described

---

[15] Criminal Procedure (Scotland) Act 1995, s. 54.

[16] *ibid.*, s.55(4).

[17] *ibid.*, s.57(2)(a).

[18] *ibid.*, s.57(2)(a)&(b).

[19] *ibid.*, s.57(2)(bb); this option was introduced under the Criminal Justice (Scotland) Act 2003 but has not been implemented yet—see later.

[20] *ibid.*, s.57(2)(c).

[21] *ibid.*, s.57(2)(d).

[22] *ibid.*, s.57(2)(e).

[23] *ibid.*, s.57(2)(a).

[24] *ibid.*, s.57(2)(b).

[25] *ibid.*, s.57A and s.59.

in Chapter 7. The interim compulsion order[26] is available primarily for the assessment of potentially "high-risk" cases (as set out in Part 1 of the Criminal Justice (Scotland) Act 2003) and, unlike the interim compulsion order after conviction[27], cannot be followed by a penal disposal.

The supervision and treatment order[28] is unique to insanity procedures and is analogous to a probation order with a condition of psychiatric treatment following conviction[29]. It is a mechanism "to secure access to supervision and assistance in the community, including medical treatment"[30]. It requires medical evidence from two approved doctors[31] and requires the person to submit to treatment, comply with instructions, maintain contact with a supervising officer and comply with residential requirements. However, none of these measures can be enforced, and breach of the conditions of the order has no meaningful consequences.

Appeal

The accused may appeal to the High Court against a finding or refusal **6–07** to make a finding of insanity in bar of trial, against an EOF finding, and against any disposal imposed. The Crown has similar rights of appeal but only on points of law.

CLINICAL ASPECTS

Assessment

The assessment of fitness to plead is concerned with the current **6–08** mental state and ability of an accused. This involves making a diagnosis of mental disorder, and determining the impact of this disorder on the ability of the accused to give instructions for his defence and follow proceedings in court. Clinicians should be aware that the mental state of an individual may change and, therefore, if some time has elapsed between a clinical examination and the accused's appearance in court then a brief re-examination may be necessary. As with other capacities, fitness to plead is task-specific and may change over time.

Problems may arise due to the terminology used. An individual who is fit to plead is described as "sane and fit to plead" and one who is not as "insane in bar of trial" or "insane and unfit to plead". These terms are specific to this capacity. The use of the words "sane" and "insane" should not be confused with "insanity at the time of the offence" (see below) or "mental illness" under the Mental Health (Care and Treatment) (Scotland) Act 2003. Although the three may be related, they are separate legal issues. If an accused is floridly psychotic but able to follow proceedings and give instruction it is customary to describe him as "sane and fit to plead" and not "insane and fit to plead". Although the latter

---

[26] Criminal Procedure (Scotland) Act 1995, s.57(2)(bb).
[27] *ibid.*, s.53.
[28] *ibid.*, s.57(2)(d) and *ibid.*, Sch.4.
[29] *ibid.*, s.230.
[30] Scottish Office circular SWSG 4/98 and Criminal Procedure (Scotland) Act 1995, Sch.4.
[31] Mental Health (Care and Treatment) (Scotland) Act 2003, s.22.

may make more sense clinically, the phrase should not be broken up into its constituents. So in a report the clinician should state whether the accused is:

- Sane and fit to plead

or

- Insane and unfit to plead (or insane in bar of trial)

Diagnoses that may be relevant to the determination of fitness to plead are:

- Dementia and other chronic organic conditions
- Delirium
- Schizophrenia and related psychoses
- Severe affective disorders (mania and depression)
- Learning disability

Features of an individual's mental state due to their disorder to be taken into consideration include the individual's:

- ability to communicate: schizophrenic thought disorder, manic flight of ideas, depressive poverty of speech, dysphasia or dementia
- beliefs: *e.g.* the individual may have delusions that they have a divine mission and that the court process is irrelevant to them
- comprehension: may be impaired in dementia, acute confusion or learning disability
- attention and concentration: may be impaired in any of the conditions listed above
- memory: as noted above, amnesia for the alleged offence is irrelevant, but short-term memory impairment due to organic impairment may be such as to make following proceedings in court impossible

The clinician must consider the impact of the features of the disorder on the patient's ability to instruct his defence and follow proceedings in court. Therefore the clinician must have some understanding of the court process. In some cases, suggestions may be made as to how the communication and understanding of the accused may be facilitated. However, such suggestions must be practicable in court.

In most cases, psychiatric evidence is unanimous and followed unquestioningly in court. A recommendation that an individual is insane in bar of trial should be reserved for cases where this is beyond doubt. In borderline cases certain measures may allow further assessment and treatment to clarify the issue:

1. An assessment order[32] either as a pre-trial court disposal or as a pre-trial transfer from prison remand.

---

[32] Criminal Procedure (Scotland) Act 1995, s.52C.

2. A treatment order[33] either as a pre-trial court disposal or as a pre-trial transfer from prison remand.
3. Bail with a condition of residence in hospital.

The first two of these measures are described in more detail in Chapter 7.

Where the index offence is relatively minor it may be appropriate for charges to be dropped and for civil detention to be initiated. In such cases procurators fiscal are usually keen to take this course.

INSANITY AT THE TIME OF THE OFFENCE

Background

Insanity at the time of an offence provides a complete defence to a **6–09** criminal charge. The principle is that a person suffering from a mental disorder who commits what would otherwise be a crime as a result of that disorder is not to blame for their actions. The definition of insanity for this purpose has shifted over time, but the current criteria (set out below) have their origins in the 18th century.

The mental element in a crime occupies an important position in law[34]. For a crime to be committed not only must there have been a criminal act (sometimes referred to as *actus reus*), there must have been the accompanying mental element. The term *mens rea* is used in this regard to refer to the mental element necessary to make an act an offence, but this was not a term originally used in Scotland. Rather Hume used the term "dole" to refer to "that corrupt and evil intention, which is essential . . . to the guilt of any crime"[35]. This concept remains influential with Scottish courts giving consideration to "evil intent" and "wickedness" although the term *mens rea* is now more commonly used. *Mens rea* is not related in any way to psychological or psychiatric concepts. It is a legal notion and for a particular offence there will be a particular mental element that is necessary to make the act an offence. This may be intent, or with some crimes, recklessness. Courts judge it objectively rather than subjectively. If there is no *mens rea* there is no offence (see "automatism" below). Insanity at the time of an offence does not necessarily negate *mens rea,* but rather excuses a person despite the presence of the necessary *mens rea*—a person may intentionally kill another person but if they were acting on psychotic delusions then they may be acquitted despite the presence of the *actus reus* (the act of killing another person) and the *mens rea* (the intention to kill the person).

In the 16th century, the test for insanity was to compare the accused to children or wild beasts[36], and in the 17th century only the "absolutely

---

[33] Criminal Procedure (Scotland) Act 1995, s.52L.

[34] Christie, M. G. A. (2001) *The Criminal Law of Scotland by Sir Gerald H. Gordon* (3rd ed.) Vol I, Edinburgh, W. Green.

[35] Hume , D. (1844) *Commentaries on the Law of Scotland respecting crimes.* Edinburgh, Bell and Bradfute.

[36] Arnot, H. (1833) *A Collection and Abridgement of Celebrated Criminal Trials in Scotland 1536–1784.* Edinburgh: William Smellie.

furious" were to be excused from punishment[37]. In the late 18th century, Hume, summarizing the Scottish case law up until then, stated that for a plea of insanity to succeed there had to be:

> "An absolute alienation of reason . . . such a disease as deprives the patient of the knowledge of the true aspect and position of things about him,—hinders him from distinguishing friend from foe,—and gives him up to the impulse of his own distempered fancy."[38]

This definition forms the basis of the current criteria for insanity. However, since it was set out there has been confusion and change in the definition of insanity in Scotland. The narrower M'Naghten rules from England were used in 1844:

> ". . . at the time of the committing of the act, the party was labouring under such a defect of reason, from disease of the mind, as not to know the nature and quality of the act he was doing; or, if he did know it, that he did not know he was doing what was wrong."[39]

However, as the 19th century progressed, a broader view of insanity was taken by some courts. By the start of the 20th century the Scottish law on insanity was largely a combination of the M'Naghten rules with the addition of an irresistible impulse criterion:

> ". . . insanity was relevant if it deprived the accused of the capacity to know he was doing wrong, or to know the nature and quality of his act, or if it deprived him of the power of controlling his actions."[40]

This broader definition of insanity in Scotland was confirmed in *Lord Advocate v Kidd* (see "criteria" below).

Before 1995 the disposal following an acquittal on the ground of insanity was an automatic committal to the State Hospital (or another hospital if there were special circumstances) on a hospital order with restrictions on discharge. As mentioned above, until the 1970s there was confusion between insanity in bar of trial and insanity at the time of the offence. In most cases where an accused was found insane this was in bar of trial. Despite this an acquittal on the ground of insanity has been more frequent in Scotland than in England and Wales, probably due to the broader concept in Scotland[41].

LEGAL ASPECTS

Criteria

6–10   Lord Strachan's charge to the jury in *Lord Advocate v Kidd* is generally accepted and used as the basis of the insanity defence:

---

[37] Mackenzie, G. (1678) *The Laws and Customs of Scotland in Matters Criminal,* Edinburgh, George Swintoun.

[38] Hume, D. (1844) *Commentaries on the Law of Scotland respecting crimes,* Edinburgh, Bell and Bradfute.

[39] *M'Naghten's Case* (1843) 10 Cl & F 200.

[40] *HMA v James Denny Scott* (1853) 1 Irv. 123.

[41] Chiswick, D. (1990) Criminal responsibility in Scotland. In *Principles and Practice of Forensic Psychiatry* (eds R. Bluglass and P. Bowden), pp.313–318, Edinburgh, Churchill Livingstone.

". . . in order to excuse a person from responsibility on the grounds of insanity, there must have been an alienation of reason in relation to the act committed. There must have been some mental defect . . . by which his reason was overpowered, and he was thereby rendered incapable of exerting his reason to control his conduct and reactions. If his reason was alienated in relation to the act committed, he was not responsible for the act, even although otherwise he may have been apparently quite rational."[42]

It was stated explicitly that this was broader than the M'Naghten rules. The Scottish insanity defence therefore has cognitive (knowing what one is doing) and volitional (controlling what one is doing) prongs, compared to the purely cognitive M'Naghten rules. The definition in *Kidd* has been likened to the American Law Institute Model Penal Code[43] which has been adopted by the majority of States in the U.S.A. Self-induced intoxication does not provide the grounds for an insanity defence (*Brennan v HMA*[44]).

PROCEDURE

Determination of Insanity at the Time of the Offence

The defence is available in both summary and solemn cases. It is a **6–11** special defence and advance notification must be given to the Crown. There are no statutory requirements regarding medical evidence, but written and oral evidence is usually presented from at least two doctors, neither of whom needs to be approved under the Mental Health (Care and Treatment) (Scotland) Act 2003. The burden of proof is a balance of probabilities. In most cases psychiatric evidence will be unanimous and unopposed, but if challenged then the issue is determined by the judge (in summary cases) or jury (in solemn cases).

If the defence is successful the individual is acquitted on the grounds of insanity. Although they do not therefore have a conviction, the finding does appear on their criminal record.

Disposal

The disposals available are identical to those available for persons **6–12** found insane in bar of trial[45]. Therefore in "high-risk" cases there will be a mandatory compulsion order with restrictions (following the implementation of the Criminal Justice (Scotland) Act 2003—see above), but in other cases there is a flexible range of disposals depending on the mental state of the acquitted person and the risk they pose.

Appeal

The individual may appeal to the High Court against a finding, or **6–13** refusal to make a finding of insanity and against the disposal made by the court. As with insanity in bar of trial, the Crown has similar rights of appeal, but only on points of law.

---

[42] *Lord Advocate v Kidd*, 1960 J.C. 61.
[43] American Law Institute (1960) *Model Penal Code*. Philadelphia: American Law Institute.
[44] *Brennan v HMA*, 1977 J.C. 38.
[45] Criminal Procedure (Scotland) Act 1995, s.57.

CLINICAL ASPECTS

6–14 The clinical examination necessitates the reconstruction of the circumstances of the offence and in particular the mental state of the accused at that time. Along with interviewing the accused it is extremely helpful to peruse witness statements, police reports and transcripts of police interviews. It is also usually helpful to speak to a relative, or someone else, who knew the accused person at the time. Occasionally the accused may have had a psychiatric assessment soon after the offence, if the police or court were sufficiently concerned about their mental state. Also, the person may have been in contact with psychiatric services at the time, and records and interviews with relevant staff can help to build up a picture of the offence.

Putting the legal criteria into clinical terms is not easy. At the time of the offence the accused should have been suffering from a severe mental disorder which was the overwhelming factor in determining the occurrence of the offence. There should be a clear relationship between the offence and the symptoms of the mental disorder. However, it should be noted that the criteria are broader than not knowing what one is doing or that it is wrong, and encompass an inability to control one's actions due to an "alienation of reason".

Diagnoses that may be relevant are:

- Dementia and other chronic organic disorders (including those secondary to alcohol or drug misuse)
- Delirium (including delirium tremens)
- Schizophrenia and related psychoses
- Severe affective disorders with psychotic symptoms
- Severe learning disability

The following diagnoses are unlikely to be relevant:

- Non-psychotic affective disorders
- Neurotic, somatoform and adjustment disorders
- Eating disorders
- Personality disorders
- Sexual deviation
- Intoxication with alcohol, drugs or solvents
- Mild to moderate learning disability

In most successful cases the diagnosis is a psychotic disorder, and delusions or hallucinations are directly relevant to the behaviour constituting the offence.

AUTOMATISM

6–15 Where individuals commit offences when their bodies are not under the control of their minds (*e.g.* when asleep) they are not guilty of an offence. Legally this is called an automatism. It should be noted that this is different from the clinical concept of automatism occurring during a complex partial seizure. Until relatively recently the law on automatism in Scotland was largely untested.

In England and Wales two legal types of automatism are recognized: insane and sane (automatism simpliciter)[46]. The distinction is based on whether the behaviour is likely to recur: if it is, it is illogically said to have an intrinsic cause and labelled insane (*e.g.* sleepwalking, brain tumours, epilepsy); if not, it is, again illogically, said to have an extrinsic cause and is labelled sane (*e.g.* confusional states, concussion, reflex actions after bee stings, dissociative states, night terrors and hypoglycaemia). The former results in an acquittal on the grounds of insanity and the latter in a complete acquittal. The distinction is less important now that there is a flexible range of disposals available for those found insane.

In Scotland *Simon Fraser*[47] killed his infant son while sleep walking in 1878. The jury found that he was not responsible due to somnambulism. He was not acquitted, but was released from court after undertaking to sleep alone in future. In *HMA v Ritchie*[48] in 1926 a defence of automatism led to a complete acquittal. In *HMA v Hayes*[49] a special defence based on temporary dissociation was successful, the jury finding both the charge of culpable homicide and the special defence proved. Hayes was released with a requirement to surrender his driving licence. Despite these cases where automatisms were not regarded as forms of insanity, any concept of sane automatism was rejected in *HMA v Cunningham*[50] in 1963. It was held that absence of *mens rea* due to a disorder of mind leading to acquittal was only relevant if there was insanity at the time of the offence. Until recently this was the leading case. Thus, sane automatism was not accepted as a defence in Scotland for many years. There were some successful hypoglycaemia cases[51], but the basis for these is unclear.

The decisions in *Ross v HMA* in 1991 and *Sorley v HMA* in 1992 have established sane automatism as a recognised legal concept in Scotland[52]. In *Ross* involuntary intoxication with drugs was accepted as a cause of absence of *mens rea* leading to a complete acquittal rather than acquittal on the ground of insanity. The finding of sane automatism is limited to cases where the automatic behaviour is not self-induced and where the factor leading to the automatic behaviour is not due to a "continuing disorder of the mind or body which might lead to the recurrence of the disturbance of . . . mental faculties". In such cases the decision in *Cunningham* would apply, with insane automatism being the only defence available. In *Sorley* the conditions required for a defence of sane automatism were set out: first that the automatic behaviour was caused by an external factor that was not self-induced; secondly this factor was

---

[46] Fenwick, P. (1990) Automatism. In *Principles and Practice of Forensic Psychiatry* (Ed.s R. Bluglass and P. Bowden), pp.313–318, Edinburgh, Churchill Livingstone.

[47] *Simon Fraser* (1878) 4 Couper 70.

[48] *HMA v Ritchie*, 1926 J.C. 45.

[49] *HMA v Hayes*, unreported, November 1949, HCJ (reported in Gane, C. H. W. and Stoddart, C. N. (1988) *A case book on Scottish Criminal Law*. Edinburgh: W. Green, Sweet & Maxwell).

[50] *HMA v Cunningham*, 1963 J.C. 80.

[51] *Stirling v Annan*, 1983 S.C.C.R. 396.

[52] *Ross v HMA*, 1991 J.C. 210; *Sorley v HMA*, 1992 S.C.C.R. 396; see also McCall Smith, R. A. A. and Sheldon, D. (1997) *Scots Criminal Law*. Edinburgh: Butterworths.

not foreseeable; and thirdly this factor caused a total alienation of reason leading to complete loss of self-control.

The current legal position in Scotland is therefore essentially similar to that in England and Wales with the recognition of sane and insane automatism. Despite the recognition of sane automatism, courts have taken a cautious approach to this defence since *Ross* and *Sorley*. With the flexibility of disposal in insanity cases the artificial divide between sane and insane automatism is perhaps less relevant.

DIMINISHED RESPONSIBILITY

Background

6–16   The insanity defence sets a high threshold for a mentally disordered offender. It has long been recognized that there may be cases where the mental disorder of an accused may be such as to have played a significant part in an offence, but may not be severe enough for an acquittal on the grounds of insanity. Prior to the abolition of the death penalty, if such a case involved murder the mandatory punishment was execution; and now in such a case there would be a mandatory life sentence imposed. Diminished responsibility sets a lower threshold than insanity, but instead of an acquittal the accused is convicted of culpable homicide instead of murder. There is no mandatory disposal for culpable homicide and the potential sentences range from absolute discharge, through community disposals to imprisonment, including the discretionary life sentence and order for lifelong restriction. Mental health disposals are also available.

Diminished responsibility is a Scottish invention. In the 17th century it first occurred to Sir George Mackenzie to moderate the punishment of those who were not "absolutely furious"[53]. In capital cases courts would recommend royal mercy following a murder conviction in these cases. In *HMA v Dingwall*[54] in 1867, Lord Deas went a step further in suggesting to the jury that they might bring a verdict of culpable homicide by taking into consideration the mental condition of the accused. This view gained ready acceptance and seems to have applied in both capital and non-capital cases. The doctrine of diminished responsibility was therefore established, although the term "diminished responsibility" was not actually used until 1939[55].

Initially there was broad interpretation, but by the start of the 20th century judges showed an increasing distrust of the concept due to the expanding number of psychiatric conditions described, a fear that many murderers might escape their just desserts and discomfort that psychiatrists were determining what should be a legal decision. Thus the interpretation of diminished responsibility was increasingly restrictive[56].

---

[53] Mackenzie, G. (1678) *The Laws and Customs of Scotland in Matters Criminal*, Edinburgh, George Swintoun.

[54] *HMA v Dingwall* (1867) 5 Irv. 466.

[55] *Kirkwood v HMA*, 1939 J.C. 36.

[56] *HMA v Smith* (1893) 1 Adam 34; *HMA v Aitken* (1902) 4 Adam 88 and *HMA v Braithwaite*, 1945 J.C. 55.

The leading case, until 2001, was *HMA v Savage*[57]:

> ". . . that there must be aberration or weakness of mind; that there must be some form of mental unsoundness; that there must be a state of mind bordering on, though not amounting to, insanity . . . there must be some form of mental disease"

Diminished responsibility within these criteria was interpreted restrictively. Psychopathic personality disorder[58] and voluntary intoxication[59] were excluded.

Diminished responsibility was imported into England and Wales in 1957:

> "When a person is party to the killing of another, he shall not be convicted of murder if he was suffering from such abnormality of mind (whether arising from a condition of arrested or retarded development of mind or any inherent causes or induced by disease or injury) as substantially impaired his mental responsibility for his acts and omissions in doing or being a party to the killing."[60]

Initially this was interpreted restrictively as in Scotland[61]. However, in *R v Byrne*[62] in 1960 the Court of Appeal gave a wide interpretation of "abnormality of mind":

> ". . . a state of mind so different from that of ordinary human beings that the reasonable man would term it abnormal. It appears to us to be wide enough to cover the mind's activities in all its aspects, not only the perception of physical acts and matters and the ability to form a rational judgement whether an act is right or wrong, but also the ability to exercise will-power to control physical acts in accordance with that rational judgement."

The English version was therefore more generous than its Scottish counterpart. Nigel Walker commented that "the adopted child had outgrown its twin"[63].

In Scotland, the narrow scope of diminished responsibility was confirmed in *Connelly v HMA*[64] and *Williamson v HMA*[65]. However, this narrow interpretation was set aside in *Galbraith v HMA (No.2)*[66] in 2001, with the Court of Criminal Appeal redefining diminished responsibility and potentially widening its scope. With this recent change we await sufficient cases and possible appeals to have a clear understanding of what is now meant by diminished responsibility in Scotland.

---

[57] *HMA v Savage*, 1923 J.C. 49.
[58] *Carraher v HMA*, 1946 J.C. 108.
[59] *Brennan v HMA*, 1977 J.C. 38.
[60] Homicide Act 1957, s.2.
[61] *R v Spriggs* (1958) 42 Cr. App. R. 69.
[62] *R v Byrne* (1960) 44 Cr. App. R. 246.
[63] Walker, N. (1968) *Crime and Insanity in England. Volume One: the Historical Perspective*, Edinburgh, Edinburgh University Press.
[64] *Connelly v HMA*, 1990 S.C.C.R. 505.
[65] *Williamson v HMA*, 1994 J.C. 149.
[66] *Galbraith v HMA (No.2)*, 2001 S.C.C.R. 551.

LEGAL ASPECTS

Criteria

6–17   As the *Galbraith* judgment was set out so recently, there has been little experience either legally or clinically of the "new" interpretation of diminished responsibility[67]. The conclusions of the court in *Galbraith v HMA* are therefore set out in full:

1. Where, on the facts found proved by the jury, the law holds that the accused's responsibility was diminished at the time when he killed his victim, the proper course is for the jury to convict the accused of culpable homicide.
2. But, precisely because diminished responsibility is a legal concept, it is for the trial judge to determine whether there is evidence on which the jury would be entitled to convict the accused of culpable homicide rather than of murder, on the ground of diminished responsibility. In determining that issue, the judge must consider the kinds of issue that we have discussed. In essence, the judge must decide whether there is evidence that, at the relevant time, the accused was suffering from an abnormality of mind which substantially impaired the ability of the accused, as compared with a normal person, to determine or control his acts.
3. The abnormality of mind may take various forms. It may mean that the individual perceives physical acts and matters differently from a normal person. Or else it may affect his ability to form a rational judgment as to whether a particular act is right or wrong or to decide whether to perform it. In a given case any or all of these effects may be operating.
4. The abnormality must be one that is recognised by the appropriate science. But it may be congenital or derive from an organic condition, from some psychotic illness, such as schizophrenia or severe depression, or from the psychological effects of severe trauma. In every case, in colloquial terms, there must, unfortunately, have been something far wrong with the accused, which affected the way he acted.
5. While the plea of diminished responsibility will be available only where the accused's abnormality of mind had substantial effects in relation to his act, there is no requirement that his state of mind should have bordered on insanity.
6. It is for the court to determine, having regard always to relevant policy considerations, whether any particular abnormality can found a plea of diminished responsibility. Thus, no mental abnormality, short of actual insanity, which is brought on by the accused himself taking drink or controlled drugs or sniffing glue, will found a plea of diminished responsibility (*Brennan*). Similarly, our law does not recognise psychopathic

---

[67] See Crichton, J. H. M., Darjee, R. and Chiswick, D. (2004) *Diminished responsibility in Scotland: new case law*, Journal of Forensic Psychiatry and Psychology 15: 552–565.

personality disorder as a basis for diminished responsibility (*Carraher*).

7. If, applying the appropriate tests, the judge concludes that the evidence is not capable of supporting a plea of diminished responsibility, he should direct the jury that, if convicting, they should convict of murder.

8. If, on the other hand, the judge concludes that there is evidence to support the plea, then he must leave it for the jury to consider. In that event the judge's directions to the jury should not simply recite the Savage formula but should be tailored, so far as possible, to the facts of the particular case. The amount of detail required will also depend on the facts of the particular case and on the precise issue in controversy between the Crown and the defence. In essence, the jury should be told that they must be satisfied that, by reason of the abnormality of mind in question, the ability of the accused, as compared with a normal person, to determine or control his actings was substantially impaired.

Thus the test is whether there is "an abnormality of mind which substantially impaired the ability of the accused . . . to determine or control his acts". Although this looks very similar to the English and Welsh version, it remains to be seen how close it is in practice. Psychopathic personality disorder and voluntary intoxication remain excluded.

Procedure

Prior to the recent changes, only a small proportion of diminished **6–18** responsibility pleas went to trial. It was common practice for the Crown to accept the plea before trial and reduce the charge to one of culpable homicide, taking into consideration not just the psychiatric evidence but also the broader aspects of the case. This will probably remain so in clear-cut cases. In cases that go to trial, proof must be established on a balance of probabilities. As in England and Wales, contested cases are unlikely to be successful for the accused.

There is flexibility in disposal. The full range of psychiatric disposals is available (compulsion orders with restriction orders, compulsion orders, hospital directions, interim compulsion orders, probation orders with conditions of psychiatric treatment) as well as community and custodial sentences. A life sentence based on the dangerousness of the accused, inferred from their mental condition, may be imposed (*Duff v HMA*[68]), and the new order for lifelong restrictions will be mandatory in high-risk cases (see Chapter 7).

Unlike England and Wales, there is no legally recognized offence of infanticide in Scotland. In such cases it is usual for the Crown to charge the woman with culpable homicide.

Appeal

There are no appeal procedures specific to diminished responsibility. **6–19** The accused may appeal against a conviction for murder following an unsuccessful diminished responsibility plea, and against the disposal

---

[68] 1983 S.C.C.R. 461.

following a conviction for culpable homicide on the grounds of diminished responsibility. Similarly, the Crown may appeal against a conviction for culpable homicide instead of for murder (but only on a point of law), and against the disposal in diminished responsibility cases.

CLINICAL ASPECTS

Assessment

6–20   The clinical assessment is identical to that concerning insanity at the time of the offence with regard to the information required. The clinician needs to assess whether the accused was suffering from an "abnormality of mind" and, if so, what the impact of that abnormality was in relation to the killing. The "appropriate science" to recognize this abnormality may be psychology or psychiatry. Therefore conditions beyond those recognized in DSM-IV and ICD-10 may be relevant. In *Galbraith v HMA* "battered spouse syndrome" and "learned helplessness" were mentioned specifically. All the conditions that may form the basis of an insanity defence (see above) are highly likely to be accepted as grounds for diminished responsibility if an insanity defence fails or, as in most cases, if the accused directly puts forward diminished responsibility as a defence. Other mental disorders that may be relevant are:

- Non-psychotic affective disorders (mania, hypomania and depression)
- Acute stress reactions and adjustment disorders
- Post-traumatic stress disorder
- Personality disorders (excluding primary antisocial personality disorder)
- Pervasive developmental disorders (including autistic spectrum disorders)
- Mild to moderate learning disability

The clinician needs to form an opinion as to the presence of a mental condition, and, considering the other factors present in the case, the relative contribution of that condition to the killing. However the clinician should resist stating that the accused was of diminished responsibility or suffering from diminished responsibility. The question of substantial impairment of ability to determine or control acts is for the jury, and this is stated explicitly in *Galbraith v HMA*.

"Psychopathic personality disorder" remains excluded. However, this is based on a judgment from 1946 when concepts of personality disorder were very different from current clinical concepts. The clinical concept of the time was Henderson's "aggressive psychopath"[69]. The closest current clinical concepts would be dissocial personality disorder according to ICD-10[70], antisocial personality disorder according to DSM-IV[71] and

---

[69] Henderson, D. K. (1939) *Psychopathic States*. London: Chapman and Hall.

[70] World Health Organization(1992) *The ICD-10 Classification of Mental and Behavioural Disorders*. Geneva, World Health Organization.

[71] American Psychiatric Association (1994) *Diagnostic and Statistical Manual of Mental Disorders* (4th ed.), Washington DC, American Psychiatric Association.

psychopathy as defined by the Psychopathy Check List-Revised[72]. However, not all homicide offenders with personality disorders have antisocial personality disorder. Are these other personality disorders excluded as grounds for diminished responsibility? This is unclear. Certainly in one case since *Galbraith* non-antisocial personality disorder has been put forward along with limited intellect as the basis of diminished responsibility. The accused was convicted of culpable homicide—but other non-psychiatric features in the case may have been influential on the jury[73]. Borderline personality disorder may be conceptualized as a long-term reaction to severe trauma in childhood. Such conditions are mentioned specifically in *Galbraith* as coming within the scope of diminished responsibility. The position of personality disorders in relation to diminished responsibility may be clarified as cases build up and if there are relevant appeals.

The effects of voluntary acute intoxication with alcohol, drugs or solvents are excluded. This exclusion goes beyond the disinhibiting effects of substances to cover hallucinatory experiences that may occur, when for example intoxicated with amphetamine, LSD, solvents or cocaine. In such cases these transient experiences have to be differentiated from the more prolonged psychotic symptoms experienced in drug-induced psychoses and co-morbid psychotic disorders. Both of the latter may form the basis for a plea of diminished responsibility. In cases where intoxication is a feature, but other mental conditions are also present, it is necessary to try to estimate the relative contribution of each to the killing. For example, a man with chronic mild depressive symptoms who kills when intoxicated after an argument, is unlikely to be successful; whereas a man with depression who feels hopeless and suicidal and is intoxicated when he kills his family before attempting to take his own life, would probably be successful in pleading diminished responsibility.

PROVOCATION AND DIMINISHED RESPONSIBILITY

Provocation is another ground on which a charge of murder may be **6–21** reduced to culpable homicide. However, the law on provocation is based on the proportionate reaction of the ordinary person, and the provocation needs to be immediate[74]. Expert evidence regarding the mental state of the accused is irrelevant to provocation as the test is to compare the accused to a non-mentally disordered ordinary man, and is to be assessed by the court objectively rather than subjectively.

If an individual with a mental disorder is provoked and the mental disorder lessens his ability to control his reactions, then the basis on which he must seek a reduction to culpable homicide is through diminished responsibility not provocation. Expert evidence therefore becomes relevant.

---

[72] Hare, R. D. (1991) *The Hare Psychopathy Checklist-Revised.* Toronto: Multi-Health Systems.

[73] *HMA v Bone*, 2002, unreported.

[74] Christie, M. G. A. (2001) *The Criminal Law of Scotland by Sir Gerald H. Gordon* (3rd ed.) Vol II., Edinburgh, W. Green.

If the provocation is chronic, and there is no provocation immediately before the killing then provocation may not be offered as a defence in itself. In this case the only way to reduce the charge to culpable homicide is if the chronic provocation has resulted in an abnormality of mind sufficient for diminished responsibility.

The above gives the strict legal interpretation. It should be noted that in reality when a jury returns a verdict of culpable homicide, or the Crown accepts a plea of guilty to culpable homicide, a number of factors may operate together, only one of which may be diminished responsibility. For example, a conviction for culpable homicide may be the result of a mixture of provocation, diminished responsibility and other factors negating the *mens rea* for murder, even though legally these should be considered separately.

DIMINISHED RESPONSIBILITY AND OFFENCES OTHER THAN MURDER

6–22   It is often stated that diminished responsibility is only relevant in murder cases. It is only in such cases that there is a mandatory life sentence so that mitigating factors, such as mental disorder, cannot be taken into consideration by the judge in determining the type of sentence to impose. For example, if a man with schizophrenia is convicted of murder he must be imprisoned, whereas a conviction for culpable homicide may result in a hospital disposal. If he is charged with attempted murder or assault and found guilty he may be hospitalized without any need to diminish his responsibility and decrease the gravity of the conviction; the nature of the conviction does not automatically determine the disposal, and discretion in sentencing is available. Therefore diminished responsibility is necessary in murder cases, but not with other offences, to provide flexibility in disposal.

In *HMA v Blake*[75] Lord Brand ruled that in a case where a man who was accused of attempted murder was unsuccessful with an insanity defence, the jury could give consideration to whether he might be "guilty of assault under deletion of attempted murder on the ground of diminished responsibility". In other cases it has been asserted that diminished responsibility is only relevant to murder[76]. In Scotland there are no fixed tariffs for offences other than murder, so mental disorder can be considered in mitigation at sentencing; therefore there would seem to be no utility in the application of diminished responsibility to other offences. However, legally it is unclear whether diminished responsibility does or does not apply to non-murder cases[77].

FREQUENCY OF USE OF INSANITY AND DIMINISHED RESPONSIBILITY

6–23   Table 1 shows the number of cases disposed of under insanity provisions (either insane in bar of trial or at the time of the offence) over the last decade. As can be seen, cases involving insanity procedures make up a

---

[75] *HMA v Blake*, 1986 S.L.T. 661 (an appeal against this decision did not proceed as Blake died).

[76] *HMA v Cunningham*, 1963 J.C. 80 and *Brennan v HMA*, 1977 J.C. 38.

[77] Scottish Law Commission (2003) *Discussion paper on insanity and diminished responsibility*, Edinburgh, The Stationery Office.

tiny minority of episodes of detention of mentally disordered offenders. There has not been a great increase in the number of insanity cases since the introduction of flexible disposals in 1995.

Table 1: Episodes of disposals under the insanity provisions of the Criminal Procedure (Scotland) Acts 1975 and 1995, compared with episodes of detention under other provisions for mentally disordered offenders, from 1992–3 to 2001–2. Figures are from the Annual Reports of the Mental Welfare Commission for Scotland[78].

	1992–1993	1993–1994	1994–1995	1995–1996	1996–1997	1997–1998	1998–1999	1999–2000	2000–2001	2001–2002
Insanity[1] (Restriction order)	–	–	–	–	4	5	2	1	4	6
Insanity[2] (Hospital order)	–	–	–	–	7	7	9	9	5	5
Insanity[3] (Total)	4	12	6	8	11	12	11	10	9	11
Hospital order with restrictions[4]	8	5	18	10	17	16	18	8	9	8
Hospital order without restrictions[5]	107	119	109	118	93	103	94	88	68	64
Hospital order (Total)	115	124	127	128	110	119	112	96	77	72
Other procedures for mentally disordered offenders[6]	289	352	330	256	385	347	345	242	283	275
Total	408	488	463	392	506	478	468	348	369	378

1. Criminal Procedure (Scotland) Act 1995, s.57(2)(b).
2. Criminal Procedure (Scotland) Act 1995, s.57(2)(a).
3. There is no breakdown available for restricted versus non-restricted hospital orders in insanity cases under ss.174 and 375 Criminal Procedure (Scotland) Act 1975, therefore only totals are given for the years covered by this Act.
4. ss.58 and 59 Criminal Procedure (Scotland) Act 1995, and previously ss.175 and 178 Criminal Procedure (Scotland) Act 1975 or ss.376 and 379 Criminal Procedure (Scotland) Act 1975.
5. s.58 Criminal Procedure (Scotland) Act 1995, and previously s.175 Criminal Procedure (Scotland) Act 1975 or s.376 Criminal Procedure (Scotland) Act 1975.
6. Remand orders, interim hospital orders and hospital directions under the Criminal Procedure (Scotland) Acts 1975 and 1995, and transfer orders and transfer directions under the Mental Health (Scotland) Act 1984.

N.B. Figures refer to episodes of detention under that provision in that year, so a patient on a particular charge or conviction may be represented more than once (*e.g.* if a patient was placed on a transfer order, then a remand order and then found insane in bar of trial he would be represented 3 times, once under each of the appropriate sections).

Research on the operation of insanity procedures over the 2 years after the introduction of the EOF and flexible disposals identified 52

---

[78] Mental Welfare Commission for Scotland (1993–2002) *Annual reports 1993–2002*, Edinburgh, Mental Welfare Commission for Scotland.

cases where insanity in bar of trial or at the time of the offence was raised[79]. Of these, 39 were in the Sheriff Court (9 on indictment and 30 summary cases) and 13 were in the High Court. In 37 cases there was a plea in bar of trial: 29 of these were found unfit to plead, 5 were found fit to plead, 2 cases were deserted by the Crown and in 1 case the plea was withdrawn. In 3 cases there was a plea in bar of trial along with an insanity defence and all 3 were successful. Of 12 insanity defences 10 were successful. There were 30 EOFs: 22 resulted in the facts being found, 3 in an acquittal on the grounds of insanity and in 5 cases the facts were not established. The disposals in the unfit to plead cases, where the facts were found, and in the insanity defence cases were: 9 hospital orders with restrictions on discharge, 26 non-restricted hospital orders, 5 supervision and treatment orders, 1 guardianship order and 3 cases where no order was made.

There are no specific figures available regarding diminished responsibility. Chiswick estimated that there were about 5 or 10 cases per year[80]. In 2000 there were 87 homicide offenders (murder and culpable homicide) dealt with by Scottish Courts: 74 received custodial disposals, 8 community disposals, 2 were admonished or absolutely discharged and 3 received mental health disposals[81]. There is no breakdown between murder and culpable homicide. Figures for 1991–2000 showed that of 1109 homicide cases, mental disorder was considered to be the motivation in 58 (5.2 per cent) cases. However the data does not allow for any conclusion as to the link between this "motivation" and a legal finding of diminished responsibility or insanity.

THE FUTURE

6–24 The consideration of the criteria for insanity in bar of trial, insanity at the time of the offence and diminished responsibility was outwith the remit of the Millan Committee[82] in its comprehensive review of mental health legislation in Scotland. However it did recommend that the Scottish Law Commission should review the law in this area. The Commission produced a discussion paper[83] and, following consultation on this, a final report[84], which included a draft Criminal Responsibility and Unfitness for Trial (Scotland) Bill.

The Commission proposed that the criteria for insanity in bar of trial, insanity at the time of the offence and diminished responsibility should be set out in statute using appropriate modern phraseology. The defence

---

[79] Burman, M. and Connelly, C. (1999) *Mentally Disordered Offenders and Criminal Proceedings*, Edinburgh, Scottish Office Central Research Unit.

[80] Chiswick, D. (1999) Mental Disorder and Criminal Justice. In *Criminal Justice in Scotland* (Ed.s P. Duff and N Hutton) Aldershot, Ashgate Dartmouth.

[81] Scottish Executive (2001) *Homicide in Scotland 2000*. Statistical Bulletin CrJ/2001/9, Edinburgh, Scottish Executive.

[82] Scottish Executive (2001) *Review of the Mental Health (Scotland) Act 1984*, Edinburgh, Scottish Executive.

[83] Scottish Law Commission (2003) *Discussion paper on insanity and diminished responsibility*, Edinburgh, The Stationery Office.

[84] Scottish Law Commission (2004) *Report on insanity and diminished responsibility*, Edinburgh, The Stationery Office.

of insanity would change to acquittal on the ground of mental disorder (as defined in the Mental Health (Care and Treatment) (Scotland) Act 2003); anti-social personality disorder would be excluded (but, surprisingly, not other personality disorders); and the defence would depend on the effect of the disorder being such that the person was unable to appreciate the nature or wrongfulness of their conduct. There would be no explicit volitional component to this definition. Diminished responsibility would retain a definition similar to that set out in *Galbraith*, and although voluntary intoxication would remain excluded, anti-social personality disorder would not. Insanity in bar of trial would become "unfitness for trial", and would be defined in terms of a mental or physical condition leading to lack of capacity to participate effectively in proceedings, with the court taking into consideration a non-exhaustive list of abilities that would contribute to this capacity. These are the ability to: understand the nature of the charge; understand the requirement to tender a plea to the charge and the effect of such a plea; understand the purpose of, and follow the course of, the trial; understand the evidence that may be given against the person; and instruct and otherwise communicate with the person's legal representative.

Case examples

Case 1. A 32-year-old woman was charged with breach of the peace **6–25** having been found naked, shouting in a busy shopping street. She had a previous history of bipolar affective disorder. When examined on remand by a psychiatrist she was disinhibited, her speech was rambling and almost incoherent, she had an inflated sense of her own abilities and was overly optimistic. She was diagnosed as suffering from mania and an opinion was given that she was insane and unfit to plead. She was placed on an assessment order at her next court appearance. Due to the relatively minor nature of the charge the procurator fiscal discontinued the case and she was then detained under civil procedure.

Case 2. A 25-year-old man was charged with the murder of his partner. He believed that she was conspiring with aliens, who had infiltrated the police and other organizations, to gather information about him so that he could be abducted and taken to their home planet to be experimented on. On remand in prison he stated that the court process was a farce and he could not subject himself to it as aliens had infiltrated the judiciary. Two psychiatrists gave opinions that he was suffering from paranoid schizophrenia, that he was unfit to plead and that he was insane at the time of the offence. He was found insane in bar of trial. At the examination of facts it was found that he had killed his partner, but he was acquitted on the grounds of insanity. He was given a compulsion order with a restriction order and admitted to the State Hospital.

Case 3. A 28-year-old woman was charged with the murder of her 3-year-old daughter. She had a history of depression following separation from her husband and had previously received anti-depressant medication and counselling. In the weeks prior to the homicide she had stopped taking her medication as she had felt well. She relapsed into depression, felt hopeless about the future and decided to kill herself. She also felt there was no hope for her daughter whom she wanted to take with her. She smothered her daughter with a pillow and then took a substantial overdose. She was placed on a pre-trial treatment order to a medium secure unit where her depression was treated. Psychiatric reports stated that she was sane and fit to plead and was not insane at the time of the offence. However, they stated that she was suffering from a depressive disorder at the time of the killing and had it not been for the presence of this it would not have occurred. A plea of guilty to culpable homicide on the grounds of diminished responsibility was accepted by the Crown and her disposal was a compulsion order to the medium secure unit.

CHAPTER 7[1]

LEGISLATION FOR MENTALLY DISORDERED OFFENDERS

INTRODUCTION

People with mental disorder may be arrested regarding, charged with **7–01** and convicted of criminal offences. Although, broadly, there is little association between mental disorder and offending, some particular types of mental disorder are associated with a greater likelihood of committing certain types of offences (see Chapter 1). Mentally disordered offenders may require assessment and/or treatment, and a number of procedures are available at the various stages of the criminal justice process allowing for the assessment and treatment of such offenders by mental health services. Such procedures are sometimes referred to as "diversion" as they allow mentally disordered offenders to be diverted, temporarily or permanently, from the criminal justice system to the health system.

Traditionally, only offenders found unfit to plead or insane at the time of an offence were given a health disposal (see Chapter 6). Mentally disordered offenders who did not reach the high threshold set by these procedures may have received psychiatric care if criminal proceedings were discontinued, but, particularly with serious crimes where discontinuation was unlikely, they would receive a criminal justice sanction. During the 20th century a number of procedures were introduced, allowing for diversion at various stages of the criminal justice process for mentally disordered offenders who were not insane, but nevertheless required health care. This culminated in what was described by Walker and McCabe, commenting on England and Wales, as the "utilitarian revolution" in the 1960s[2]. By this they were referring to the move from the legalistic approach of insanity to an approach based on the clinical needs and welfare of mentally disordered offenders. This "revolution" occurred in Scotland too, with the introduction of the Mental Health (Scotland) Act 1960. Under this act several procedures for mentally disordered offenders were introduced, which were based on similar criteria to those for civil procedure and which continue today (although amended by subsequent legislation).

The procedures in the 1960 Act were incorporated into the Criminal Procedure (Scotland) Act 1975; amended and added to by the Mental Health (Scotland) Act 1984; set out anew in the Criminal Procedure

---

[1] Chapter author: Dr Rajan Darjee MPhil.
[2] Walker, N. and McCabe, S. (1973) *Crime and Insanity in England. Volume Two: New Solutions and New Problems*, Edinburgh, Edinburgh University Press.

(Scotland) Act 1995; and were amended and added to again by the Crime and Punishment (Scotland) Act 1997 and the Adults with Incapacity (Scotland) Act 2000.

Procedures to be used by criminal courts for mentally disordered offenders continue to be set out under Part 6 of the Criminal Procedure (Scotland) Act 1995 (referred to in this chapter as "the 1995 Act"), but have been substantially amended by two new acts: the Mental Health (Care and Treatment) (Scotland) Act 2003 (referred to in this chapter as "the 2003 Act") and the Criminal Justice (Scotland) Act 2003. The changes brought about by Part 8 of the 2003 Act bring the various orders available into line with new civil procedure. However, an important difference between patients subject to civil procedure and those subject to criminal procedure is that the "impaired decision-making ability" criterion for compulsion does not apply. Parts 9 to 12 of the 2003 Act set out the procedure to be followed after a person has been made subject to a final mental health disposal made by a criminal court. Part 1 of the Criminal Justice (Scotland) Act 2003 amended the 1995 Act introducing measures for the assessment and sentencing of high-risk violent and sexual offenders, following the recommendations of the MacLean Committee[3]. Amended procedures for such offenders who suffer from mental disorder are also introduced by this act.

When assessing a person with mental disorder at any stage of the criminal justice process, the following need to be borne in mind:

- There should be a sound clinical assessment utilising as many sources of information as are available within the practical constraints imposed by the particular situation. As in any psychiatric assessment consideration needs to be given to

  ○ Diagnosis
  ○ Care and treatment needs
  ○ Prognosis
  ○ Risk to self and others

- Specific consideration needs to be given to the pertinent legal issues, *e.g.*:

  ○ Fitness to plead
  ○ Mental state at the time of the offence
  ○ Whether the person fulfils the criteria for a particular order

- The criminal justice context must be considered, *e.g.*:

  ○ Can this person be managed safely in police custody or prison?
  ○ Why did this person offend in this way at this time?
  ○ What role has mental disorder played in current and previous offending?
  ○ Is further assessment required to clarify any of the clinical or legal issues?

---

[3] Scottish Executive (2000) *Report of the Committee on Serious Violent and Sexual Offenders*, Edinburgh, Scottish Executive.

o If so, should this be in an inpatient setting (perhaps in a secure setting)?

The various stages of the criminal justice process are outlined in Chapter 5. In this chapter the various criminal procedures for mentally disordered offenders are set out in detail. Legal provisions relating to detention in secure hospitals are also described.

Measures introduced under the 2003 Act will commence in October 2005, at the same time as the various civil procedures. Appeals against being held in conditions of excessive security will commence in May 2006. The Criminal Justice (Scotland) Act 2003 will not commence until 2006; the measures to be introduced by this Act are set out at the end of this chapter. There is also a brief description of relevant provisions of the Sexual Offences Act 2003.

The procedures available at the various stages of the criminal justice process are illustrated in Figure 1. Table 1 indicates the sections of legislation that provide for the various procedures, showing analogous procedures prior to the Acts of 2003. Table 1 also sets out analogous procedures in England and Wales and Northern Ireland, which may be particularly useful for readers used to UK legislation outwith Scotland.

Table 1: Procedures available for the assessment and treatment of mentally disordered offenders at the various stages of the criminal justice process.

	Scotland		Analogous procedure in other UK jurisdictions	
	Previous procedure before the 2003 Act	**Current procedure following the 2003 Act**	**England & Wales**	**Northern Ireland**
Police				
Detention of mentally disordered person found in public place	s.118 MH(S)A 1984	s.297 MH(CT)(S)A 2003	s.136 MHA 1983	art.130 MH(NI)O 1986
Detention of mentally disordered person in private premises	s.117 MH(S)A 1984	s.293 MH(CT)(S)A 2003	s.135 MHA 1983	art.129 MH(NI)O 1986
Pre-trial				
Remand to hospital for assessment	s.52 CP(S)A 1995	s.52B–J CP(S)A 1995	s.35 MHA 1983	art.42 MH(NI)O 1986
Remand to hospital for treatment	–	s.52K–S CP(S)A 1995	s.36 MHA 1983	art.43 MH(NI)O 1986

	Scotland		Analogous procedure in other UK jurisdictions	
	Previous procedure before the 2003 Act	**Current procedure following the 2003 Act**	**England & Wales**	**Northern Ireland**
Transfer of untried prisoner to hospital	s.70 MH(S)A 1984	s.52B–J CP(S)A 1995 or s.52K–S CP(S)A 1995	s.48 MHA 1983	art.54 MH(NI)O 1986
Trial				
Criteria for fitness to plead	*HMA v Wilson Stewart v HMA*	*HMA v Wilson Stewart v HMA*	*R v Pritchard*	*R v Pritchard*
Procedure relating to a finding of unfitness to plead	ss.54–57 CP(S)A 1995	ss.54–57 CP(S)A 1995	ss.2–3 & Sch. 1–2 CP(IUP)A 1991	Arts 49 & 50A MH(NI)O 1986
Criteria for insanity at the time of the offence	*HMA v Kidd*	*HMA v Kidd*	*M'Naghten* Rules	CJA(NI)1966
Procedure relating to a finding of insanity at the time of the offence	ss.54 & 57 CP(S)A 1995	ss.54 & 57 CP(S)A 1995	ss.1&3 & Schs 1–2 CP(IUP)A 1991	Arts 50 & 50A CJ(NI)O 1996
Criteria for diminished responsibility	*Galbraith v HMA*	*Galbraith v HMA*	s.2 Homicide Act 1957	CJ(NI)O 1996
Post-conviction but pre-sentence				
Remand to hospital for assessment	s.200 CP(S)A 1995	s.52B–J CP(S)A 1995 s.200 CP(S)A 1995	s.35 MHA 1983	art.42 MH(NI)O 1986
Remand to hospital for treatment	–	s.52K–S CP(S)A 1995	s.36 MHA 1983	art.43 MH(NI)O 1986
Interim hospital/ compulsion order	s.53 CP(S)A 1995	s.53 CP(S)A 1995	s.38 MHA 1983	–
Transfer of unsentenced prisoner to hospital	s.70 MH(S)A 1984	s.52B–J CP(S)A 1995 or s.52K–S CP(S)A 1995	s.48 MHA 1983	art.54 MH(NI)O 1986

	Scotland		Analogous procedure in other UK jurisdictions	
	Previous procedure before the 2003 Act	**Current procedure following the 2003 Act**	**England & Wales**	**Northern Ireland**
Sentence				
Compulsory treatment in hospital under MHA	s.58 CP(S)A 1995	s.57A CP(S)A 1995	s.37 MHA 1983	art.44 MH(NI)O 1986
Restriction order	s.59 CP(S)A 1995	s.59 CP(S)A 1995	s.41 MHA 1983	art.47 MH(NI)O 1986
Hybrid order (hospital disposal with prison sentence)	s.59A CP(S)A 1995	s.59A CP(S)A 1995	s.45A–B MHA 1983	–
Compulsory treatment in community under MHA	–	s.57A CP(S)A 1995	–	–
Guardianship	s.58(1A) CP(S)A 1995	s.58(1A) CP(S)A 1995	s.37 MHA 1983	art.44 MH(NI)O 1986
Intervention order for incapable adult	s.60B CP(S)A 1995	s.60B CP(S)A 1995	–	–
Psychiatric probation order	s.230 CP(S)A 1995	s.230 CP(S)A 1995	Sch.2 (para.5) Powers of Criminal Courts (Sentencing) Act 2000	Sch.1 (para.4) CJ(NI)O 1996
Post-sentence				
Transfer of sentenced prisoners to hospital	s.71 MH(S)A 1984	s.136 MH(CT)(S)A 2003	s.47 MHA 1983	art.53 MH(NI)O 1986
Restriction direction for transferred prisoner	s.72 MH(S)A 1984	*	s.49 MHA 1983	art.55 MH(NI)O 1986

'a' = article; 'p' = paragraph; 's' = section; 'sch' = schedule; 'CJA(NI)1966' = Criminal Justice Act (Northern Ireland) 1966; 'CJ(NI)O1996' = Criminal Justice (Northern Ireland) Order 1996; 'CP(IUP)A1991' = Criminal Procedure (Insanity and Unfitness to Plead) Act 1991; 'CP(S)A1995' = Criminal Procedure (Scotland) Act 1995; 'MHA' = Mental Health Act (in the relevant jurisdiction); 'MHA1983' = Mental Health Act 1983; 'MH(CT)(S)A2003' = Mental Health (Care and Treatment) (Scotland) Act 2003; 'MH(NI)O1986' = Mental Health (Northern Ireland) Order 1986; 'MH(S)A1984' = Mental Health (Scotland) Act 1984; '-' = no such procedure in this jurisdiction; * = all s.136 MH(CT)(S)A2003 transfer directions in Scotland are restricted.

Figure 1:

A schematic overview of procedures for people with mental disorders at the various stages of the criminal justice process.

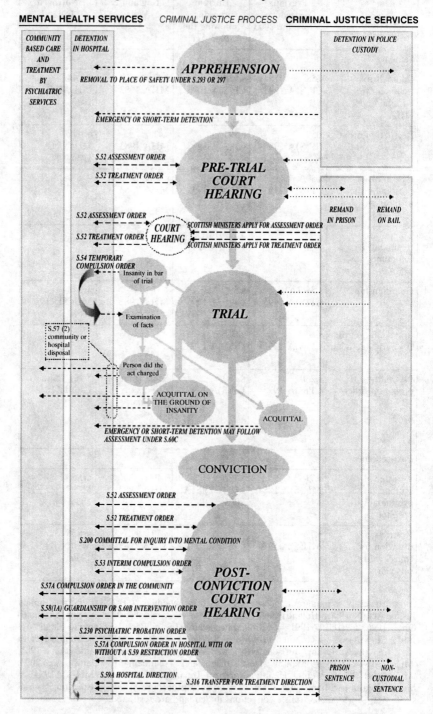

SPECIFIC PROCEDURES FOR MENTALLY DISORDERED OFFENDERS

Detailed information on the various procedures available for mentally **7–02** disordered individuals subject to the criminal justice process is set out in this section. The various procedures are summarised in Table 2.

Table 2: Summary of criminal procedures for mentally disordered offenders.

Name of provision	Section of CP(S)A1995	Criminal justice issues	Psychiatric issues	Effects
Assessment order	52B–J	Unconvicted or unsentenced. Sheriff court or High Court. Application can be made to court by prosecutor, Scottish Ministers or court may make order on own initiative.	Evidence from one doctor. Reasonable grounds to believe: there is mental disorder, detention in hospital necessary to determine if meets criteria for treatment order & if not assessed in hospital would pose a significant risk to self or others. Suitable hospital bed available within seven days.	Detention in hospital for up to 28 days for report to be prepared by RMO. Can be extended once for 7 days. Compulsory treatment can only be given after getting an opinion from an approved doctor who is not the RMO.
Treatment order	52K–S	Unconvicted or unsentenced. Sheriff court or High Court. Application can be made to court by prosecutor, Scottish Ministers or court may make order on own initiative.	Evidence from two doctors (one approved). There is mental disorder, treatment which would be likely to prevent worsening of or alleviate aspects of the disorder is available; without such treatment the person would pose a significant risk to their health, safety or welfare or to others. Suitable hospital bed available within seven days.	Detention in hospital until conviction (if made pre-conviction) or until court makes final disposal (if made pre-sentence). Compulsory treatment can be given. May be terminated early by the court at the request of the RMO.
Interim compulsion order	53	Convicted in High Court or sheriff court of offence punishable by imprisonment but for which the sentence is not fixed by law (*i.e.* not murder). Must appear to pose a considerable risk such that consideration is being given to a compulsion order with a restriction order or a hospital direction.	Evidence from two doctors (one approved). There is mental disorder & reasonable grounds to believe: treatment which would be likely to prevent worsening of or alleviate aspects of the disorder is available, without such treatment the person would pose a significant risk to their health, safety or welfare or to others. Suitable hospital bed available within seven days.	Detention in hospital for up to 12 weeks. Compulsory treatment may be given. Renewable for 12 weeks at a time up to 1 year. At the end of the interim compulsion order the court may impose any disposal it sees fit (penal or mental health).

Name of provision	Section of CP(S)A1995	Criminal justice issues	Psychiatric issues	Effects
Remand to hospital for inquiry into mental condition	200	Convicted in High Court or sheriff court of offence punishable by imprisonment.	Evidence from one doctor. Appears to be suffering from mental disorder.	Detention in hospital for three weeks. Compulsory treatment may not be given. May be renewed once for further three weeks.
Compulsion order	57A	Convicted in High Court or sheriff court of offence punishable by imprisonment but for which the sentence is not fixed by law (*i.e.* not murder).	Evidence from two doctors (one approved). There is mental disorder, treatment which would be likely to prevent worsening of or alleviate aspects of the disorder is available, without such treatment the person would pose a significant risk to their health, safety or welfare or to others. If hospital detention is to be authorised: the treatment must be such that it could only be provided in hospital & a suitable hospital bed must be available within seven days.	May authorise compulsion in hospital or the community for six months initially. Compulsory treatment may be given. If in the community may also require: attendance for treatment and to receive other services, residence at specified place, access to be given to RMO, MHO and other relevant staff. Care plan must be prepared by RMO. May be extended by six months following application to MHT. Subsequently may be renewed for 12 months at a time. MHT must review at least every two years and patient may appeal to MHT annually. RMO may revoke order, but must apply to MHT to vary order.
Restriction order	59	Compulsion order authorising detention in hospital has been made. Having regard to the nature of the offence, the antecedents of the person and the risk of his committing further offences if set at large; it is necessary for the protection of the public from serious harm to impose special restrictions on the patient. Interim compulsion order should be imposed first unless it is clearly not appropriate to do so.	Oral evidence from one of the doctors recommending the compulsion order must be heard.	Restriction order is applied without limit of time. The compulsion order does not need to be renewed. Only MHT may revoke (absolute discharge) or conditionally discharge patients. Leave and transfer (but not discharge) must be approved by Scottish Ministers.

Name of provision	Section of CP(S)A1995	Criminal justice issues	Psychiatric issues	Effects
Hospital direction	*59A*	Convicted in High Court or sheriff court on indictment of offence punishable by imprisonment. Interim compulsion order should be imposed first unless it is clearly not appropriate to do so. Should be imposed in cases where there is little or no link between the mental disorder and the offence and/or the risk of further offending.	Evidence from two doctors (one approved). There is mental disorder, treatment which would be likely to prevent worsening of or alleviate aspects of the disorder is available, without such treatment the person would pose a significant risk to their health, safety or welfare or to others. A suitable hospital bed must be available within seven days.	'Hybrid order' allowing detention in hospital in parallel with imposition of a prison sentence. Patient remains a restricted patient whilst in hospital as long as the prison sentence lasts. If patient no longer requires treatment in hospital then transferred to prison. If remains in hospital at end of prison sentence then may be discharged or detained under civil order.
Guardianship order	*58(1A)*	Convicted in High Court or sheriff court of offence punishable by imprisonment but for which the sentence is not fixed by law (*i.e.* not murder).	Evidence from two doctors (one approved) that there is mental disorder and the person has incapacity in relation to the relevant personal welfare issues.	Guardianship order under sections 57–76 Adults with Incapacity (Scotland) Act 2000.
Intervention order	*60B*	Convicted in High Court or sheriff court of offence punishable by imprisonment but for which the sentence is not fixed by law (*i.e.* not murder).	Evidence from two doctors (one approved) that there is mental disorder and the person has incapacity in relation to the relevant personal welfare issue.	Intervention order under sections 53–56 Adults with Incapacity (Scotland) Act 2000.
Psychiatric probation order	*230*	Convicted in High Court or sheriff court. The offender and the supervising officer (a criminal justice social worker) must agree to the order.	Evidence from one approved doctor and, if this doctor will not be responsible for the treatment, from the doctor or psychologist who will. There is a mental condition which requires or may be susceptible to treatment, but a compulsion order is not warranted. Relevant services are appropriate and available.	Treatment as inpatient or outpatient under direction of registered doctor or chartered psychologist. Maximum period three years. Compulsory treatment may not be given.

The criteria for the application of the various orders available for mentally disordered persons involved in criminal proceedings are best understood with reference to the criteria for the application of compulsory treatment orders (CTOs) for civil compulsion. Section 57 of the 2003 Act states:

"(3) This subsection applies where each of the medical practitioners who carries out a medical examination mentioned in subsection (2) above is satisfied-:

(a) that the patient has a mental disorder;
(b) that medical treatment which would be likely to-

(i) prevent the mental disorder worsening; or
(ii) alleviate any of the symptoms, or effects, of the disorder,

is available for the patient;

(c) that if the patient were not provided with such medical treatment there would be a significant risk-

(i) to the health, safety or welfare of the patient; or
(ii) to the safety of any other person;

(d) that because of the mental disorder the patient's ability to make decisions about the provision of such medical treatment is significantly impaired; and
(e) that the making of a compulsory treatment order is necessary."

In this section, (a) will be referred to as the 'mental disorder' criterion; (b) as the 'treatability' criterion; (c) as the 'civil risk' criterion; (d) as the 'impaired decision-making ability' criterion; and (e) as the 'necessity of the order' criterion. The main difference between the criteria for all the orders for mentally disordered offenders and theses criteria is that the 'impaired decision-making ability' criterion does not apply.

ASSESSMENT ORDER AND TREATMENT ORDER (S.52 OF THE 1995 ACT)

Background

7–03   The assessment order[4] and treatment order[5] allow for the detention in hospital of a mentally disordered person at the pre-trial or pre-sentence stage. They should be seen as part of the same process, which allows for the hospital assessment and treatment of mentally disordered offenders who are facing criminal charges. Previously a remand to hospital under s.52 was only available pre-trial and did not allow for treatment. Now there are provisions allowing for assessment and treatment, and the orders are available either pre-trial or pre-sentence. Another change is that previously there was a separate procedure allowing for the transfer of remand prisoners to hospital for treatment, but not assessment[6]; the assessment and treatment order replace this as, along with being made at a court hearing as part of the criminal justice process, either may also be made following an application by the Scottish Ministers where a person is remanded in custody.

In most cases an assessment order would usually be applied first, with the patient then moving onto a treatment order if necessary. However there is nothing to stop a treatment order being applied directly, without the assessment order first, if the required evidence is available.

---

[4] Criminal Procedure (Scotland) Act 1995, s.52B–J.
[5] *ibid.*, s.52M–S.
[6] Mental Health (Scotland) Act 1984, s.70.

At What Stage of the Criminal Justice Process are the Assessment Order and the Treatment Order Available?

These orders can be made at any stage of the criminal justice process **7–04** between the first court appearance after arrest and the final sentence being imposed, *i.e.* pre-trial or post-conviction/pre-sentence. They can be made at a court hearing as part of the criminal justice process, or where a person is on remand in custody a specific court hearing can occur following an application for an order to be made. These orders may be made in a sheriff court or in the High Court.

Who Applies for an Assessment Order or a Treatment Order?

At a pre-trial court appearance an application for either order may be **7–05** made by the prosecutor or a judge may make an order on his own initiative. Post-conviction/pre-sentence an order can be made by the judge on his own initiative. Where a prisoner is on remand in custody the application must be made by the Scottish Ministers.

What Evidence is Required?

Assessment order

There must be written or oral evidence from one registered medical **7–06** practitioner. On the basis of this evidence the court must be satisfied that there are reasonable grounds to believe:

- The 'mental disorder' criterion is met
- Detention in hospital is necessary to determine if the patient meets criteria for a treatment order (see below)
- The 'civil risk' criterion is met
- A suitable hospital bed is available within seven days
- The assessment could not be undertaken if the person were not detained in hospital

The court must also consider the making of the assessment order to be appropriate after considering:

- All the circumstances (including the nature of the offence)
- Any alternative means of dealing with the person

Treatment order

There must be written or oral evidence from two registered medical practitioners, one of whom must be approved[7]. On the basis of this evidence the court must be satisfied that:

- The 'mental disorder' criterion is met
- The 'treatability' criterion is met
- The 'civil risk' criterion is met
- A suitable hospital bed is available within seven days

---

[7] Mental Health (Care and Treatment) (Scotland) Act 2003, s.22.

As with the assessment order the court must also consider the making of the treatment order to be appropriate after considering:

- All the circumstances (including the nature of the offence)
- Any alternative means of dealing with the person

What Happens When a Person is Subject to an Assessment Order?

Admission to hospital

7–07   The person must be admitted to the hospital specified in the order within seven days. He may be kept in a place of safety pending admission; this could be in prison. However, in most cases patients will be admitted to hospital on the day the court makes the order. If during these seven days it becomes apparent, due to emergency or special circumstances, that it is not reasonably practical to admit the person to the original hospital, then alternative arrangements may be made for admission elsewhere if authorised by the court or Scottish Ministers. For example, the person's mental state may deteriorate and the risk posed may increase so that they require a more secure hospital placement.

The person may be conveyed to hospital by the police, a person employed by or authorised by the hospital, or by another specified person. New arrangements for the transportation of patients to and from court, in line with those for prisoners, by private contractors, are to be introduced.

When in hospital

7–08   An assessment order allows detention in hospital for 28 days, which may be extended on one occasion for a further 7 days. If the patient does not have a RMO or MHO these must be appointed. A multi-disciplinary assessment should be undertaken. The RMO has a statutory duty[8] to submit a *report* to the court before the end of the assessment order addressing whether the patient meets the criteria for a treatment order. In addition the RMO should address any other issues that may have been specified by the court when the assessment order was made.

It should be noted that in effect there are two processes occurring in parallel: (1) the assessment order to treatment order process, via the s.52G report, which in some ways mirrors the short-term detention to compulsory treatment order process under civil procedure; and (2) the criminal justice process, which in the case of mentally disordered offenders requires the court to consider specific issues such as fitness to plead, responsibility, risk and appropriate disposal. In summary cases it is unlikely that the remand period (which is up to 40 days) will extend beyond the period of the assessment order, so it is likely that both processes will be considered together. In solemn cases, where the remand period (of up to 110 days) may extend far beyond the assessment order period, it is likely that these processes will be considered separately.

When a patient is admitted on an assessment order the MHO has a statutory duty to produce a *Social Circumstances Report* (SCR) within 21

---

[8] Criminal Procedure (Scotland) Act 1995, s.52G.

days, unless it is considered that it would serve no useful purpose. The main reason for the latter would be where a SCR had recently been submitted in relation to a previous order.

Emergency *treatment* under s.243 of the 2003 Act may be given, but medical treatment under Part 16 of that Act may only be given if this is determined to be in the patient's best interests by an approved medical practitioner who is not the patient's RMO and this determination is recorded in writing[9].

If the patient *absconds* they may be detained, taken into custody and returned to hospital. The court and the Scottish Executive should be notified. The court may, perhaps with the advice of the RMO, MHO and clinical team, wish to revoke or vary the order under such circumstances.

Periods of leave may be arranged using *suspension of detention* procedures[10]. A certificate authorizing leave may only be issued by the RMO with the consent of the Scottish Ministers. The certificate may specify where the patient may go, for how long and that an escort is required.

The RMO may apply to the court at any stage for the assessment order to be *revoked* or *varied*. Revocation may be requested, for example, where it becomes clear that the person does not suffer from a mental disorder. Variation may perhaps be requested where it becomes clear that the hospital is not secure enough for the assessment to continue.

The end of the order

The assessment order ends at any of the following stages: **7–09**

- After 28 days, or 35 days if extended by 7 days by the court
- When revoked by the court
- When the court makes a treatment order
- At the pre-trial stage when the person is convicted or acquitted or, in some cases, where proceedings are dropped
- At the post-conviction stage where the court defers sentence, makes an interim compulsion order, or makes a final disposal (whether mental health or penal)

What Happens When a Person is Subject to a Treatment Order?

In many ways what happens after a treatment order is made is very **7–10** similar to that for an assessment order. The main differences are:

- Treatment under Part 16 of the 2003 Act may be given.
- There is no time-limit for a treatment order; it ends:
  - When revoked by the court, or
  - At the pre-trial stage when the person is convicted or acquitted or, in some cases, where proceedings are dropped, or

---

[9] Mental Health (Care and Treatment) (Scotland) Act 2003, s.242(5).
[10] *ibid.*, s.221.

    ○ At the post-conviction stage where the court defers
    sentence, makes an interim compulsion order, or makes a
    final disposal

During a treatment order further reports will have to be prepared by
the RMO, and perhaps the MHO, as requested by the court. These
should address the pertinent issues at the relevant stage of the criminal
justice process, whether pre-trial or pre-sentence.

The following issues are dealt with in an identical way as for
assessment orders:

- Admission to hospital
- Absconding
- Revocation and variation

Provisions for suspension of detention are similar, but not identical[11].
The main difference is that specific time limits are set out as to the
amount of leave allowed. (These leave procedures for treatment orders
are identical to those for interim compulsion orders, compulsion orders
with restriction orders, hospital directions and transfer for treatment
directions which are also covered by s.224; see below.)

PRE-SENTENCE INQUIRY INTO MENTAL OR PHYSICAL CONDITION (S.200 OF
THE 1995 ACT)

Background

7–11   Section 200 allows a court to remand a convicted person in custody or
on bail for an assessment of his mental or physical condition. Where this
assessment is of his mental condition then it also allows for a remand in
hospital. This procedure has been available for over 50 years and is not
changed by the 2003 Act. However, previously this was the only
procedure available for the assessment of mentally disordered offenders
in hospital pre-sentence; s.52 procedures were not available post-
conviction. Now that the new s.52 procedures (the assessment and
treatment orders) are also available post-conviction, although s.200
continues to allow inpatient assessment of mentally disordered
offenders, its use for this purpose will be unusual. It will continue to be
the procedure used by courts to allow an assessment of a person's mental
condition on bail or on remand in prison, where a hospital based
assessment is not indicated or is not possible; and it will also continue to
allow courts to seek assessment of a person's physical condition, again
whilst on bail or on remand in prison.

What are the Criteria for a s.200 Order?

7–12   A remand on bail or in custody may be ordered by a court where:

- The person has been convicted of an offence punishable with
imprisonment

---

[11] Mental Health (Care and Treatment) (Scotland) Act 2003, s.224.

- It appears to the court that inquiry should be made into his mental or physical condition

Hospital detention may be ordered if:

- The person appears to be suffering from mental disorder according to the evidence of one registered medical practitioner
- There is a suitable hospital placement available

The criteria for detention in hospital under s.200 are therefore less stringent than for an assessment order, although in practice there may be little difference between the two. In most circumstances an assessment order should be used.

What Happens When a Person is Subject to a s.200 Order?

Hospital committal

The duration of the order is three weeks, which can be renewed on **7–13** one occasion for a further three weeks. In most cases instead of renewal, if further detention in hospital is required before final disposal, it would be more appropriate to recommend an assessment or treatment order.

There are no specific statutory procedures relating to the process of admission to hospital, appointment of a RMO and MHO, treatment in hospital, absconding or leave. It would be good practice to adopt a similar approach as applies to assessment orders.

During the period in hospital the court will usually request that further psychiatric reports are prepared to inform subsequent disposal. If it becomes clear that continued detention in hospital is no longer required (for example the person does not have a mental disorder) then an application may be made to the court, before the order expires, for the order to be revoked.

Remand on bail

The person must attend to be assessed by one or two medical **7–14** practitioners, as specified by the court. It may be a condition of bail that the person resides in hospital to be assessed, but in cases where the assessment of mental disorder is at issue hospital committal, as set out above, or more usually an assessment order (see above) should be the preferred option.

Remand in custody

This can be used where mental disorder is an issue, but where the court does not have the required medical evidence for an assessment order or committal to hospital, or where there is conflicting evidence and further assessment is required. A medical practitioner should not recommend that a person is remanded in prison. When a person is remanded in custody under s.200 one or two psychiatric reports will usually be requested in the same way as set out above for remands on bail.

INTERIM COMPULSION ORDER (S.53 OF THE 1995 ACT)

Background

7-15   The interim compulsion order under s.53 is the new term for the interim hospital order. It allows for the inpatient assessment and treatment of mentally disordered offenders who have been convicted of serious offences and/or where there is concern that the person might pose a serious risk in the future. The order may last from 3 to 12 months and allows for a thorough assessment of diagnosis, risk, treatment needs and response to treatment.

The main changes from the previous interim hospital order are:

- The order may be renewed for up to 12 weeks at a time rather than 4 weeks
- It is no longer specified that the order is to be made in cases where a final disposal to the State Hospital is being considered
- Previously, except under special circumstances, the State Hospital had to be the hospital specified for detention under an interim hospital order—this is no longer the case
- It is now specified as being only for cases where the final disposals being considered are a compulsion order with a restriction order or a hospital direction
- These disposals may not be made unless the person has been on an interim compulsion order first, except where not appropriate

At What Stage of the Criminal Justice Process is the Interim Compulsion Order Available?

7-16   An interim compulsion order may be made by a sheriff court or the High Court, where a person has been convicted of an offence punishable by imprisonment, but not where the sentence is fixed by law (*i.e.* murder).

What Evidence is Required?

7-17   There must be written or oral evidence from two registered medical practitioners, one of whom is approved[12]. On the basis of this evidence the court must be satisfied that:

- The 'mental disorder' criterion is met
- There are reasonable grounds for believing that

  ○ The 'treatability' criterion is met
  ○ The 'civil risk' criterion is met

- There are reasonable grounds to believe that the final disposal should be a compulsion order with a restriction order or a hospital direction
- A suitable hospital bed is available within seven days

---

[12] Mental Health (Care and Treatment) (Scotland) Act 2003, s.22.

As with other orders, the court must also consider the making of the interim compulsion order to be appropriate after considering:

- All the circumstances (including the nature of the offence)
- Any alternative means of dealing with the person.

What Happens When a Person is Subject to an Interim Compulsion Order?

Admission to hospital

Procedures relating to admission to hospital are identical to **7–18** assessment and treatment orders (see above).

In hospital

An interim compulsion order allows detention in hospital for up to 12 **7–19** weeks, which may be extended on three occasions up to a total of 12 months. If the patient does not have a RMO or MHO these must be appointed and a multi-disciplinary assessment should be undertaken. The RMO has a statutory duty[13] to submit a *report* to the court before the expiry of the interim compulsion order addressing:

- The type(s) of mental disorder present
- Whether the 'treatability' and 'civil risk' criteria are met
- Whether extension of the interim compulsion order is necessary

Where renewal is recommended, a recommendation may be made for the patient to be admitted to a different hospital, if this is necessary (for example, because the person requires a more or less secure unit).

Interim compulsion orders allow a thorough, prolonged inpatient assessment of serious offenders with mental disorder. During the order the following issues will need to be assessed:

- What is the prognosis of the mental disorder and what will be the response to treatment?
- What is the relationship between the mental disorder and the offence?
- What risk does the offender pose and what is the contribution to this risk made by mental disorder?

These issues should be addressed in the final report(s) submitted during the interim order, which should set out whether the final disposal should be a compulsion order with a restriction order or a hospital direction (or perhaps another mental health disposal).

When a patient is admitted on an interim compulsion order the MHO has a statutory duty to produce a *Social Circumstances Report* (SCR) within 21 days, unless he considers that it would serve no useful purpose.

Medical *treatment* under Pt 16 of the 2003 Act may be given.

If the patient *absconds* they may be detained taken into custody and returned to hospital. The court and the Scottish Executive should be

---

[13] Criminal Procedure (Scotland) Act 1995, s.53B(1).

notified. The court may, perhaps with the advice of the RMO, MHO and clinical team, wish to revoke or vary the order under such circumstances.

Periods of leave may be arranged using *suspension of detention* procedures[14]. A certificate authorizing leave may only be issued by the RMO with the consent of the Scottish Ministers. The certificate may specify where the patient may go, for how long and that an escort is required. Specific time limits are placed on the amount of leave allowed.

There is no specific statutory procedure allowing for the *revocation or variation* of the interim compulsion order outwith the hearings at which the court may consider renewal of the order. In the unlikely circumstance that revocation or variation seems necessary before the court is due to reconsider the case, then the RMO should write to the court requesting that the hearing be brought forward.

End of the interim compulsion order

7–20   An interim compulsion order ends when the court makes:

- A compulsion order (with or without a restriction order)
- A hospital direction
- Any other final mental health disposal
- Any penal disposal (including imprisonment or a deferred sentence)

COMPULSION ORDER (s.57A OF THE 1995 ACT)

Background

7–21   The compulsion order under s.57A replaces the old hospital order[15], in the same way that the CTO replaces long-term detention for treatment[16] under civil procedure. In line with changes to civil procedure, the compulsion order allows a court to impose hospital or community based treatment on a mentally disordered offender. The effect of a compulsion order is almost identical to that of a CTO.

At What Stage of the Criminal Justice Process can a Compulsion Order be Made?

7–22   A compulsion order may be made by a sheriff court or the High Court, where a person has been convicted of an offence punishable by imprisonment, but not where the sentence is fixed by law (*i.e.* murder).

What Evidence is Required?

7–23   There must be written or oral evidence from two registered medical practitioners, one of whom is approved[17]. On the basis of this evidence the court must be satisfied that:

---

[14] Mental Health (Care and Treatment) (Scotland) Act 2003, s.224.
[15] Criminal Procedure (Scotland) Act 1995, s.58 (prior to amendment by Mental Health (Care and Treatment) (Scotland) Act 2003).
[16] Mental Health (Scotland) Act 1984, s.18.
[17] Mental Health (Care and Treatment) (Scotland) Act 2003, s.22.

- The 'mental disorder' criterion is met
- The 'treatability' criterion is met
- The 'civil risk' criterion is met
- If a hospital based order is to be made

    o A suitable hospital bed is available within seven days
    o In a case where detention at a state hospital is to be authorised the person must meet the statutory criteria for this (see below)

The court should also in all but exceptional cases consider a report by the MHO[18] setting out:

- The personal circumstance of the patient relevant to the recommendation for a compulsion order
- Any other relevant information, which may include similar matters to those to be considered in an MHO report for a CTO under civil procedure

The MHO must prepare this report unless he considers this to be impracticable.

As with other orders, the court must consider the making of the compulsion order to be appropriate after considering:

- All the circumstances (including the nature of the offence)
- Any alternative means of dealing with the person

It must also consider the making of the compulsion order to be necessary.

The relevant issues should be addressed by the medical practitioners and MHO in the same way as they would be addressed in determining the appropriateness of a CTO under civil procedure. If a hospital-based order is recommended then reasons should be given why a community-based order is not appropriate, and the level of security of the hospital or unit should be no more than is necessary to manage the risk the person poses to himself or others.

If a community-based order is recommended then the personnel and services required should be put in place before the recommendation is made, and should be specified in the reports. The medical recommendations and the MHO report should set out the compulsory measures which it is considered should be authorised by the order (see below).

What Happens When a Person is Subject to a Compulsion Order?

Hospital-based order

A hospital-based compulsion order allows identical procedures for the **7–24** admission of a person to hospital as for assessment and treatment orders. The person may be detained in the specified hospital and may be

---

[18] Criminal Procedure (Scotland) Act 1995, s.57C.

given medical treatment for mental disorder under Part 16 of the 2003 Act. This is identical to measures available where a hospital-based CTO is made.

Community-based order

A community-based compulsion order may authorise any of the following (as is the case with a community-based CTO):

- Medical treatment under Part 16 of the 2003 Act
- A requirement to attend specific or directed places for medical treatment, on specific or directed dates or at specific or directed intervals
- A requirement to attend community care services, relevant services, or any treatment, care or service, on specific or directed dates or at specific or directed intervals
- A requirement to reside at a specific place (if this is a care home service then the court must be satisfied that this is willing to receive the person)
- A requirement to allow the MHO, RMO and/or other relevant mental health personnel authorised by the RMO access to visit the person
- A requirement that the person obtain the permission of the MHO before changing address
- A requirement to inform the MHO of any change of address before it happens

Procedures relating to non-compliance and non-attendance are identical to those for CTOs.

Matters to be addressed soon after the compulsion order is made

If not already designated, then a RMO and MHO should be appointed. The RMO should prepare a 'Part 9 Care Plan'. This care plan should be similar to that for a CTO. This should have been considered before recommendations for a compulsion order were made, although there is no statutory obligation to produce a proposed care plan before the compulsion order is made, unlike the CTO. The criminal court making the compulsion order does not need a proposed care plan before it, although components of the future care plan will have to be considered when the court sets out the relevant compulsory measures authorised by the order. The Part 9 Care Plan should contain the same core information as the care plan for a CTO, but it will also include the details of the index offence and, for certain patients, details of whether they may be subject to further notification and supervision requirements on transfer or discharge (for example Schedule 1 offenders and sex offenders).

Review and renewal

The process for the renewal and review of a compulsion order are virtually identical to those for a CTO (see Chapter 3), noting the following differences:

- The criteria to consider when making or renewing a CO are identical to those for the making of a CTO, except that for a CO the 'impaired decision-making ability' criterion does not apply.
- A patient subject to a CO must be reviewed by the Tribunal if the order is to be renewed after the first six months, whereas renewal of a CTO may proceed without such a hearing. This is because the Tribunal will not have reviewed a patient subject to a CO at the time of the making of the order as this will have been made by a criminal court. Further renewals may be made without referral to a Tribunal as for a CTO.

As with the CTO the compulsion order lasts six months, may be extended by a further six months, and then may be renewed annually.

RESTRICTION ORDER (S.59 OF THE 1995 ACT)

Background

A restriction order may be made by a court when making a hospital-based compulsion order. It is applied in cases where there is felt to be the potential for serious future risk to others, and allows for extra scrutiny and control of patients as they progress through mental health services from secure hospital care towards the community. A restriction order takes decisions regarding leave, transfer and discharge of patients away from the RMO, giving them instead to the Tribunal and Scottish Ministers. The criteria for making a restriction order are not changed by the 2003 Act, but there are changes to the procedure to be followed when a patient is subject to a restriction order. **7–25**

Criteria for Making a Restriction Order

The court making the compulsion order (to hospital), in addition to which the restriction order will be made, must hear oral evidence from at least one medical practitioner who recommended the compulsion order. The medical practitioner may or may not recommend that a restriction order be made, but the court may make the order anyway[19]. If there has not been a period of assessment on an interim compulsion order, then there should be a good reason for not making such an order first. **7–26**

The court must be satisfied that the criteria for making a restriction order[20] are met:

(a) having regard to the nature of the offence with which he is charged;
(b) the antecedents of the person; and
(c) the risk that as a result of his mental disorder he would commit offences if set at large,

---

[19] For example the decision in *Thomson v HMA*, Appeal Court, High Court of Justiciary, June 25, 1999 *http://www.scotcourts.gov.uk/opinionsv/c18399.html*.

[20] Criminal Procedure (Scotland) Act 1995, s.59(1).

that it is necessary for the protection of the public from serious harm so to do, the court may, subject to the provisions of this section, further order that the person shall be subject to the special restrictions set out in Part 10 of the 2003 Act, without limit of time.

For a restriction order to be made there should be a significant link between the mental disorder specified in the compulsion order and the risk of further offending. If this is not the case then a more appropriate disposal may be a hospital direction (see below).

What Happens When a Person is Subject to a Compulsion Order with a Restriction Order?

7–27   A compulsion order with a restriction order leads to the detention of the offender in hospital (a compulsion order in the community cannot be made with a restriction order) and instead of the compulsion order lasting only six months the duration of compulsion is indefinite— sometimes described as *"without limit of time"*. A restriction order cannot be made for a time-limited period. There is no requirement that a patient on a restriction order be admitted to a secure hospital, but in practice this is almost always the case.

The procedure to be followed where a patient is subject to a compulsion order with a restriction order is set out under Part 10 of the 2003 Act.

REVIEW

7–28   A compulsion order with a restriction order can only be changed (*i.e.* discharge from hospital or the restriction order terminated with continuation of the compulsion order) by the Tribunal. Previously the Scottish Ministers also had this power, but this is no longer the case. The Scottish Ministers still have the power to authorise leave and transfer between hospitals (see below). Unlike a compulsion order without a restriction order, the RMO and the MWC have no power to change the order directly.

RMO Duty to Review

7–29   The RMO, in consultation with the MHO and other members of the clinical team, must review the restriction order annually[21] and submit a report[22]. This report must consider whether the criteria for the restriction order and compulsion order continue to be met and whether the patient should continue to be detained in hospital. These criteria are the same as those that a Tribunal must consider when reviewing the case of a patient subject to a compulsion order with a restriction order (see below). The report should also describe the patient's progress over the last year and developments relevant to the understanding of the index offence, the risk of further offending and future rehabilitation.

In addition the RMO should review the order *"from time to time"*[23] submitting a report if it appears that the patient's legal status should change.

---

[21] Mental Health (Care and Treatment) (Scotland) Act 2003, s.182.
[22] *ibid.*, s.183.
[23] *ibid.*, s.184.

When a report making a recommendation for a change in the legal status of a patient is submitted by an RMO, the Scottish Ministers must then refer the case to the Tribunal[24]. Notification of the making of the reference will be given by the Scottish Ministers to the patient, the named person, any guardian, any welfare attorney, the RMO, the MHO and the MWC.

MWC Initiated Review

A similar process may be initiated by the MWC[25]. Where it appears to be appropriate to the MWC that a Tribunal should review a patient, then they may send a notice in writing to the Scottish Ministers requiring them to make a reference to the Tribunal and giving the MWC's reasons for this. The reference by the Scottish Ministers under such circumstances[26] proceeds in an identical way to that following an RMO recommendation[27].   **7–30**

Scottish Ministers' Duty to Review

The Scottish Ministers have a duty to keep a compulsion order with a restriction order under review[28]. If it appears that there should be a change in the legal status of the patient, the Ministers must make an application to the Tribunal[29]. This proceeds in an identical way to a reference following an RMO recommendation[30].   **7–31**

Application for Review by Patient or Named Person

A patient or his named person may make an application[31] to the Tribunal requesting that the tribunal make an order[32] changing the order or granting discharge. Such an application cannot be made within six months of the making of the compulsion order or within three months of the last determination by the Tribunal. Only one such application may be made in any 12 months. If the application is made by the named person then he must give notice to the patient.   **7–32**

Automatic Tribunal if No Hearing in Last Two Years

Where no reference or application has been made to the Tribunal in any of the following ways during a two year period starting with the making of the order or subsequently in any two year period ending with the anniversary of the making of the order, then the Ministers must make a reference to the tribunal[33]:   **7–33**

---

[24] Mental Health (Care and Treatment) (Scotland) Act 2003, s.185.
[25] *ibid.*, s.186.
[26] *ibid.*, s.187.
[27] *ibid.*, s.185.
[28] *ibid.*, s.188.
[29] *ibid.*, s.191.
[30] *ibid.*, s.185.
[31] *ibid.*, s.192.
[32] *ibid.*, s.193.
[33] *ibid.*, s.189.

- By Ministers following a RMO recommendation[34]
- By Ministers following notice from the MWC[35]
- By Ministers on their own initiative[36]
- Following an application by a patient or named person[37]

(A previous reference under s.189 will be disregarded if it was in the first year of the two year period under consideration.) In practice no patient should go without a Tribunal for more than two years. The persons listed above for s.185 will be notified of such a reference.

Powers of Tribunal

7–34   Tribunals for restricted patients must be chaired by a sheriff. The Tribunal may make one of the following orders when reviewing a compulsion order with a restriction order[38]:

- No order (the compulsion order and restriction order remain in place).
- An order revoking the compulsion order (and therefore the restriction order) *i.e.* absolute discharge.
- An order revoking the restriction order (but keeping the compulsion order in place). The compulsion order may remain as it was, or it may be varied. The compulsion order continues as set out under Part 9, as if it had been made on the date of revocation of the restriction order.
- An order that the patient be conditionally discharged. This may be deferred by the Tribunal until the necessary arrangements have been made. The Tribunal may attach any conditions it sees fit to the discharge.

The criteria to be considered are set out in Box 1 and the outcomes depending on which criteria are met are set out in Box 2. Where a person continues to have a mental disorder but there appears to be a risk of serious harm to others all other issues are irrelevant in considering continued detention; the person must remain detained in hospital. This measure was introduced under the Mental Health (Public Safety and Appeals) (Scotland) Act 1999 following the high profile case of a personality disordered homicide offender who gained his absolute discharge from the State Hospital on appeal. He successfully argued that although he was mentally disordered and perhaps posed a serious risk he was nevertheless untreatable. It remains in place under the 2003 Act[39]

---

[34] Mental Health (Care and Treatment) (Scotland) Act 2003, s.185(1).

[35] *ibid.*, s.187(2).

[36] *ibid.*, s.191.

[37] *ibid.*, s.192(2).

[38] *ibid.*, s.193.

[39] See Crichton, J., Darjee, R., McCall-Smith, A. and Chiswick, D. (2001) *Mental Health (Public Safety and Appeals) (Scotland) Act 1999: Detention of Untreatable Patients with Psychopathic Disorder*, Journal of Forensic Psychiatry 3: 647-661 and Darjee, R., McCall-Smith, A., Crichton, J. and Chiswick, D. (1999) *Detention of Patient with Psychopathic Disorder in Scotland: 'Canons Park' called into Question by House of Lords*, Journal of Forensic Psychiatry 10: 649-58. The relevant legal cases are *Ruddle v Secretary of State for Scotland* 1999 G.W.D. 29–1395 and *R. v Secretary of State for Scotland* [1999] 2 W.L.R. 28.

and has not been found to breach the European Convention on Human Rights[40].

Before making its decision the Tribunal must hold a hearing, and allow representations from the patient, named person, primary carer, guardian, welfare attorney, *curator ad litem* appointed by the tribunal, Scottish Ministers, RMO, MHO or any other person appearing to have an interest. It is important to note that the onus of proof is on the "authorities" to show that an order should continue rather than on a patient to show that they no longer meet the criteria[41].

Any order made by the Tribunal under s.193 does not come into effect until the expiry of the appeal period (where no appeal has been made during that period) or (where an appeal has been made) the end of the appeal process[42].

Box 1: Criteria to be considered at review of a compulsion order with a restriction order.

The criteria to be considered when reviewing a compulsion order with a restriction order

- "Mental disorder criterion": Does the patient continue to suffer from a mental disorder?
- "Treatability criterion": Is medical treatment which would be likely to prevent the mental disorder worsening, or alleviate any of the symptoms, or effects, of the disorder available?
- "Civil risk criterion": If the patient were not provided with such medical treatment would there be a significant risk to the health safety or welfare of the patient, or to the safety of any other person?
- "Serious risk to others criterion": As a result of the patient's mental disorder is it necessary for the protection of another person from serious harm for the patient to be detained in hospital, regardless of medical treatment?
- "Compulsion order necessary criterion": Is it necessary for the patient to continue to be subject to a compulsion order?
- "Restriction order necessary criterion": Is it necessary for the patient to continue to be subject to a restriction order?
- "Variation of compulsion order criterion": If the restriction order is no longer necessary, should the compulsion order be varied?

---

[40] See Darjee, R. and Crichton, J. (*in press*) *Reid v the United Kingdom: Restricted patients and the European Convention on Human Rights*, Journal of Forensic Psychiatry and Psychology. The relevant legal cases are *Anderson, Doherty and Reid v The Scottish Ministers*, 2000 S.L.T. 873 and *Anderson, Doherty and Reid v The Scottish Ministers*, 2001 S.L.T. 1331.

[41] See *Lyons v The Scottish Ministers*, 17 January 2002, First Division of the Court of Session and *Reid v The United Kingdom* (2003) 37 E.H.R.R., ECHR.

[42] Mental Health (Care and Treatment) (Scotland) Act 2003, s.196.

- "Hospital necessary criterion": If the restriction order is still necessary, is it still necessary for the patient to be detained in hospital?

Box 2: Changes that should be made at review of a compulsion order with a restriction order

- If the "mental disorder criterion" is not met the *compulsion order (and therefore the restriction order) must be revoked—absolute discharge.*
- If the "mental disorder criterion" is met, but the "treatability criterion" or the "civil risk criterion" or the "compulsion order necessary criterion" is not met, and the "serious risk to others criterion" is not met then the *compulsion order (and therefore the restriction order) must be revoked—absolute discharge.*
- If the "mental disorder criterion", the "treatability criterion", the "civil risk criterion" and the "compulsion order necessary criterion" are met, but the "serious risk to others criterion" and the "restriction order necessary criterion" are both not met then the restriction order should be revoked, but the compulsion order continues. Under these circumstances if the "variation of compulsion order criterion" is met then the *compulsion order must be varied.*
- If the "mental disorder criterion", the "treatability criterion", the "civil risk criterion", the "compulsion order necessary criterion" and the "restriction order necessary criterion" are met, but the "serious risk to others criterion" and the "hospital necessary criterion" are both not met, then the *patient may be conditionally discharged.*
- If the "mental disorder criterion", the "treatability criterion", the "civil risk criterion", the "compulsion order necessary criterion", the "restriction order necessary criterion" and the "hospital necessary criterion" are met, whether or not the "serious risk to others criterion" is met or not, the *patient will remain subject to a compulsion order with a restriction order.*
- If the "mental disorder criterion" and the "serious risk to others criterion" are met, whether any of the other criteria are met or not, then the *patient will remain subject to a compulsion order with a restriction order.*

Leave

7–35　　Section 224 of the 2003 Act sets out procedures for suspending the detention of a patient detained under a compulsion order with a restriction order (these procedures also apply to the following: treatment order, interim compulsion order, hospital directions and transfer for treatment directions). This was previously called "leave of absence". Suspension of detention may be requested for a number of reasons: rehabilitation including pre-transfer visits to other hospitals; quality of life visits; compassionate visits; treatment in hospital; attendance at

Court. During the suspension of detention the patient is allowed to leave the hospital to travel to, take part in and return from the specified activity, and must comply with any conditions that are imposed.

The RMO should apply to the Scottish Ministers for any period or periods of suspension of detention. The application should set out the duration, nature and purpose of the proposed suspension(s) of detention and any conditions to be attached. Any further information as may be required by the Scottish Ministers should also be included in the application. After receiving the approval of the Scottish Ministers the patient's RMO may grant a certificate specifying period(s) during which the relevant order does not authorise detention in hospital and any conditions attached to this suspension of detention. The period specified may be the duration of an event or series of events with or without any associated travel. The total duration of the period must not exceed 3 months and the total amount of leave during any 12-month period must not exceed 9 months.

Conditions may be included on the certificate, if necessary, in the interests of the patient or for the protection of any other persons, including that the patient be kept in the charge of a person authorised in writing by the RMO. If the period of leave exceeds 28 days then the RMO must notify the patient, the patient's named person, the patient's general practitioner and the MHO to give notice of the proposed leave before it occurs. Under such circumstances the RMO must also notify the MWC within 14 days of the granting of the certificate.

The certificate may be revoked by the RMO[43] or the Scottish Ministers[44] if either is satisfied that it is necessary in the patient's interests or for the protection of any other person. Revocation authorises immediate conveyance back to hospital by staff of the hospital and/or the police. If the certificate is revoked by the RMO then as soon as practicable the patient, the patient's named person, the patient's general practitioner (if the leave was for more than 28 days), any person in whose charge the patient may have been, the MHO and the Scottish Ministers should be notified.

Transfer

There are provisions for the transfer of restricted patients[45] and **7–36** relevant appeal procedures[46]. Usually a transfer will be planned well in advance. However under certain circumstances (*e.g.* the need for urgent medical treatment for physical illness or the need for a rapid transfer to a more secure hospital) a quick transfer will be necessary without such planning having occurred. Transfer for urgent medical treatment would usually be achieved via suspension of detention procedure (see above); urgent transfer to a more secure hospital can be achieved via urgent transfer procedures[47].

---

[43] Mental Health (Care and Treatment) (Scotland) Act 2003, s.225.
[44] *ibid.*, s.226.
[45] *ibid.*, s.218.
[46] *ibid.*, s.219.
[47] *ibid.*, s.218(5).

Restricted patients may only be transferred to another hospital by the managers of the current hospital with the consent of the managers of the receiving hospital and the Scottish Ministers. At least seven days' notice must be given to the patient (unless the patient consents to the transfer) and the named person. If the proposed transfer does not occur within three months of this notice being given, then the transfer may only go ahead if the managers of the receiving hospital and the Scottish Ministers still consent, and at least seven days' notice has been given to the patient (unless the patient consents to the transfer) and the named person again of the postponed date of transfer.

Usually the patient would initially visit the second hospital under suspension of detention provisions (see above). If following these the transfer seems feasible and appropriate then a formal request would be made by the RMO to the Scottish Ministers for consent to the transfer stating the approximate date of the proposed transfer, that there is an appropriate bed available and that an RMO in the next hospital has been identified and has consented to the transfer (he will be acting on behalf of the managers of the receiving hospital).

An urgent transfer differs from a non-urgent transfer in that notification need not be given to the patient and named person at least seven days before the transfer[48], but such notification must be given as soon as practicable, either before or after the transfer has occurred[49]. As with non-urgent transfer, no notification to the patient is required if the patient consents to the transfer. The requirements as to the consent of the Scottish Ministers and the managers of the receiving hospital still apply.

Discharge

Conditional discharge

7-37   Conditional discharge allows a period of formal supervision in the community with appropriate supervision, support and limits placed on patients. Patients on conditional discharge may be recalled to hospital by the Scottish Ministers if there are concerns about them. Most patients subject to a compulsion order with a restriction order will return to the community on conditional discharge.

Plans for conditional discharge need to be made well in advance, involving appropriate local health and social work services. A supervising RMO and MHO must be identified and consideration will need to be given to where the patient will reside; the individuals who will be involved in providing care, treatment and services; the places where the person will need to attend (*e.g.* clinics, hospitals, day-hospitals, day-centres, work placements); and treatment to be given (*e.g.* medication, psychological therapies). In some cases the police may be involved in planning conditional discharge; mentally disordered offenders subject to certain requirements will require to register with the police following discharge (*e.g.* sex offenders).

In most cases prior to conditional discharge there will be periods of suspension of detention, during which patients will start spending time in

---

[48] Mental Health (Care and Treatment) (Scotland) Act 2003, s.218(5).
[49] *ibid.*, s.218(6).

the community engaging with elements of their conditional discharge care package.

The conditions imposed by the Tribunal[50] may include: residence at a stated address; supervision by a social worker; psychiatric supervision; attendance at specific places (*e.g.* clinics, hospitals, day-hospitals, day-centres, work placements); allowing access to specified people (*e.g.* psychiatrist, social worker, community psychiatric nurse); taking medication; complying with other treatments (*e.g.* attending for psychological treatment); restrictions on use of alcohol and illicit substances including submitting to urine drug testing; prohibition from going to certain areas or places (*e.g.* to prevent contact with victims). The Scottish Ministers may vary these conditions as they think fit[51]. Within 28 days of receiving the notification of variation from the Ministers the patient or their named person may appeal against the variation to the Tribunal[52].

A conditionally discharged patient may be recalled to, and detained in, hospital if the Scottish Ministers are satisfied that this is necessary and issue a warrant to this effect[53]. This may be to a different hospital than that specified in the compulsion order[54]. In an emergency, where there has not been time for the warrant to be issued, a conditionally discharged patient may be admitted to hospital voluntarily or under civil procedure if there is a deterioration in his mental state. Recall from conditional discharge may then be initiated. Where a patient is recalled he is subject to detention under a compulsion order with a restriction order, as had been the case prior to the conditional discharge. Within 28 days of the patient returning to hospital, the patient or their named person may appeal against the recall to the Tribunal[55].

Absolute discharge

This is the revocation of a compulsion order and restriction order. In most cases it will follow a period in the community under conditional discharge. Non-compulsory treatment and contact with services would continue in most cases. In a few cases patients may be absolutely discharged from hospital by a Tribunal. In such cases aftercare for the patient should be organized, even though this would not be subject to compulsion.

7–38

Absconding

If a restricted patient absconds he may be apprehended by hospital staff or the police and either returned to hospital or taken into police custody. The Scottish Executive should be notified immediately if a restricted patient absconds. In some cases consideration may have to be given to transferring the patient to a more secure unit.

7–39

---

[50] Mental Health (Care and Treatment) (Scotland) Act 2003, s.193(7).
[51] *ibid.*, s.200.
[52] *ibid.*, s.201.
[53] *ibid.*, s.202.
[54] *ibid.*, s.203.
[55] *ibid.*, s.204.

HOSPITAL DIRECTION (s.59A OF THE 1995 ACT)

Background

7–40   The hospital direction is a relatively new addition to the range of disposals available for mentally disordered offenders, introduced by the Crime and Punishment (Scotland) Act 1997. It is also known as the "hybrid order" as it combines hospital detention with a prison sentence. The patient is admitted to hospital and then, when no longer requiring detention in hospital, may be transferred to prison to serve the rest of his sentence. If the patient is still in hospital when the sentence ends, then he may be placed on a civil compulsory order. The hospital direction was originally conceived in England and Wales as a measure for personality disordered offenders, allowing psychiatric services to try to treat patients without them becoming stuck in hospital inappropriately. In Scotland it applies to all categories of mental disorder.

Initially there was opposition to the introduction of the hospital direction[56], but research has shown that psychiatrists and sentencers feel it is a useful disposal in some cases[57]. It is only available in the most serious cases (those dealt with on indictment). It is the appropriate disposal where there does not appear to be a significant link between the offender's mental disorder and the index offence and/or the risk of further serious offending. Although this is not set out in statute, this is the policy intention and is set out in the Code of Practice[58]. It should be seen as an alternative to a compulsion order with a restriction order.

At What Stage of the Criminal Justice Process can a Hospital Direction be Made?

7–41   A hospital direction may be made by a sheriff court or the High Court, where a person has been convicted on indictment of an offence punishable by imprisonment. Unlike the compulsion order, there is no exception for an offence where the sentence is fixed by law (*i.e.* murder). So, in murder cases a hospital direction may be imposed along with a life sentence.

What Evidence is Required?

7–42   The evidence required is identical to that for a hospital based compulsion order (see above). Although there is no such statutory requirement, as with a compulsion order with a restriction order, an interim compulsion order should be made first, unless there are good reasons not to do so. Although this is not set out in statute, it is clearly

---

[56] See Thomson, L. D. G. (1999) *The Crime and Punishment (Scotland) Act 1997: relevant provisions for people with mental disorders*, Psychiatric Bulletin 23: 68–71.

[57] See Darjee, R., Crichton, J. and Thomson, L. (2000) *Crime and Punishment (Scotland) Act 1997: A study of psychiatrists' views towards the hospital direction*, Journal of Forensic Psychiatry 11: 608–620 and Darjee, R., Crichton, J. and Thomson, L. (2002) *Crime and Punishment (Scotland) Act 1997: A study of sentencers' views towards the hospital direction*, Medicine Science and the Law 42: 76–86.

[58] See Scottish Executive (2001) *New Directions. Report of the review of the Mental Health (Scotland) Act 1984.* Edinburgh, Scottish Executive; Scottish Executive (2001) *Renewing mental health law. Policy statement*, Edinburgh, Scottish Executive.

the policy intention that cases where a hospital direction would be appropriate, rather than a compulsion order with a restriction order, are those where serious offences have been committed but the link between the specified mental disorder and the index offence and/or the risk of further serious offending is weak. When the hospital direction was first introduced, guidance stated that psychiatrists should not recommend this disposal as it is attached to a prison sentence. This guidance no longer applies, so psychiatrists may recommend a hospital direction.

What Happens When a Person is Subject to a Hospital Direction?

The court imposes a prison sentence and directs that the patient be **7–43** admitted to a specified hospital. Procedure relating to the admission of a patient to hospital is identical to that for a hospital-based compulsion order. While the patient is subject to the hospital direction they are treated as a restricted patient. Procedures for leave, absconding and transfer are identical to those set out above for restricted patients.

Review

The review process is similar to that for patients subject to compulsion **7–44** orders with restriction orders. It is set out under Part 11 of the 2003 Act. Part 11 also applies to patients subject to transfer for treatment directions (see below). Both types of order are referred to as "directions" and their effects are identical, in that an offender serving a prison sentence is subject to a period of detention in hospital. Directions end when revoked or when the term of imprisonment ends.

The review process is similar to that described above for the compulsion order and restriction order, except for the following:

- The options on reviewing a direction are more limited: continued detention in hospital or revocation and transfer to prison. This is reflected in the criteria to be considered at review (see Box 3) and the outcomes related to these (see Box 4). During a direction a patient may not be discharged to the community.
- The Scottish Ministers, as well as the Tribunal, have the power to revoke a direction.
- Patients subject to directions who are serving life sentences, if they are to remain with mental health services rather than going to prison before release, will usually be released on life license via the Parole Board. This is like conditional discharge, but is not covered by mental health legislation.

Box 3: Criteria to be considered at review of a hospital direction.

The criteria to be considered when reviewing a compulsion order with a restriction order:

- 'Mental disorder criterion': Does the patient continue to suffer from a mental disorder?

- 'Treatability criterion': Is medical treatment which would be likely to prevent the mental disorder worsening, or alleviate any of the symptoms, or effects, of the disorder available?
- 'Civil risk criterion': If the patient were not provided with such medical treatment would there be a significant risk to the health safety or welfare of the patient, or to the safety of any other person?
- 'Serious risk to others criterion': As a result of the patient's mental disorder is it necessary for the protection of another person from serious harm for the patient to be detained in hospital, regardless of medical treatment?
- 'Hospital direction necessary criterion': Is it necessary for the patient to continue to be subject to a hospital direction?

Box 4: Changes that should be made at review of a hospital direction

- If the 'mental disorder criterion' is not met the *hospital direction must be revoked—transfer to prison for remainder of sentence.*
- If the 'mental disorder criterion' is met, but the 'treatability criterion' or the 'civil risk criterion' or the 'hospital direction necessary criterion' is not met, and the 'serious risk to others criterion' is not met then the *hospital direction must be revoked— transfer to prison for remainder of sentence.*
- If the 'mental disorder criterion', the 'treatability criterion', the 'civil risk criterion' and the 'hospital direction necessary criterion' are met then the *hospital direction continues.*
- If the 'mental disorder criterion'and the 'serious risk to others criterion' are met, whether or not the other criteria are also met, the *hospital direction continues.*

It should be noted that the 'public safety' test applies to these patients, but needs to be considered in a different way than for patients on compulsion orders with restriction orders. The risk that has to be considered is the risk to the narrower section of the public in prison (*i.e.* prisoners and prison staff) rather than the risk to the public in the community[59].

Discharge

Revocation of direction whilst prison sentence is still running

7–45   When a person is subject to a direction, his prison sentence continues to run until the earliest date of liberation (EDL) (for determinate sentence prisoners) or until he is granted parole (for some long-term prisoners and for life prisoners). During this time the direction may only be revoked by the Scottish Ministers; either on their own initiative[60],

---

[59] See *Anderson, Doherty and Reid v The Scottish Ministers*, 2000 S.L.T. 873 and *Anderson, Doherty and Reid v The Scottish Ministers*, 2001 S.L.T. 1331.
[60] Mental Health (Care and Treatment) (Scotland) Act 2003, s.212.

following a recommendation by an RMO[61] or when directed to do so by the Tribunal[62]. When the direction is revoked the Scottish Ministers will issue a warrant directing that the person be admitted to prison and at the point that the person is admitted there the direction ceases to have effect[63].

Termination of direction on date that person would have been released from prison

If a patient remains detained in hospital under a direction at the point **7–46** when he would have been released had they not been admitted to hospital, then the direction will cease to have effect[64]. For most persons serving determinate sentences this will be the EDL. For some long-term determinate sentence prisoners and for all life prisoners this will be the date on which they are released on licence after consideration by the Parole Board. If the person meets criteria for a compulsory treatment order then an application should have been made for this to be imposed at the end of the direction (see below). Otherwise the person must be discharged from hospital or may remain as an informal patient.

Continued detention of patient beyond date that person would have been released from prison

Schedule 3 of the 2003 Act allows an application to a Tribunal for a **7–47** CTO to be made to have effect immediately after the direction ceases to have effect. The CTO must be made during the period of 28 days before the expiry of the direction, and takes effect on the day that the direction ceases to have effect. As with any CTO, the authorised treatment may be in hospital or in the community, and the duration of the CTO will be for six months before it must be renewed.

Early release of determinate sentence prisoners

The EDL is the date on which all determinate sentence prisoners must **7–48** be released. In most cases where a patient on a direction is serving a determinate sentence, the date on which the direction falls will be the EDL. However, in some cases, where patients who have determinate sentences are serving long-term sentences (*i.e.* four years or more), they may be released on licence at any point between the parole qualifying date (PQD) and the EDL. If this happens then the direction ends. The fact that a person is subject to a direction does not preclude him from being considered for parole.

In circumstances where the RMO is of the view that a patient meets or is likely to meet the criteria for discharge during the period between the PQD and the EDL, he or she may recommend to Scottish Ministers that release on licence direct from hospital should be considered. The Parole and Life Sentence Review Division (PLSRD) of the Scottish

---

[61] Mental Health (Care and Treatment) (Scotland) Act 2003, s.210.
[62] *ibid.*, s.215.
[63] *ibid.*, s.216.
[64] *ibid.*, s.217.

Executive will then consider whether or not the individual's case should be referred to the Parole Board to consider his suitability for early release.

Release on licence of patient detained in hospital under direction serving a life sentence

7–49 A patient subject to a direction who is serving a life sentence may be discharged in one of two ways: (1) returning to prison through revocation of the direction under s.216 (see above); or (2) release directly from hospital on life licence under s.2(4) of the Prisoners and Criminal Proceedings (Scotland) Act 1993. On the date of release the direction falls.

After the "punishment" period, which a life-sentenced prisoner must serve before being considered for parole has been served the patient may require the Scottish Ministers to refer his case to the Parole Board, who will consider the level of risk the patient might present to the public. If that risk is considered by the Life Prisoner Tribunal to be acceptable, it will decide that he should be released on life licence (with simultaneous revocation of the direction). If that is the decision, it will direct Scottish Ministers to release the patient. Scottish Ministers are statutorily obliged to release the person as soon as practicable. The Parole Board will also decide on any special conditions to include in the life licence.

If the Parole Board considers that the level of risk is unacceptable the person remains subject to imprisonment and therefore the direction. The Parole Board may also make recommendations about the steps that could be taken to reduce the risk before the next hearing. The Parole Board will fix the date for the hearing no later than two years from the current disposal. The right of a life prisoner to require Scottish Ministers to refer his case to the Parole Board is not affected by being subject to a direction.

Where the opinion of the RMO is that the patient subject to a direction should not be returned to prison on medical grounds, he may propose that the individual is prepared for eventual release on life licence direct from hospital. The preparatory period for such release can be lengthy and Scottish Ministers should be made aware of the RMO's views on this at an early stage. Scottish Ministers will normally expect the person to progress gradually through less secure settings to reintroduction into the community, with testing through a programme of increasing unescorted freedoms, in a similar way as for conditional discharge for restricted patients. Suitable accommodation and supervision arrangements should also be in place in the community.

The Scottish Executive Health Department issues detailed guidance on procedures to be followed with restricted patients[65]. This should be consulted by any clinician involved in the care of such patients.

---

[65] The most recent version of this available at the time of writing is Scottish Executive Health Department (2002) *Memorandum of procedure on restricted patients*, Edinburgh, Scottish Executive. This version obviously refers to previous legislation and a new version covering procedures under new legislation should become available.

PROBATION ORDER WITH REQUIREMENT OF TREATMENT OF MENTAL CONDITION (s.230 OF THE 1995 ACT)

Background

A probation order requiring treatment for a mental condition is for **7–50** cases where a person with a mental condition is convicted of an offence, but the mental condition does not warrant a compulsion order, and the circumstances do not lead the court to conclude that imprisonment is warranted. Medical or psychological treatment for the mental condition is made a requirement of the probation order.

There are two minor changes to this order made by the 2003 Act: the 12–month time limit has been removed, so the potential maximum duration is now the full three years for which any probation order may apply; and the court must be satisfied on the evidence of the medical practitioner or psychologist under whom the treatment will be given that the relevant services are available and appropriate.

What are the Criteria for Making a Probation Order with Requirement of Treatment of Mental Condition?

To make a probation order with a requirement of treatment for a **7–51** mental condition the court should be satisfied:

- That suitable arrangements for the supervision of the person can be made[66]
- On the evidence of an approved medical practitioner[67]
  - that the person has a mental condition
  - this mental condition requires and may be susceptible to treatment
  - but a compulsory treatment order or a compulsion order is not warranted

- On the written or oral evidence of the registered medical practitioner or chartered psychologist by whom or under whose direction the treatment will be provided that the treatment is appropriate[68] and arrangements have been made for the treatment, including reception in hospital if treatment as a resident inpatient in hospital is to be specified[69].

Such an order should not be made unless the offender and the supervising officer (a criminal justice social worker) agree to it. A probation order cannot be made unless the court has received a Social Enquiry Report and is satisfied that a local authority can make suitable arrangements for the supervision of the person. Before such a course of action is recommended there should be liaison between criminal justice social work and mental health services, and this needs to continue during the order.

---

[66] Criminal Procedure (Scotland) Act 1995 s.228(2).
[67] *ibid.*, s.230(1).
[68] *ibid.*, s.230(3)(a).
[69] *ibid.*, s.230(3)(b).

When making the order the court must have regard to:

- The circumstances, including the nature of the offence and the character of the offender
- The Social Enquiry Report (this is a pre-sentence report produced by a criminal justice social worker; it is not the same as a SCR—see above and Chapter 3)

Treatment

7–52   A probation order does not provide any compulsory powers of detention or treatment under the 2003 Act. The alternative types of treatment which may be specified in the order are[70]:

- Treatment as a resident patient in hospital (excluding a state hospital) where the patient has the status of a voluntary patient
- Treatment as a non-resident patient
- Treatment by or under the direction of a registered medical practitioner or chartered psychologist

The duration of the requirement of treatment should be specified in the report by the registered medical practitioner or chartered psychologist by, or under, whom the treatment will be given. This may be any length of time between six months and three years.

Effects

7–53   The offender should attend for the specified treatment. However, the order does not give the power to convey the person forcibly to a hospital or clinic and does not give the power to compel a person to take medication, nor does it provide power to detain the person or require them to remain resident at a location. Part 16 of the 2003 Act concerning medical treatment does not apply to persons made subject to an order under s.230.

Non-compliance with the Conditions of the Order by the Probationer

7–54   If a person fails to comply with the treatment specified in the order this should be reported by the registered medical practitioner or chartered psychologist to the supervising officer. A decision will need to be made as to whether the non-compliance warrants notification to the court[71]. The court may find that a person has not been non-compliant with an order under s.230 if a refusal to submit to treatment is deemed to be reasonable[72].

If the order specifies that the treatment should be as an inpatient in hospital and the person either fails to attend or leaves, then consideration may be given to using civil compulsory measures under the 2003 Act if there has been sufficient change in the mental condition of

---

[70] Criminal Procedure (Scotland) Act 1995, s.230(2).
[71] *ibid.*, s.232.
[72] *ibid.*, s.232(5).

the offender. This may also be the case where a probationer is in the community.

Variation of the Conditions Specified in the Order

If the registered medical practitioner or chartered psychologist is of **7–55** the opinion that the probationer requires different treatment, then he may make alternative arrangements for the treatment of the probationer[73]. These alternative arrangements may only be made if: the probationer and the supervising officer agree; the alternative treatment will be given by or under a registered medical practitioner or a chartered psychologist who has agreed to accept the probationer as his patient; and, if the alternative involves treatment in hospital, then arrangements have been made for admission[74]. When such arrangements are made the supervising officer must notify the court and the alternative treatment is deemed to be treatment to which the person should submit in pursuance of the order under s.230[75].

DISPOSALS UNDER ADULTS WITH INCAPACITY (SCOTLAND) ACT 2000
(SS.58(1A) AND 60B OF THE 1995 ACT)

Before the Adults with Incapacity (Scotland) Act 2000 (referred to **7–56** here as "the 2000 Act"), the 1995 Act allowed guardianship under the Mental Health (Scotland) Act 1984 to be imposed where a person had been found insane[76] (see Chapter 6) or where a mentally disordered person had been convicted[77]. Guardianship under the 1984 Act was replaced by new measures set out in the 2000 Act. Instead of guardianship under the 1984 Act, either an intervention order[78] or a guardianship order[79] under the 2000 Act, may be applied. The 2003 Act makes little change in this area. The intervention order and guardianship order are described in Chapter 4.

A court may make an intervention order or guardianship order where:

- A person has been found insane or has been convicted of an offence punishable with imprisonment
- He is suffering from mental disorder
- A compulsion order is not warranted
- In the case of a convicted mentally disordered offender, penal measures are not deemed appropriate
- The person has incapacity in relation to the relevant matters
- The circumstances are such that decisions need to be made about personal welfare

---

[73] Criminal Procedure (Scotland) Act 1995, s.230(4).
[74] *ibid.*, s.230(6).
[75] *ibid.*, s.230(7).
[76] *ibid.*, s.57(2)(c) (prior to amendment by the Adults with Incapacity (Scotland) Act 2000).
[77] *ibid.*, s.58 (prior to amendment by the Adults with Incapacity (Scotland) Act 2000).
[78] *ibid.*, s.60B.
[79] *ibid.*, s.58(1A).

This may authorise the relevant measures as set out in the 2000 Act (see Chapter 4). The requirements as to medical evidence and evidence from a MHO are identical to those for these orders where they are made out with criminal proceedings.

A guardianship order or an intervention order made through criminal proceedings may only be made in relation to matters of personal welfare, and may not be made in relation to financial matters.

CASES WHERE CRIMINAL PROCEEDINGS END UNEXPECTEDLY

Background

7–57   In some cases the criminal justice process may terminate, perhaps unexpectedly or prematurely, and therefore the current mental health order may end (*e.g.* an assessment order ends if a case is deserted) or the proposed mental health order may not be made (*e.g.* in a case where a compulsion order has been recommended, if a person is acquitted, other than on account of insanity, then this recommendation may not be acted on).

The reason for the termination of proceedings will be based on criminal justice grounds (such as lack of evidence or prosecution not being in the public interest). In some circumstances, through liaison between the prosecutor and/or court and mental health services, it may be appropriate for this to happen in a planned way, with care and treatment being put in place either informally or through compulsion under civil procedure. However, there are circumstances where a termination in the criminal justice process is unexpected and does not allow the recommended disposal to be made, but with no contingency arrangements in place. Previously, in such cases, a person could not be held to allow for a medical practitioner to examine him with a view to potential emergency detention.

At What Stage of the Criminal Justice Process can this Procedure be Applied?

7–58   Section 134 of the 2003 Act inserts s.60C into the 1995 Act, allowing for the urgent detention of a person acquitted of an offence, where there are medical recommendations for a mental health disposal which cannot be acted on by the court as the person has not been convicted. Section 60C allows for a further medical assessment with a view to potential emergency or short-term detention under civil procedure.

What are the Criteria for Urgent Detention of Acquitted Person?

7–59   For the detention of a person under s.60C:

- The person must have been acquitted of an offence
- There must be medical evidence from two medical practitioner (one of whom is approved) satisfying the court regarding the:
  - 'Mental disorder' criterion
  - 'Treatability' criterion
  - 'Civil risk' criterion

- The court must be satisfied that it is not practicable to secure the immediate examination of the person by a medical practitioner

The criteria for detention under s.60C are such that two medical recommendations for the following orders may allow a court to detain a person under this section if they are acquitted: treatment order, interim compulsion order (in some circumstances), compulsion order or hospital direction. The criteria for an interim compulsion order are less stringent than those for the other orders listed. But in some cases, despite this, the medical recommendations may be such that the court is satisfied that the s.60C criteria are met.

Effects of Detention Under s.60C

Detention in place of safety

The person may be held in a place of safety for up to six hours. The **7–60** most appropriate place of safety is the hospital where the person was due to be admitted but six hours may be too short a time period for this, and therefore in many cases detention will be at the court holding cells or perhaps a police station.

The medical examination during detention under s.60C

Ideally, the doctor assessing the person should be one of the doctors **7–61** who made a recommendation for disposal if the person had been convicted, but this may not be practical within the available timescale. In general, as the s.1 principles of the 2003 Act apply equally to offender and non-offender patients, the hospital in which a person should be detained under the potential emergency or short-term detention order, should be the same as the one where they would have gone if convicted. An exception to this would be where the acquittal changes the assessment of the risk the person poses.

Treatment

Medical treatment under Part 16 of the 2003 Act cannot be given, and **7–62** as the person is not detained in hospital (but is detained in a place of safety, which may happen to be a hospital) urgent treatment cannot be given under s.243 of the 2003 Act. If a person does require emergency treatment during detention under s.60C then common law principles apply.

TRANSFER FOR TREATMENT DIRECTION (s.136 OF THE 2003 ACT)

Background

A significant number of prisoners have mental disorders. In some **7–63** cases it may be appropriate for prisoners to receive voluntary treatment in prison (in a similar way to patients receiving voluntary outpatient treatment in the community). However, in other cases treatment in hospital may be necessary. Health care centres and hospitals in prisons are not hospitals in which patients may be detained for treatment under the 2003 Act. If a prisoner requires treatment for mental disorder in hospital then he should be transferred using the appropriate legislation. Compulsory treatment under a community based CTO or compulsion order cannot be enforced whilst a person is in prison.

Any prisoner who has not yet been sentenced (either pre-trial or post-conviction) may be transferred to hospital under an assessment order or treatment order (see above)[80]. Previously s.70 of the Mental Health (Scotland) Act 1984 provided for the transfer of unsentenced prisoners to hospital. This has now been incorporated into s.52 of the 1995 Act.

Section 136 of the 2003 Act provides a "transfer for treatment direction" (TTD) allowing for the transfer of sentenced prisoners with mental disorder to hospital. It replaces s.71 of the Mental Health (Scotland) Act 1984 Act. Previously, a restriction direction[81] could be made in addition to an order under s.71. Now all such patients are restricted patients for the duration of the order.

What are the criteria for a TTD?

7–64 A TTD may be made by the Scottish Ministers having considered written reports from two medical practitioners, one of whom must be approved[82].

The criteria for making a TTD are identical to those for a hospital-based CTO except that, as with other procedures for mentally disordered offenders, the 'impaired decision-making ability' criterion does not apply. So the criteria to be considered are:

- The 'mental disorder criterion' is met
- The 'treatability criterion' is met
- The 'civil risk criterion' is met
- The making of the TTD is necessary

There must be a suitable hospital available to admit the prisoner within seven days of the making of the order. The reports should then be submitted to the Scottish Ministers by the prison governor or his representative.

It should be remembered that although there is no legal bar to the transfer of a prisoner to hospital for voluntary treatment (as happens when a prisoner requires treatment for physical illness), this should not happen where hospital treatment is required for mental disorder. In such cases prisoners should be transferred under a TTD. If a patient consents to treatment in hospital then a TTD can still be made.

The assessing doctor should bear in mind that the person is in prison, and therefore that treatment in the community as an alternative to hospital is not an option that is available. In these cases the options are voluntary treatment in prison or compulsory treatment in hospital.

---

[80] Criminal Procedure (Scotland) Act 1995, s.52.
[81] Mental Health (Scotland) Act 1984, s.72.
[82] Mental Health (Care and Treatment) (Scotland) Act 2003, s.22.

What Happens When a Person is Subject to a Transfer for Treatment Direction?

The measures authorised by the making of a TTD are: **7–65**

- Within seven days of the making of the order the person may be removed to the specified hospital by the police, someone employed by or authorised by the hospital, or another specified person.
- The detention of the prisoner in the specified hospital.
- The giving of medical treatment under Part 16 of the 2003 Act.
- The removal of the prisoner to and detention in a place of safety pending transfer to the hospital. Usually the prisoner would remain in prison until transferred to hospital.

Procedures for the review, renewal, transfer and discharge are identical to those set out above for the hospital direction (see above; p.212).

DETENTION IN SECURE SETTINGS

Background

As set out in Chapter 1, there are psychiatric wards, units and **7–66** hospitals in Scotland which offer different levels of security. Not all patients detained in secure settings are mentally disordered offenders as many are detained under civil procedures, but the specific legislation referring to secure settings is described here as many secure units and hospitals are managed as part of forensic mental health services, and mentally disordered offenders who have committed more serious offences will usually be managed in such settings initially.

Section 1(4) of the 2003 Act sets out the principle that when a person is carrying out a function under the Act this should be done in such a "manner that involves the minimum restriction on the freedom of the patient that is necessary in the circumstances". This is an important principle to be followed when a patient is detained in, or considered for detention in, any secure setting. Whether a patient should be admitted to a secure ward or unit will depend on the risk he poses to others, and/ or perhaps himself, and whether this could be managed safely in a less secure setting.

STATE HOSPITALS

Provision of State Hospitals

Section 102 of the National Health Service (Scotland) Act 1978, as **7–67** amended, sets out the legal basis for the provision of "state hospitals":

(1) The Scottish Ministers shall provide such hospitals as appear to them to be necessary for persons subject to detention under the 1995 Act or the 2003 Act who require treatment under

conditions of special security on account of their dangerous, violent or criminal propensities.

(2) Hospitals provided by the Scottish Ministers under subsection (1) are referred to in this Act as "state hospitals".

In effect this refers to the State Hospital, Carstairs, although in theory it would allow for the provision of other such hospitals.

Admission to a State Hospital

7–68   The criteria to be satisfied for a patient to be admitted to the State Hospital under a compulsion order, interim compulsion order, hospital direction or transfer for treatment direction are that it appears:

(a) that the patient requires to be detained in hospital under conditions of special security; and

(b) that such conditions of special security can be provided only in a state hospital.

The same criteria must be considered in an appeal to the Tribunal against transfer to the State Hospital (see below). These criteria are not specified as having to be met when a patient on a CTO requires to be transferred to the State Hospital, but as these are the criteria to be considered if an appeal is made against such a transfer, it would seem sensible that these criteria should be referred to when considering such a transfer.

For other orders these criteria are not specified. Patients may still be admitted to and detained in the State Hospital under these other orders (emergency detention, short-term detention, assessment order, treatment order, temporary compulsion order (see Chapter 6) and committal to hospital for inquiry into mental condition). All these orders are time-limited orders used for assessment. During such an assessment period, attention must be given to whether the person fulfils the criteria above if a longer-term order is being considered. Generally, admission under emergency and short-term civil procedure would be unusual, but may be necessary in rare situations where immediate risk of serious violence is such that the only option is detention at the State Hospital.

It is difficult to translate the criteria into anything that is clinically meaningful. "Special security" appears to refer to the State Hospital and other hospitals (such as medium secure units perhaps), as the second criterion implies that under some circumstances conditions of special security could be provided outwith the State Hospital. The wording used is such that, with the regional variation in provision of local secure services, it could be argued in an area with no medium secure facilities, that a patient requiring medium security could only receive care under suitable conditions of security if admitted to the State Hospital, even though this could not be argued in another region where medium secure facilities are available. Whether this approach will be accepted by Tribunals or appeal courts awaits legal testing.

Appeal Against Transfer to a State Hospital

7–69   The procedures relating to the transfer of a patient to another hospital are set out in Chapter 3 for patients detained under CTOs and above for restricted patients. Where that transfer is to the State Hospital, s.126 of the 2003 Act sets out the procedure for appealing against this where the person is subject to a CTO or a compulsion order (*i.e.* is not a restricted patient). Similar measures for patients subject to a compulsion order with a restriction order, a hospital direction or a transfer for treatment direction (*i.e.* for restricted patients) are set out under s.220 of the 2003 Act. The transfer and appeal procedures are similar for restricted and non-restricted patients, and are similar to analogous appeal procedures relating to transfers to other hospitals[83]; the only significant difference being that for transfers to the State Hospital the time limit for the appeal is 12 weeks rather than 28 days.

A patient, or their named person, may appeal to the Tribunal against transfer to the State Hospital either before the transfer has taken place, where they have been given notification of such a transfer, or after the transfer has occurred. The patient or their named person must lodge the appeal within 12 weeks of receiving the notification of a proposed transfer or of the actual transfer taking place. If they have not been transferred when the appeal is made, then the transfer cannot go ahead until the appeal has been heard, unless the Tribunal is satisfied that pending the determination of the appeal the patient should be transferred as proposed.

When considering such an appeal the Tribunal must be satisfied:

(a) that the patient requires to be detained in hospital under conditions of special security; and

(b) that such conditions of special security can be provided only in a state hospital.

If not then the transfer cannot go ahead, or if the transfer has already occurred the patient must be returned.

APPEAL AGAINST BEING HELD IN EXCESSIVELY SECURE SETTING (PART 17, CHAPTER 3: ss.264–273 OF THE 2003 ACT)

Patients have the right to appeal against detention in conditions of **7–70** excessive security in the State Hospital[84] or another hospital[85] if they are detained six months after the commencement of a CTO, compulsion order, a hospital direction or a transfer for treatment direction. The patient, the named person, any guardian, any welfare attorney or the Mental Welfare Commission can apply to the Tribunal. No more than one application can be made in any 12-month period.

The Tribunal can make an order declaring that the patient is being detained in conditions of excessive security and specifying a period, not exceeding three months, during which the relevant health board shall identify a hospital, with the agreement of Scottish Ministers in the case of restricted patients, which the health board and managers of the

---

[83] Mental Health (Care and Treatment) (Scotland) Act 2003, s.125 (for non-restricted patients) and s.219 (for restricted patients).

[84] *ibid.*, s.264–267.

[85] *ibid.*, s.268–271.

potential receiving hospital agree is appropriate to the patient's security needs, and where a bed is available. All involved have the right to make representations to the Tribunal and to lead or produce evidence.

If the relevant Health Board fails to give notice to the Tribunal that the patient has been transferred during the period specified in the order a further hearing will be heard before the Tribunal. The Tribunal, if satisfied that the patient continues to be held in excessively secure conditions, can extend the order for a period of between 28 days and 3 months, for consideration to be given to finding an appropriate placement in the same way as set out above for the initial hearing. If the patient again fails to be transferred, a further hearing is held and the order can be extended again. The Act does not specify what happens at the end of this third period if the patient has still not been transferred.

Orders made by the Tribunal under these provisions can be recalled if the Tribunal is satisfied, on application by the relevant Health Board, the Scottish Ministers (for restricted patients) or the RMO (for non-restricted patients), that the patient requires to be detained under the conditions of security in which they are currently detained.

Where the appeal is against being detained at the State Hospital, the criteria to be considered by the Tribunal are the same as those set out above for admission to the State Hospital and appeals against admission to the State Hospital.

The policy intention behind these legal provisions is clearly that patients should not be held in excessively secure conditions, and in particular patients should not be detained at the State Hospital if they do not require to be held in a high security hospital. Appeals against detention in conditions of excessive security will be available from May 2006, although it is unlikely that there will be sufficient secure beds outwith the State Hospital for the 100 or so patients who do not require high security care. The clinical and legal implications will not be clear until then.

PART 1 CRIMINAL JUSTICE (SCOTLAND) ACT 2003: NEW MEASURES FOR 'HIGH-RISK' OFFENDERS

Background

7–71   In Scotland, as in several other jurisdictions, there has been concern about serious offenders who are considered to pose a continuing risk[86]. The MacLean Committee[87] was established by the Scottish Office:

> "To consider experience in Scotland and elsewhere and to make proposals for the sentencing disposals for, and the future management and treatment of serious sexual and violent offenders who may present a continuing danger to the public, in particular:

---

[86] For example see Heilbrun, K., Ogloff, J. R. P. and Picarello, K. (1999) *Dangerous offender statutes in the United States and Canada: Implications for risk assessment*, International Journal of Law and Psychiatry 22, 393–415 and Home Office and Department of Health, (1999) *Managing dangerous people with severe personality disorder*. London, Home Office and Department of Health.

[87] Scottish Executive (2000) *Report of the Committee on Serious Violent and Sexual Offenders*, Edinburgh, Scottish Executive.

- to consider whether the current legislative framework matches the present level of knowledge of the subject, provides the courts with an appropriate range of options and affords the general public adequate protection from these offenders;
- to compare practice, diagnosis and treatment with that elsewhere, to build on current expertise and research to inform the development of a medical protocol to respond to the needs of personality disordered offenders;
- to specify the services required by this group of offenders and the means of delivery;
- to consider the question of release/discharge into the community and service needs in the community for supervising those offenders."

The proposals of the MacLean Committee were well received by government[88], and have been enacted under Part 1 of the Criminal Justice (Scotland) Act 2003, which amends the 1995 Act. This has introduced provisions for the assessment and sentencing of high-risk offenders, whether or not they suffer from mental disorder. Most of these provisions are unlikely to commence until 2005/6.

Risk Assessment Order

If a person is convicted of a sexual offence, a violent offence, an **7–72** offence which endangers life, or an offence the nature or circumstances of which indicate a propensity to commit such offences, and it appears that the risk criteria (see below) may be met, then the court may make a risk assessment order. The risk assessment order allows the offender's detention for up to 90 days (which may be extended by a further 90 days, and may exceptionally be extended even further) so that a risk assessment report may be prepared. If the offender suffers from mental disorder and the criteria for making an interim compulsion order are met, then the court may instead make an interim compulsion order (see above) during which a risk assessment report must be prepared. If the person has been found insane in bar of trial or acquitted on the grounds of insanity having been charged with an offence such as one of those mentioned above, and it appears that the risk criteria may be met, then the court should make an interim compulsion order during which a risk assessment report must be prepared.

The risk assessment report, whether the person is assessed in prison or hospital, must be submitted by an individual accredited by the Risk Management Authority (RMA), and the assessment must follow the guidance issued by the RMA. At the time of writing the RMA is newly established, so the details relating to these matters are unclear. The MacLean Committee favoured structured clinical approaches to risk assessment (see Chapter 1). We wait to see whether this will be the favoured approach of the RMA.

---

[88] Scottish Executive (2001) *Serious violent and sexual offenders. Criminal Justice.* Edinburgh, Scottish Executive.

Risk Criteria

7–73   The purpose of the preparation of the risk assessment report is to assist the court in determining whether the 'risk criteria' are met[89]:

> ". . . the nature of, or the circumstances of the commission of, the offence of which the convicted person has been found guilty either in themselves or as part of a pattern of behaviour are such as to demonstrate that there is a likelihood that he, if at liberty, will seriously endanger the lives, or physical or psychological well-being, of members of the public at large."

Order for Lifelong Restriction (OLR)

7–74   If the court is satisfied on a balance of probabilities that these criteria are met, then in the case of an offender who does not suffer from mental disorder warranting a mental health disposal, the court will make an OLR, which is an indeterminate prison sentence. A punishment part will be imposed by the court, based on the punishment that the court deems applicable. After this period of imprisonment has been served, release will depend on the risk assessment and management plan, and the Parole Board will impose licence conditions in the community.

Following release, a risk management plan approved by the RMA would be implemented. Supervision would be intensive, with strict licence conditions, announced and unannounced visiting, alcohol and drug testing, and surveillance, including electronic monitoring. Non-compliance with licence conditions or concerns about an escalation in the risk posed would lead to rapid and predictable recall to custody. The lead agencies in the community management of such offenders would be criminal justice social work and the police. Mental health services should also be involved where there are relevant issues, and would play a key role in cases where such individuals suffer from mental disorder (see below).

Mentally Disordered 'High-Risk' Offenders

7–75   If the court is satisfied regarding the s.210E criteria in the case of a convicted offender who suffers from mental disorder, then if the criteria for a hospital direction are met, a hospital direction may be made at the same time as the OLR. In such cases no other mental health disposal is available. If the court is so satisfied, in the case of a person who has been found insane, then the mandatory disposal is a compulsion order with a restriction order (see Chapter 6). This replaces homicide offenders as the group of insane offenders who must receive a restriction order.

Thorough assessment of risk, diagnosis and the relationship between the offence, the risk posed and the mental disorder present, is important in all cases where a serious offence has been committed and/or there appears to be a significant risk of further serious offending. This would include potential s.210E cases.

The differences between the restriction order criteria[90] and those for high-risk offenders[91] are:

---

[89] These criteria are set out in the Criminal Procedure (Scotland) Act 1995, s.210E.
[90] Criminal Procedure (Scxotland) Act 1995, s.59.
[91] *ibid.*, s.210E.

- The restriction order criteria set a lower threshold: a mentally disordered offender may be assessed as not posing a high enough risk to qualify for an OLR with a hospital direction, but may still nevertheless meet the criteria for a restriction order
- For the imposition of a restriction order the risk posed must be due to the specified mental disorder, whereas the risk criteria for high-risk offenders do not specify any link to mental disorder, and they are also applicable to non-mentally disordered offenders

Risk Management Authority (RMA)

The RMA has been established under s.3 of the Criminal Justice 7–76 (Scotland) Act 2003. Its primary function is to ensure the effective assessment and management of risk of violent or sexual offending. It is responsible for:

- Policy and research
- Education, training and accreditation
- Guidelines and standards
- Approving risk management plans

The risk management plans are to be prepared by:

- Scottish Ministers for prisoners
- Hospital managers for hospital inpatients
- The local authority for offenders in community

Risk management plans will:

- Set out an assessment of risk
- Include measures to address the risk
- Be reviewed periodically and when circumstances change

SEXUAL OFFENCES ACT 2003

The Sexual Offences Act 2003 has superseded the Sex Offenders Act 7–77 1997 in setting out, among other matters, specific notification requirements for sex offenders. These apply to mentally disordered sex offenders who have been convicted, acquitted on the ground of insanity or found insane in bar of trial with the facts found. Aspects of this legislation relevant for clinicians or services managing mentally disordered offenders are set out briefly below.

Qualifying Offences

Schedule 3 of the Sexual Offences Act 2003 lists specific sexual 7–78 offences, a conviction for any of which will make the person subject to special notification requirements. Other, apparently "non-sexual", offences qualify if the court determines that there was a significant sexual aspect to the offender's behaviour in committing the offence. On an application by a chief constable of police, such notification requirements may be imposed on people convicted of equivalent offences in other jurisdictions when they move to Scotland.

Notification Period

7–79   The period of time for which a person is subject to the notification requirements of the Act depends on the sentence imposed by the court. For individuals receiving a mental health disposal the notification period is: an indefinite period where they receive a compulsion order with a restriction order; seven years where they receive a compulsion order alone; the period of the probation order where they receive a probation order with a requirement for treatment for a mental condition; dependent on the prison sentence imposed where the patient is on a hospital direction or transfer for treatment direction; and five years for any other disposal. The notification period commences on the day of conviction, or in the case of offenders found insane, the date where they are found to have committed the act charged.

Notification to the patient and service

7–80   The person will receive a copy of a certificate of conviction and a notice explaining the notification requirements. Both are copied by the court to the police and the service to which the patient is disposed. Where a patient is transferred from prison to mental health services, the notice should be passed on by the prison or local authority.

On receiving this notice the hospital records should be endorsed so that appropriate action can be taken, *e.g.* reminding the patient of the notification requirements when they leave hospital. It is suggested that it may be good practice to discuss the notification requirements with a patient on admission to hospital.

Persons subject to the notification requirements of the 1997 Act become subject to those of the new Act. It should be noted that the notification requirements of the 1997 Act, and therefore the new Act, apply to offenders convicted of relevant offences before 1997.

Notification requirements

7–81   Within three days of being discharged to the community, the person must notify the police of the following: date of birth, national insurance number, name and any aliases at the time of conviction and currently, home address at the time of conviction and currently, any other address where the person regularly stays. Any changes in circumstances must be notified within three days of the change. During the notification period the person must make a notification to the police annually. At notification, the police may verify identity by taking photographs or fingerprints. Breach of the notification requirements is a criminal offence for which the person may be imprisoned.

A patient must notify the police if they are on leave from hospital for a period lasting for seven days or more. This notification must also be made within three days of the commencement of leave. This will, therefore, need to be taken into account where periods of suspension of detention in the community are planned.

The role of mental health services in notification

Mental health services should remind patients of their notification **7–82** duties prior to leave or discharge. The need to comply with registration requirements needs to be borne in mind when planning discharge and leave. Guidance on the Sex Offenders Act 1997 suggested that mental health services should seek patients' consent to notify the police when the patient leaves. If the patient refused then clinicians would need to consider whether, in a particular case, public interest justified overriding this refusal. The guidance suggested that usually the balance in such cases would favour informing the police. In such circumstances, in line with general guidance on confidentiality, only the minimum information necessary should be divulged and the patient should be informed of the decision to override their refusal.

The Secretary of State may make regulations potentially requiring, amongst others, RMOs to give notice to the police about leave or discharge[92].

Sexual Offence Prevention Orders (SOPOs)

A SOPO allows specific restrictions to be placed on a sex offender in **7–83** the community. It may be made on application by a chief constable in respect of a convicted sex offender (or one who has been found insane) to a sheriff court. The court must be of the opinion that the person's behaviour makes it necessary to make such an order to protect others from serious sexual harm. The SOPO forbids the person from doing anything described in the order (*e.g.* approaching specific potential victims, going to places such as schools) and lasts for a fixed period of time which will be at least five years. The restrictions placed on the person may only relate to the prevention of serious sexual harm to others. Breach of the conditions of the order is a criminal offence for which the person may be imprisoned.

In England and Wales and Northern Ireland SOPOs may be imposed by a court when convicting a sex offender (or making a finding in relation to insanity or unfitness to plead) without a specific application being made by a senior police officer. This is not permitted in Scotland.

---

[92] Sexual Offences Act 2003, s.96.

CHAPTER 81

COURT REPORTS AND THE EXPERT WITNESS

INSTRUCTING AND WRITING REPORTS

8–01 Each time a doctor or a clinical psychologist writes a court report they should be aware that they are creating a potentially public document that may have to be defended in court. The purpose of the court report is to provide a professional opinion on the accused in criminal cases, or the pursuer or defender in civil cases. The professional who writes the report must understand the clinical and legal issues to be addressed and present the report in a comprehensive and standardised manner. The report must be accurate, factual, unbiased and independent. It must not be influenced by the interests of the instructor nor omit evidence that may be contrary to a final opinion.

Courts or lawyers requesting a report must give clear instructions on their reasons for doing so, and have an expectation and understanding of the general content of the report to be received. They may specifically request that certain issues be addressed.

Reports can also be requested by many other bodies such as the Driver and Vehicle Licensing Authority, professional bodies, the Scottish Executive, the Parole Board and Tribunals. Social circumstances and social enquiry reports are discussed in Chapters 3 and 7.

Court Report Instructions

8–02 Court reports can be requested by solicitors, advocates, the prosecution services (Procurators Fiscal and the Crown Office), or the Sheriff or Judge via the Clerk of Court. Box 1 outlines the information which must be given to an expert when instructing a report.

Box 1: Instructions to Obtain a Court Report

Name, D.O.B., Address/Location of subject
Charge(s)/Nature of civil case
Expertise required
Reason(s) for report request
Background information
Details of available documents
Current legal status of case
Instruction on issues to be addressed
Authority to pay estimated fees *e.g.* Legal Aid
Date report required
Court date if known / relevant

---

[1] Chapter author: Dr L.D.G. Thomson M.D.

In criminal cases the prosecution has a duty to bring to the attention of the court any concerns or information that suggests the accused has a mental disorder. Reports may be requested pre-trial, or post-conviction but pre-sentencing:

- To provide an explanation of behaviour
- To assess suspected illness and need for further assessment or treatment
- To outline any mitigating factors
- To comment on fitness to be interviewed at time of arrest and/ or suggestibility
- To determine fitness to plead
- To ascertain the presence of factors required for a psychiatric defence, such as insanity or diminished responsibility (see Chapter 6)
- To assess future risk
- To recommend suitable psychiatric disposal (see Chapter 7)

Court reports *in civil law* vary greatly depending on the issue being pursued; for example detention under mental health legislation, or a personal injury claim.

An issue which often causes confusion for a non-clinician is the difference between a psychiatrist and a psychologist. A clear understanding of this is important in issuing instructions for a court report. A psychiatrist is a medical doctor and has completed a five-year medical undergraduate degree. He will have worked for a minimum of one year in medicine and surgery before commencing psychiatric training. Often he will have completed training in other fields such as general practice or medicine. He has a minimum of three years of clinical experience and academic study in psychiatry and during that time undertakes examinations to become a member of the Royal College of Psychiatrists. At this stage he is eligible to complete his higher psychiatric training, lasting between three to five years, as a specialist registrar. During this period, psychiatrists may elect to train in a specific sub-speciality. These include general adult psychiatry, forensic psychiatry, learning disability, liaison psychiatry, child and adolescent psychiatry, psychiatry of old age, neuropsychiatry and psychotherapy. All members of the Royal College of Psychiatrists are entitled to obtain s.22 approval under the Mental Health (Care and Treatment) (Scotland) Act 2003. This states that the practitioner has been approved by a Health Board as having special experience in the diagnosis and treatment of mental disorder, and such approval is required to carry out functions under the Act.

A consultant forensic psychiatrist is specifically trained in the assessment and management (pharmacological, psychotherapeutic and social) of mentally disordered offenders. Risk assessment and management are part of routine practice. He has specialist knowledge of the relevant legislation, the relationship between mental disorders and crime, and the criminal justice process and services. He works in prisons, courts, police stations and hospitals of varying degrees of security. He has expertise in the diagnosis of mental disorders, psychiatric defences and disposals, and the treatment of mentally disordered offenders combining both mental health and criminological therapeutic approaches. The forensic psychiatrist will have access to beds in psychiatric hospitals of varying levels of security. All s.22–approved psychiatrists can recommend any of the disposals under the Mental Health (Care and Treatment) (Scotland) Act 2003, the Criminal Procedure (Scotland) Act 1995 or the Crime and Punishment (Scotland) Act 1997. Court reports primarily address issues of diagnosis, treatment needs, applicability of mental health legislation, risk assessment and public safety, fitness to plead, psychiatric defences and recommendations for disposal.

A clinical psychologist works in the area of mental health having completed an undergraduate degree in psychology, and a three-year Doctorate (prior to 1994 this was a Masters degree) in Clinical Psychology comprising both clinical experience and academic study[2]. Following this, many will have undertaken further study to gain chartership with the British Psychological Society in subspecialites such as forensic or neuropsychology. Clinical Psychologists practising in a forensic setting possess expertise in the assessment and psychological treatment of mental disorders and offending behaviours, and their interface. Court requested reports are commonly in the fields of risk assessment, intellectual assessment and competency to understand proceedings, suggestibility, and suitability for treatment in a wide range of areas such as sexual or violent offending, personality disorder or addictions. Clinical psychologists work in both the criminal justice system and health service but, unlike psychiatrists, do not have a statutory responsibility for disposals under the Mental Health Act.

Conducting a Psychiatric Report

8–03   At the beginning of the interview the clinician, having introduced himself, must make it clear that the content of the interview will not be confidential and will be used to provide a court report. This is particularly important for doctors. People generally assume that information given to a doctor will remain confidential. It must be stated that the normal rules of the doctor-patient relationship do not apply.

Box 2: Summary Psychiatric Court Report—Criminal Case

Name
Date of birth
Address / Location
Charge
Interview(s)—place, date, length, requested by, sources of information (written and verbal)
Brief description of interviewee and capacity to understand the purpose of the interview

---

[2] Dr Suzanne O'Rourke, Lecturer in Forensic Clinical Psychology, The University of Edinburgh.

Personal history: birth and development, childhood, physical/sexual abuse, schooling, employment, sexual and marital relationships, social situation

Family history: medical, psychiatric, criminological

Substance abuse history

Past medical/psychiatric history

Criminological history

Current charge(s)

Examination

Additional information

Opinion

Recommendations

Mental Health Act approval

Soul and Conscience statement

Name and Qualifications

Civil Reports

Civil reports are requested from a variety of sources and the content **8–04** will vary depending on the issues to be addressed. For example, civil reports may be required in appeals against use of mental health legislation, in medical negligence cases, in personal injury cases and by the Parole Board. The content of these reports is not dissimilar to that of a psychiatric report in criminal cases. In reports for the Parole Board as well as the standard information, there will be a description of the index offence, information on the prisoner's conduct since conviction, a risk assessment and a description of the prisoner's plans post-release. It is these latter factors, along with considerations of public safety, which are most influential in the Parole Board decision-making process.

Personal Injury Report

The content of a personal injury report is not dissimilar to that of a **8–05** psychiatric report in criminal cases. Instead of a crime, there will be an incident or alleged events to describe and discuss, concentrating particularly on their psychological and psychiatric consequences. The format of a personal injury report is set out in Box 3.

Box 3: Summary Psychiatric Court Report—Personal Injury Case

Name, Date of Birth, Address

Reason for request, Source of request, Information Available and Date, Number and Length of Interviews with Pursuer or Defender

Information on Accident / Events

Patient's Perspective on Accident / Events

Psychological and Psychiatric Consequences
Personal History
Family History
Psychiatric History
Medical History
Substance Abuse History
Any other Relevant Information
Mental State Examination
Opinion
Soul and Conscience statement
Name and Qualifications / Brief C.V.

THE EXPERT WITNESS

8–06 The Scottish legal system is described in Chapter 2. An expert witness must understand the legal process and the different types of court where evidence may be called.

Types of Witness

8–07   There are three types of witness. First, a witness to fact: this is someone who has witnessed something relevant to the court case, such as a car crash. Second, a professional witness: this is someone who has a professional relationship to the accused, for example a general practitioner. He can give technical information but must limit his opinion to his areas of expertise and experience. Third, an expert witness who must have special knowledge, skill, training or experience that enables him to supply information and opinion on the relevant issue and questions that lie beyond the experience and general knowledge of the ordinary person, including judge and jury.

Preparing for Court

8–08   Prior to court, an expert witness will receive a witness citation stating the name of the accused or the parties in a civil case, and the location and date of the trial. The witness must be very clear who he is going to court about, where it is and why he is being asked to attend. Many psychiatric reports are presented to the court without it being necessary for the psychiatrist to give evidence in person. Oral evidence is likely to be required in cases where clarification of a report is needed or there are conflicting expert opinions. Oral evidence is mandatory for psychiatric defences such as insanity at the time of the offence, and for restriction orders.

   Cited witnesses may be precognosed by either side. A precognition is a statement taken by a precognition officer (often a retired policeman) covering the facts of the case known to that witness. This statement cannot be used as evidence because the information has been passed through a third party. The issue of confidentiality remains important and the witness must not add detail that is not contained within the original report and agreed with the patient.

Often, the date given on the witness citation is that of the commencement of the trial rather than the day on which the witness is required to give evidence. Liaison with the person who instructed the preparation of the report will obtain precise details. It is often possible to be on standby for the court for an agreed period, for example, if an expert witness can get to court within one hour of being notified that he is required. If a witness is unable to attend he must contact the person issuing the citation in order to be formally excused. A failure to do so may lead to arrest.

Sometimes, prior to the commencement of the case, there may be a conference to review the issues. For instance, if there is a disputed insanity case then all psychiatrists involved may be asked to reconsider their views in the light of other opinions.

Prior to the trial/hearing the expert witness must prepare thoroughly by rereading his report and the papers provided, and reviewing any appropriate references. He must ensure that he is able to substantiate his opinions, and anticipate and prepare for likely questions. For example, if it is stated that the accused has schizophrenia, the witness must be able to describe to the court in lay terms what schizophrenia is.

Attendance at Court

On the day of the court appearance, the expert witness should dress **8–09** conservatively and smartly. Whatever your personal views on this, there is no doubt that the court takes more seriously the views of someone dressed in such a manner. It is often appropriate to have a brief interview with the accused prior to court commencing and this is essential in cases of insanity in bar of trial. The accused must be unfit to plead on the day of the trial rather than when last interviewed.

Occasionally, an expert witness may be invited to sit in court to listen to other witnesses to see if he would modify his opinion in light of what is said, or if he can respond to some of the points raised. This is very uncommon in Scotland.

Finally, appearing in court means sitting around for hours so the expert witness should take a good book. Mobile telephones are not allowed in court buildings.

Procedure in Court

When the judge, sheriff or Justice of the Peace enters, all those present **8–10** in court stand. Usually an expert witness will be in the witness room at this stage. In the High or Sheriff Courts the judge and sheriff are addressed as "My Lord" or "My Lady". In the District Court the correct term is "Your Honour".

The layout of courts does vary but, in criminal cases, the Judge is usually raised above the court; the clerk of the court sits lower down and in front of the presiding official; the accused is in the dock opposite to the Judge; the Jury box is to one side of the Judge and the witness box to the other side. The charge or indictment is read out by the Clerk of the Court. The Jury, if a solemn case, is sworn in. The prosecution presents its witnesses. Witnesses are examined by the side calling them, cross-examined by the opposite side and then re-examined, if required, by their own side. This is the adversarial system. An expert witness, however, must give an accurate, unbiased, professional opinion and not become caught up in the adversarial nature of the proceedings and bias his evidence accordingly. At the end of the prosecution case the defence has the right in all courts to make a submission of "no case to answer". This is a submission that, even if all the evidence presented by the prosecution is accepted, there is insufficient to justify a conviction. If the submission is not accepted, or no such submission is made, the defence will then present their witnesses in a similar manner. The prosecution and the defence can make closing speeches outlining respectively the facts in favour or against the prosecution case. The judge instructs the jury, if present, on the law as it applies to the facts of the case heard. The jury can reach a verdict of guilty, not guilty or not proven. Sentencing can be that day or deferred for further psychiatric or social work reports.

In civil cases there are only brief opening speeches by both sides if a jury is present. The pursuer's witnesses are examined, cross-examined and re-examined as before, followed by the defender's witnesses. Counsel for the defender addresses the judge on legal and factual matters as does the pursuer's counsel. In civil cases the judgement depends on a balance of probabilities.

In the Witness Box

8–11   It is perfectly normal to be anxious about appearing in court. This is a setting that the witness does not control, with which they are often not familiar and in which they will not have the last word. Indeed, if there is not some performance anxiety then the replies will not be as sharp as they otherwise could be. The usher shows the witness to the witness box. It is advisable for the witness to have a copy of his report with him because not infrequently the report cannot be found. He should not encumber himself with bags, briefcases, coats or umbrellas. He can ask staff where he can leave these items securely. Often, this will be in the witness room, so do not leave keys or wallets. Ensure that any mobile telephones or beepers are switched off.

Once in the witness box, the witness can take the oath or affirm that he will tell the truth. The witness should inform the usher of his intention. Usually, the sheriff or judge asks the witness to raise his right hand and starts to say the oath that s/he will be asked to repeat. At this stage, if the witness wishes to affirm s/he must say so clearly. Do not worry that interrupting the Judge will give a bad impression; it is often viewed as a sign of confidence in the witness.

When giving evidence the witness must speak clearly and more slowly than usual. The judge and/or a shorthand writer or stenographer will be noting what is said. It is important to give them time to take notes. The witness will be asked questions by the prosecution or defence counsel, or occasionally the judge will intervene and ask a question directly. However, at all times it is the judge that he is addressing, although in a jury trial, it is the jury that he is trying to influence. Questions should be answered using no jargon and any technical terms should be explained.

Short sentences are advisable. The witness should keep to the opinion given in his report and give reasons why he can or cannot accept an alternative argument. Even the lawyers who instructed the preparation of the report will ask testing questions. This is to establish the credibility of a witness in the court. The opposing side may attempt to question that credibility, disparage or denigrate an opinion. The witness must not become upset. He should address the judge and, if he thinks that his words have been taken out of context, then ask the judge for an opportunity to clarify what he was saying.

Box 4: Appearing in the Witness Box

- The key to success is an accurate, factual, unbiased and independent report
- Prepare thoroughly by rereading your report and relevant documents
- Predict and prepare for likely questions
- Dress conservatively and smartly
- Be familiar with court procedure
- Do not encumber yourself with belongings in the witness box
- Be wary of the steps into (and out of) the witness box
- Listen to questions carefully
- Address the judge and/or jury but not counsel
- Speak slowly and clearly
- Avoid medical terminology or be prepared to explain it
- Ask permission to refer to the medical file if required
- If you make a mistake apologise and correct yourself
- Do not argue with counsel but refer to the judge if you think there is a need to clarify your response
- Be aware of the techniques used by counsel to discredit you as a witness

---

Techniques used by Advocates

Advocates when cross-examining an expert witness can attempt to **8–12** discredit the witness or to give an alternative interpretation of the evidence presented[3]. For example the advocate may:

Concentrate on age and length of experience of a younger expert witness.
Response: if appropriate repeat qualifications and job title but do not sound defensive.

Ask questions, not directly relevant to the case, beyond the expertise of the witness to make the witness look ignorant.
Response: Acknowledge your ignorance and state that you do not think the questions are directly relevant to your evidence.

Harass a witness to try and get him to make a mistake or to contradict himself.

---

[3] Brockman B., Carson D., Lader M. and Thompson C. (1997) *Psychiatrists in the Box. A practical guide for the expert witness*, Phase IV Communications.

Response: Take your time. If you are unsure what you are being asked seek clarification from the judge or, if you make a mistake, apologise to the judge and correct it.

Interrupt the witness to stop the witness from making an important point.

Response: Turn to the judge and ask to continue.

Use a technique called "pinning out". Even the most carefully prepared report can contain a small mistake. In pinning out, counsel asks a number of questions to establish how much care and attention the witness used in preparing the report and then undermines his credibility by highlighting a mistake.

Response: Address the judge, apologise for the error, point out that it is minor and state that there are no major mistakes in your report.

Phrase questions to obtain a "yes" or "no" response when this may be too simplistic for the concepts to be communicated.

Response: Address the Judge and ask permission to clarify your answer or to explain your difficulty in giving a "yes' or "no" response.

Focus on the definition of a word and assume it is an all-or-nothing concept or too vague to be worthwhile employing.

Response: Turn to the judge and explain the use of a word.

Ask a series of innocuous questions and then obtain a "yes but" response which the barrister stops before a full explanation is given.

Response: Repeat the relevant part of the question and progress to the required explanation thereby avoiding the "yes but" response.

Comment

8–13   As an expert witness your duty is to be independent and to provide clear and concise written or oral evidence to assist the court. An accurate report with a clear opinion and recommendations is the key factor. You should ensure that you are familiar with Scottish legal proceedings and with court room practice. Attendance at court to observe proceedings and an expert witness skills course will be beneficial.

SAMPLE PSYCHIATRIC REPORTS FOR CRIMINAL CASES

8–14   A detailed fictional psychiatric report for a criminal case is presented, followed by abbreviated sample reports addressing the issues of the insanity defence, insanity in bar of trial and use of a compulsion order. Lastly, a full civil psychiatric report is set out.

Confidential Psychiatric Report

Ms C. Gray
Procurator Fiscal Office
10 Baker Street
Gotham City
GC1 5AC

JOHN SMITH (d.o.b. 21.05.83)
C/o HM Prison Gotham
Charge: Assault
Breach of the Peace
Possession of an offensive weapon
Gotham Sheriff Court 22.11.2005

In response to your letter of 15 November 2005 I examined the above named in HM Prison, Gotham on 17 November for one hour. In addition, I had the opportunity to peruse his Gotham Prison Service medical notes and a summary of the alleged offences, and to speak to Practitioner Nurse S. Morse of HMP Gotham, and to Mrs Smith, mother of the accused.

Mr Smith is a 22-year-old, single, unemployed man, who understood the purpose of the interview and was fully co-operative.

Background History

Mr Smith was born and brought up in Aberdeen and described his **8–15** birth and development as normal. His childhood was happy and there was no history of abuse.

He attended Robin Primary School and Gotham Academy. He enjoyed school and left at the age of 17 with 5 standard grades and 3 highers.

He subsequently attended Gotham College to study for an HNC in electronics. He made several friends and joined the college photography club. He worked two evenings per week as a waiter.

He met his first girlfriend at college and this relationship lasted for five months before they parted in a non-acrimonious manner. This was his only sexual experience and he has no children.

During his second year at college he became more withdrawn. He began to spend long periods in his bedroom, attended college intermittently and gave up his job.

Prior to his imprisonment he lived with his mother and younger sister in a three-bedroom private house.

Family History

His parents separated when he was 12. His father is a 52-year-old car **8–16** salesman and his mother is 48 years old and a doctor's receptionist. His father remarried two years ago, remains in Gotham city and has a one-year-old son. His mother has a new partner who lives locally. Both parents are supportive of Mr Smith. His younger sister is 17 and still at school. There is no known family history of mental illness, drug or alcohol abuse, or criminal behaviour.

Alcohol and drug use

Mr Smith stated that he drank approximately five pints once per week **8–17** in the college bar but had not done so in recent months. He admitted to using cannabis from the age of 17 and that whilst at college he had used this on a daily basis. He said, however, that this stopped in the weeks prior to his imprisonment because he had not been leaving the house.

He admitted to using ecstasy on three occasions and magic mushrooms on one occasion but not during the last year. There was no history of intravenous drug abuse.

Medical History

8–18   At the age of 8 Mr Smith fell from his bicycle and sustained a fractured skull. He was observed in hospital for 72 hours but required no further intervention.

He has no physical conditions of note and receives no prescribed medication.

Seven months ago Mr Smith, persuaded by his mother, attended his GP and stated that he felt depressed. He was prescribed fluoxetine 20 mgs (an antidepressant) which he took for a few days only.

He has never previously seen a psychiatrist and denied any history of self harm.

Criminological History

8–19   Nil.

Current charges

8–20   I note the police summary stating that Mr Smith allegedly opened the door of his house after the postman had delivered some letters and threw them at him whilst shouting and screaming that the postman must leave him alone. Mr Smith then allegedly rushed towards the postman and punched him several times. The postman ran away and contacted the police who attended Mr Smith's house and found him to be in an aroused state. He had a makeshift spear of a knife tied to a broom handle behind his front door. Mr Smith was able to give a clear account of the alleged events on 13.11.03. He denied consuming any alcohol or drugs at that time. He described being fearful for his life and believed that the postman was delivering a parcel bomb.

Examination

8–21   Mr Smith was slim, casually dressed with shoulder-length straggly brown hair. He made intermittent eye contact throughout the interview. He was initially calm and co-operative but became distressed and began to pace the interview room when discussing some of his delusional beliefs. His speech was coherent but the content was bizarre. He described his current mood as low although he was eating and sleeping well. Objectively, his emotional responses appeared blunted. He denied any intent to harm himself or others.

He said that at the beginning of his second year at college he began to feel down. He felt that his friends had no interest in him and that his tutors thought he was useless. He believed that other students were laughing at him although he was uncertain why. Then on 4 December 2002 he saw some students assembling apparatus and he knew instantly that his course was preparing people to be spies (delusional perception). He thought it was probably MI5 or MI6 that had organised the course but realised that his friends had withdrawn from him because he was not a spy. He believed that he was being followed and bugged to stop him giving away information about the spy course (persecutory delusions). He began to hear voices at the beginning of 2003. These were unrecognisable but talked about him to each other and made derogatory comments (third person auditory hallucinations). He became convinced that the security forces wanted to kill him to stop him revealing information about the course and he retreated to his room and began to carry a knife. At this time he gathered confirmatory evidence of his suspicions from the television and radio, and news reports directed specific messages to him about the activities of the security forces (delusions of reference).

He denied any grandiose or religious delusions. He denied any feelings of being controlled or of thought insertion, withdrawal or broadcasting.

He was fully orientated in time, place and person. Tests of his memory and concentration were normal.

Mr Smith was convinced all his experiences were real and was unable to accept the suggestion that he was ill and in need of treatment.

Additional Information

Mr Smith's mother confirmed his account of events. She said that his **8–22** family had been very concerned when he began to withdraw from college and family life in his second year. Any attempts to discuss this with him had been unsuccessful. On several occasions she had seen him talking to himself. He had made electronic alarms for his bedroom and was very angry if anyone entered his room although he had never been physically violent.

Practitioner Nurse Morse of HMP Gotham reported that Mr Smith refused to leave his cell and was reluctant to converse. He seemed very suspicious and was noted by officers to talk to himself.

Opinion

1. Mr Smith understood the charges against him, can distinguish **8–23** between a plea of guilty and not guilty, can instruct his defence and follow the proceedings in court. He is therefore sane and fit to plead.
2. Mr Smith is a 20-year-old man with a 12-month history of gradual social withdrawal, decline in functioning and the development of psychotic symptoms such as persecutory delusions, delusions of reference and third party auditory hallucinations as described previously. These symptoms are suggestive of the development of paranoid schizophrenia. This is a mental disorder within the meaning of the Mental Health (Care and Treatment) (Scotland) Act 2003.
3. He has a history of drug abuse, particularly cannabis, but not in the two months prior to the alleged offence. Cannabis can cause a drug-induced psychosis but can also trigger and maintain a major mental illness in those with a predisposition. The latter seems more likely in this case.
4. At the time of the alleged offence Mr Smith believed that the security forces were attempting to kill him.

5. This is a first episode of a major mental illness. His delusional beliefs are likely to respond to antipsychotic medication. The removal of these beliefs will decrease the risk of any further incidents. He has no history of previous violence. He requires further assessment in hospital.

Recommendations

8–24   1. Mr Smith is sane and fit to plead.
2. He suffers from a mental disorder within the meaning of the Mental Health (Care and Treatment) (Scotland) Act 2003. The form of this mental disorder is a mental illness, most likely to be paranoid schizophrenia. Treatment is available for his mental disorder and without this there is a significant risk to his health and safety, and to the safety of others.
3. He requires further assessment in hospital and I recommend that he is committed to hospital under an assessment order— Section 52 B-J of the Criminal Procedure (Scotland) Act 1995.
4. I can confirm that a bed is available for him in the Royal Gotham City Hospital.
5. I confirm that I am not related to Mr Smith nor do I have any pecuniary interest in his admission to hospital.
6. I confirm that I am approved by Gotham Health Board under Section 22 of the Mental Health (Care and Treatment) (Scotland) Act 2003 as having special experience in the diagnosis and treatment of mental disorder.
7. This report is given on Soul and Conscience.

Dr M. Docherty MB ChB MRCPsych
Consultant Psychiatrist

8–25 Sample Report—Insanity Defence

Confidential psychiatric report
Jane Brown (d.o.b. 17.11.62)
C/o Gotham High Security Hospital
Charge: Murder
Currently detained under Section 52 K–S Criminal Procedure (Scotland) Act 1995—17.10.05
Gotham High Court 10.02.06

8–26 *Opinion*

1. Mrs Brown understood the charge against her, can distinguish between a plea of guilty and not guilty, can instruct her defence and follow proceedings in court. She is therefore sane and fit to plead.
2. She suffers from psychotic depression. Evidence for this can be found in her psychiatric history with three previous admissions for psychotic depression each requiring treatment with electroconvulsive therapy (ECT), her long standing lithium and anti-depressant treatment, and her current presentation. She described a three-month period of low mood which was worse

in the morning (positive diurnal variation), early morning wakening, poor concentration, lack of enjoyment of life, an inability to see a future, and suicidal thoughts. In addition, she experienced psychotic symptoms and believed that her husband had a rotting mass inside of him which was killing him and emanating evil to all those in contact with him. For example, Mrs Brown blamed a neighbour's recent car crash on the evil from the growth inside her husband.

3. She stabbed her husband to prevent, in her view, his further suffering and to stop the evil coming from the mass from harming others. Given these factors, it appears that there was an alienation of reason in relation to the act committed and that her reason was overpowered and she was rendered incapable of controlling her conduct. She was insane at the time of the alleged offence.

Recommendations

1. Mrs Brown is sane and fit to plead. **8–27**
2. She suffers from a mental disorder in the form of a mental illness, namely recurrent depressive disorder, within the meaning of the Mental Health (Care and Treatment) (Scotland) Act 2003. Treatment is available for her mental disorder and without this there is a significant risk to her health and safety, and to the safety of others.
3. At the time of the alleged offence Mrs Brown was suffering from an alienation of reason in relation to the act committed and was insane.
4. I recommend that in the event of Mrs Brown being found not guilty by reason of insanity that she is committed to hospital under an interim compulsion order [Section 57(2)(bb) of the Criminal Procedure (Scotland) Act 1995] to allow for a period of further treatment and assessment.
5. In view of Mrs Brown's alleged dangerous, violent and criminal propensities I recommend that she is sent to Gotham High Security Hospital.
6. I confirm that a bed will be made available for Mrs Brown in the Gotham High Security Hospital.
7. I confirm that I am not related to Mrs Brown nor do I have any pecuniary interest in her admission to hospital.
8. I confirm that I am approved by Gotham Health Board under Section 22 of the Mental Health (Care and Treatment) (Scotland) Act 2003 as having special experience in the diagnosis and treatment of mental disorder.
9. This report is given on Soul and Conscience.

Dr Richard Marple MBChB MRC Psych MPhil
Consultant Forensic Psychiatrist

8-28 Sample Report—Insanity in Bar of Trial

Mr Frederick Holmes—(d.o.b. 25/10/69)
C/o Gotham High Security Hospital
Charge: Murder
Currently detained under Section 52 B–J of the Criminal Procedure
(Scotland) Act 1995
Court: Gotham High Court 25.04.06

Opinion

8-29
1. Mr Holmes has a ten-year history of paranoid schizophrenia. This is characterised by unshakeable beliefs that cannot be argued against and which are out of keeping with his cultural background (delusions), for example that aliens have taken over the Gotham City Council; disorder in the form of his thinking such that his speech is difficult to follow; hearing voices instructing him to attack named members of staff or other patients (command auditory hallucinations); and believing that his thoughts and movements are controlled by an alien space ship (passivity phenomena).

2. Mr Holmes denies any involvement in the death of his fellow patient, and indeed denies that his fellow patient has died, believing it to be part of an alien plot. In view of this, I do not believe that Mr Holmes fully understands the charge against him. He can distinguish between a plea of guilty or not guilty. In view of his delusional beliefs however, I do not think that he can properly instruct his defence. In addition, because of the interference in his thought processes, it is unlikely that he would adequately follow the proceedings in court. In my view he is insane and unfit to plead.

Recommendations

8-30
1. Mr Holmes is insane in bar of trial.

2. Mr Holmes suffers from a mental disorder within the meaning of the Mental Health (Care and Treatment) (Scotland) Act 2003. This is a mental illness, namely paranoid schizophrenia. Treatment is available for his disorder and without this there is a significant risk to his health and safety, and to the safety of others.

3. If the court is satisfied that Mr Holmes is insane in bar of trial, then I recommend that he is made subject to a Temporary Compulsion Order under Section 54(2A) of the Criminal Procedure (Scotland) Act 1995 until the conclusion of the examination of facts.

4. In view of his alleged dangerous and violent propensities he should be sent to Gotham High Security Hospital.

5. I confirm that a bed will be made available for Mr Holmes in the Gotham High Security Hospital.

6. I confirm that I am not related to Mr Holmes nor do I have any pecuniary interest in his admission to hospital.

7. I confirm that I am approved by Gotham Health Board under Section 22 of the Mental Health (Care and Treatment) Act

2003 as having special experience in the diagnosis and treatment of mental disorder.

Dr Richard Marple MBChB MRC Psych MPhil
Consultant Forensic Psychiatrist

Sample report—Compulsion Order   8–31

Confidential Psychiatric Report
James Poirot—(d.o.b. 09.01.55)
C/o The Royal Gotham City Hospital
Charge: Assault to severe injury
Currently detained under Section 52 B–J Criminal Procedure
(Scotland) Act 1995
Gotham Sheriff Court 20.04.05

Opinion

1. Mr Poirot understands the charges against him. He can dis- 8–32 tinguish between a plea of guilty and not guilty, instruct his defence and follow the proceedings in court. He is therefore sane and fit to plead.
2. Mr Poirot has a 20-year history of manic depression and is currently manic. Evidence for this is found in his belief that he is married to Madonna, that he is extremely intelligent and that he has made millions of pounds in a recent T-shirt-selling business. In addition, at interview he speaks very quickly (pressure of speech), has periods of elation and sometimes irritability, and denies the need to sleep.
3. In my opinion Mr Poirot was suffering from mania at the time of the alleged assault. He was explaining to a friend his business success and when his friend laughed at his exaggerated accounts, he became irritable. I do not think, however that this amounted to alienation of reason and therefore to insanity at the time of the offence. He is, however, in need of further treatment as a detained patient.
4. There is no evidence that he had abused any substances at the time of the alleged offence.
5. Previous episodes of mania have not been associated with violence and he has responded well to treatment.

Recommendations   8–33

1. Mr Poirot is sane and fit to plead.
2. He suffers from a mental disorder within the meaning of the Mental Health (Care and Treatment) (Scotland) Act 2004. The form of this mental disorder is a mental illness, namely manic depression—currently manic. Treatment is available for his disorder and without this there is a significant risk to his health and safety, and to the safety of others.
3. I recommend that Mr Poirot is admitted to hospital under a compulsion order (Section 57A of the Criminal Procedure (Scotland) Act 1995).

4. I confirm that a bed is available for him in the Royal Gotham City Hospital.
5. I confirm that I am not related to Mr Poirot nor do I have pecuniary interest in his admission to hospital
6. I confirm that I am a Medical Practitioner approved by Gotham Health Board for the purposes of Section 22 of the Mental Health (Care and Treatment) (Scotland) Act 2003 as having special experience in the diagnosis or treatment of mental disorder.
7. This report is given on Soul and Conscience.

Dr Paul Whimsey MB ChB MRCPsych MD
Consultant Forensic Psychiatrist

8–34   Sample Report—Civil Case

Ms M. Begg
Begg, Steel and Cheatham Solicitors
36 North Street
Gotham City

Psychiatric Report
Emile Chandler—(d.o.b. 25.08.57)
42 West Street, Falkirk, FK4 9VG
Emile R. Chandler v Gotham University NHS Trust
Court of Session Edinburgh 24.04.05
Incident Date 05.04.00

I have been instructed by Mary Begg of Begg, Steele and Cheatham Solicitors, agents for Emile Chandler, to prepare an independent psychiatric report on the client. Mr Chandler is pursuing a personal injury compensation claim arising from an incident in April 2000, when an abdominal wound post-laparotomy opened and required emergency corrective surgery. For the purpose of providing this report I examined Mr Chandler on the 22nd February 2005 and had the opportunity of interviewing his wife. I have read a photocopy of his hospital and general practice case notes, a copy of the closed records and a number of reports prepared on Mr Chandler, in particular reports by Professor Robertson Justice dated 23rd August 2002 and 27th January 2005. Mr Chandler was a co-operative informant who understood the nature and purpose of my interview with him.

Mr Chandler's Account Of the Index Accident And its Sequelae

8–35   Mr Chandler was admitted in April 2000 for a laparotomy to release adhesions causing intestinal obstruction. The adhesions resulted from abdominal surgery 10 years earlier required for abdominal trauma secondary to a road traffic accident. Adhesions are a recognised complication of major abdominal surgery. He remembers being generally anxious about his stay in hospital on this occasion and soon after the operation mentioned to nursing and medical staff that there appeared to be a swelling in his lower abdomen, a feeling of fullness and that the wound was weeping. After returning home these symptoms continued.

On Thursday 5th April the district nurse removed the staples sealing the wound at lunchtime. Mr Chandler remembers feeling frightened about getting the staples removed. He remembers falling asleep after the removal of the staples and his wife returning home from work and preparing a meal. He recalls going to wash his hands prior to eating and experiencing a 'horrific pain' in his back. He put his hands to his front and felt something crawling through his hands and saw that his abdominal operative wound was approximately a third open with his bowels protruding. Initially he remembers feeling panicky and confused, and thought he was going to die. He shouted to his wife for assistance. He remembers that he was holding his intestines and his wife screamed when she saw him but then called an ambulance.

Mr Chandler has no memory of how he got from the bathroom to hospital but his wife stated that an ambulance was swiftly on the scene after about ten minutes. He was initially taken to the casualty department and then to a surgical ward. His bowels were still outside his body and he remembers that saline solution needed to be poured over them to keep them moist. He was taken to theatre and his wound repaired.

Very soon after the accident Mr Chandler had a number of adverse psychological symptoms. He felt low in mood and was distressed. He was fearful of going to the bathroom or taking a bath in his home for a number of weeks. He required the presence of his wife when he went into the bathroom. He had frequent vivid re-experiencing of the incident, when he would feel his abdomen tighten and remember the physical sensations, as though it was all happening again. This initially occurred many times each day. He describes poor sleep and nightmares associated with the incident. In particular there started to be a recurrent nightmare of his being subject to an abdominal operation without anaesthesia. He describes frequent intrusive memories of the incident. From an early stage he also describes an exaggerated response when surprised. He also described an increase in general irritability.

Mr Chandler gives a clear account that these symptoms have slowly and gradually improved since the time of the incident. However, he still continues to have symptoms of increased response when surprised and increased general irritability. He continues to have very vivid dreams and will have nightmares three or four times a week. He describes vividly re-experiencing the incident and the tight feeling across his stomach occurring about once a fortnight—this experience is consistent with flashback phenomena. He avoids all news items or television programmes involving hospitals and health care. He used to enjoy watching *Casualty*. He continues to have intrusive memories about the incident although an occasional day can now go by without his thinking about it.

In addition to these symptoms Mr Chandler gives an account of recurrent depression since the time of the incident. He found it difficult to give clear estimates of when the episodes of depression began and finished. A possible precipitant to depressive episodes appears to be dealings with regards to the court case. The most recent episode of depression began at New Year and thoughts about the upcoming court case are to the fore in his mind. He has been unable to work since then. Currently he describes poor sleep, getting to bed at about 10pm and often waking in the early hours of the morning unable to go back to sleep. He describes a pervasive low mood which he likens to "a big weight on you". He is labile in his mood and takes no enjoyment in the things he used to take enjoyment in. He has feelings of guilt that he cannot explain and feelings of worthlessness. His wife is his major source of support. Currently Mr Chandler is on the antidepressant, fluoxetine, at a dose of 40mg per day.

Mr Chandler has been on other antidepressants in the past. He first saw a psychiatrist in July 2002 who recommended that he remain on antidepressants commenced by the general practitioner. He was seen by a counsellor last year and found those sessions helpful.

Background History

8–36   Mr Chandler was born and brought up in Gotham City. He described his birth and development as normal and his childhood as happy. He attended his local primary school and enjoyed this. He was bullied during his first two years at secondary school. There were no major behavioural problems. He left school at the age of 16 years with 4 "O" grades in english, arithmetic, technical drawing and geography.

He attended his local further education college for one year before commencing his apprenticeship as an electrician. He completed this and has worked for a variety of companies until his recent health problems commenced.

He married at the age of 30 and had a few brief relationships with girlfriends prior to this. He describes his wife as a "larger than life character who just bowled me over". They are clearly very fond of each other. It has been a major regret that they have not been able to have children. They were not keen to discuss this issue.

Family History

8–37   Mr Chandler's father died following a heart attack when his son was 13 years of age. He was a labourer. His mother is 72 and a retired cleaner. She is in good health and he visits her weekly. He has one older sister, aged 51, and he is close to her. He describes her as like a second mother.

There is no family history of mental disorder.

Current Social Circumstances

8–38   Mr and Mrs Chandler own their own home. They have struggled with their finances since he stopped work. Mrs Chandler has increased her working hours as a care assistant. He used to keep pigeons but has given this up since the incident.

Alcohol and Drug History

8–39   Mr Chandler shares a bottle of wine with his wife once or twice per week. Prior to the incident he smoked 10 cigarettes per day, but this subsequently increased to between 20–30 cigarettes per day. He denied any history of drug abuse.

Past Medical and Psychiatric History

8–40   Mr Chandler's medical history is unremarkable except for his history of abdominal surgery as outlined previously. He has no history of head injury or of fits.

There was no psychiatric history prior to this incident. He denies any history of self harm.

Examination of the Post Incident General Practitioner Record

Low mood and withdrawal are documented at an early point in the **8–41** General Practice records, for example on the 27th June, 17th July, 31st July 2000. Initially Mr Chandler was persuaded to take the antidepressant lofepramine on 27th June 2000. By September 2000 he was back at work and much improved in his mood. In December 2002 he presented with tiredness, low mood and insomnia. His lofepramine was restarted as it had been discontinued in February of that year. By April 2002 it is noted that he was still depressed and anxious and this was linked to the incident in 2000. A different antidepressant was considered and a referral made to a Community Psychiatric Nurse.

In July 2003 Mr Chandler was seen by a consultant psychiatrist, at that time he was apparently on the antidepressant paroxetine and his mood was back to normal. He was advised to continue with an antidepressant for a very long period.

Personality Assessment

Mr Chandler described himself as a quiet, reserved person and this **8–42** was how he presented. He said he had always preferred his own company until he met his wife after which he enjoyed more social activities with her until this incident. There was no evidence of any personality disorder.

Current Mental State

Mr Chandler was smartly presented at interview and fully cooperative. **8–43** His speech was logical and coherent. He described a number of depressive and anxiety symptoms. His low mood was apparent at interview. He described symptoms of post traumatic stress: intrusive memories, flashbacks, nightmares, avoidance, startle response and irritability. There was no evidence of any psychotic illness. He was fully orientated in time, place and person but on cognitive examination there were some deficits in his attention and concentration which would be consistent with a depressive illness.

Summary

Mr Chandler is a 47-year-old electrician, currently on sick leave, who **8–44** experienced a frightening incident when his abdominal wound opened in April 2000. He meets the diagnostic criteria for post-traumatic stress disorder, which has slowly and gradually improved through time but nevertheless continues to be sufficiently severe to cause day-to-day problems. Mr Chandler also describes recurrent depression from the time of the accident. The depression appears to be remitting and relapsing but he only feels he has been completely back to normal as far as his mood is concerned for periods of not longer than six weeks. Given that there is no past history of recurrent depression and there appear to be no factors independent of the incident to cause distress since its occurrence, I think that his recurrent depressive illness has also been caused by his psychological reaction to the incident. Although Mr Chandler is on an appropriate anti-depressant, he has not received specialist treatment for this condition. I think that cognitive behavioural therapy for his post-traumatic stress disorder would be of assistance.

I think that the ongoing court case has been a major maintaining factor to Mr Chandler's low mood. Following the resolution of the court case and with perhaps the possibility of specific cognitive behavioural therapy for depressive symptoms I would expect Mr Chandler to recover from this episode of depression. I think it is likely that he is now vulnerable to developing other episodes of depression in the future. I would hope that he would be well enough to return to work within six months.

Findings and Recommendations

8–45
1. As a direct result of the incident in April 2000 Mr Chandler developed post-traumatic stress disorder (ICD-10 F43.1) and continues to satisfy the diagnostic criteria for post traumatic stress disorder.
2. As a direct result of the incident in 2000 Mr Chandler has suffered episodes of recurrent depression (ICD-10 F 33.1); a major maintaining factor to his depression is the ongoing court case and ongoing post-traumatic stress symptoms.
3. Given the natural improvement in Mr Chandler's condition already, his co-operation with his General Practitioner, and the provision of specialist cognitive behavioural therapy, I am confident of a substantial improvement in his symptoms within a six to twelve month period following the resolution of the court case and I have made specific treatment recommendations above.
4. I confirm that I am approved by Gotham Health Board under Section 22 of the Mental Health (Care and Treatment) (Scotland) Act 2003 as having special experience in the diagnosis and treatment of mental disorder.
5. This report is given on Soul and Conscience.

Dr Ellen Queen MB, CHB; FRCPsych
Consultant Psychiatrist

List of Useful Addresses

For copies of the legislation

Stationery Office Bookshop
71 Lothian Road
Edinburgh
EH3 9AZ
Tel: 0870 606 5566
Fax: 0870 606 5588
www.scotland-legislation.hmso.gov.uk

Executive and Public Bodies

Mental Health Law Team
Scottish Executive Health Department
St Andrew's House, 3:E(N)
Edinburgh
EH1 3DG
e-mail: *mentalhealthlaw@scotland.gsi.gov.uk*
www.scotland.gov.uk/health/mentalhealthlaw

Public Guardian
Hadrian House
Callendar Business Park
Falkirk
FK1 1XR
Tel: 01324 678300
www.publicguardian-scotland.gov.uk

Mental Welfare Commission for Scotland
Argyle House
3 Lady Lawson Street
Edinburgh
EH3 9SH
Tel: 0131 222 6111
www.mwcscot.org.uk

Mental Health Tribunal Scotland
E-mail:*mts@scotland.gsi.gov.uk*
Room 1N01
St Andrews House
Regents Road
Edinburgh
EH1 3DG

Mental Health and Wellbeing Support Group secretary
The Scottish Executive
Room 2N.08
St. Andrews House
Regent Road
Edinburgh
EH1 3DG
Fax: 0131 244 2970

Scottish Commission for the Regulation of Care/Care commission
Compass House
11 Riverside Drive
Dundee
DD1 4NY
Tel: 01382 207 100
Fax: 01382 207 289

Scottish Public Services Ombudsman
4 Melville Street
Edinburgh
EH3 7NS
Tel: 0870 011 5378
Fax: 0870 011 5379
Email: *enquiries@scottishombudsman.org.uk*

Forensic Mental Health Services Managed Care Network
The State Hospital
Lanark
ML11 8RP
Tel: 01555 840295

Risk Management Authority
St James's House,
25 St James Street
Paisley
PA3 2HQ

Courts

Scottish Court Service
Hayweight House
23 Lauriston Street
Edinburgh EH3
Tel: 0131 229 9200
www.scotcourts.gov.uk

Solicitors

Law Society of Scotland
26 Drumsheugh Gardens
Edinburgh
EH3 7YR
Tel: 0131 226 7411
www.lawscot.org.uk

Psychiatrists

Royal College of Psychiatrists (Scottish Division)
9 Queen Street
Edinburgh
EH2 1JQ
Tel: 0131 220 2910
Fax: 0131 220 2915

Voluntary Sector

Alzheimer Scotland—Action on Dementia
22 Drumsheugh Gardens
Edinburgh EH3 7RN
Tel: 0131 243 1453
www.alzscot.org

Dementia Helpline Freephone 0808 808 3000

ENABLE
6th Floor
7 Buchanan Street
Glasgow
G1 3HL
Tel: 0141 226 4541

Capability Scotland
22 Corstorphine Road
Edinburgh
EH12 6HP
Tel: 0131 337 9876
www.capability-scotland.org.uk

Scottish Association for Mental Health
Cumbrae House
15 Carlton Court
GLASGOW
G5 9JP
Tel: 0141 568 7000

Sense Scotland
5th Floor
45 Finnieston Street
GLASGOW
G3 8JU
Tel: 0141 564 2444
www.sensescotland.org.uk

Citizen's Advice Scotland
26 George Square
Edinburgh
Tel: 0131 667 0156
www.cas.org.uk

National Schizophrenia Fellowship Scotland
Claremont House
130 East Claremont Street
Edinburgh
EH7 4LB
Tel: 0131 557 8969
Fax: 0131 557 8968
email: *info@nsfscot.org.uk*

INDEX

[all references are to paragraph number]